S0-BLE-569

MODERN REVOLUTION

Social Change and Cultural Continuity in Czechoslovakia and China

Daniel Brook

University Press of America,® Inc.
Lanham · Boulder · New York · Toronto · Oxford

University Press of America,® Inc.
4501 Forbes Boulevard
Suite 200
Lanham, Maryland 20706
UPA Acquisitions Department (301) 459-3366

PO Box 317
Oxford
OX2 9RU, UK

Printed in the United States of America
British Library Cataloging in Publication Information Available

Library of Congress Control Number: 2005924860
ISBN 0-7618-3192-4 (clothbound : alk. ppr.)
ISBN 0-7618-3193-2 (paperback : alk. ppr.)

Table of Contents

"[One day totalitarianism will] simply disappear, leaving no other trace in the history of [hu]mankind than exhausted peoples, economic and social chaos, a political vacuum and a spiritual tabula rasa"

— Hannah Arendt, 1951[1]

"[O]ne day there may be real and successful modern revolutions directed against regimes with Marxist-Leninist titles and formal political organization"

— John Dunn, 1972[2]

"How well we know all this! How often we have witnessed it in our part of the world! The machine that worked for years to apparent perfection, faultlessly, without a hitch, falls apart overnight. The system that seemed likely to reign unchanged, world without end, since nothing could call its power in question amid all those unanimous votes and elections, is shattered without warning. And, to our amazement, we find that everything was quite otherwise than we had thought"

— Václav Havel, 1975[3]

"[T]he same dictatorships that appeared so strong can quickly become the site of modern revolutions"

— Jack Goldstone, 1994[4]

---

[1] Hannah Arendt, *The Origins of Totalitarianism*, Second Enlarged Ed. (Cleveland, OH and New York: Meridian Books, 1951, 1958)

[2] John Dunn, *Modern Revolutions* (London and New York: Cambridge University Press, 1972), p. 253

[3] Václav Havel, "Open Letter to Gustav Husak" [1975] cited in Grzegorz Ekiert, "Democratization Processes in East Central Europe: A Theoretical Reconsideration", *British Journal of Political Science*, July 1991, p. 285

[4] Jack A. Goldstone, "Revolutions in Modern Dictatorships" in Jack A. Goldstone, ed., *Revolutions: Theoretical, Comparative, and Historical Studies*, Second Ed. (Fort Worth, Texas: Harcourt Brace College Publishers, 1994), p. 77

Preface and Acknowledgments

It should be noted here, at the beginning, that, in general, I side with the revolutionaries against their regimes throughout time and space. The sheer energy, exuberance, camaraderie, creativity, freedom, liberation, democracy, and potential that revolutions give rise to are worth the problems and pain that they engender. As a radical democrat, a radical humanist, I can plainly see the limitations and unfulfilled promises of revolutions and their leaders throughout history, yet these are still to be preferred to the limitations and unfulfilled realities of the authoritarian and illegitimate governments they replaced. Even when a revolutionary government becomes odious, it is often less so than its predecessor. The historian Howard Zinn reminds us that the cries of the powerless are not always just, but if we ignore those cries we will never know what justice is. Likewise with the cries of rebels and would-be revolutionaries.

This book is designed so that the footnotes are optional for any given reader. Readers interested in a particular point can easily look to the bottom of the page for further information and direction to other sources. Readers interested only in the main points can just as easily skip the added notes and cross-references without sacrificing any core issues and concepts. They will, of course, miss certain nuances and other bits of interest, but that is the price to be paid in the balance between swiftness and comprehensiveness in the reading of texts and in the navigating of history.

I would like to express gratitude to my advisorial committee—Jack A. Goldstone, Ming-cheng Lo, and David J. Boyd—for working with me on this project and for giving me their good advice and enduring support. This is especially true of Jack, the chair of the committee, who was my major Ph.D. advisor. Jack has been inspirational and supportive on this project and in various other valuable ways as well. It is through reading one of Jack's books as an undergraduate—long before we met each other—that I became truly inspired about the study of revolution. It has been an honor to have had this opportunity to work with him on a subject we both care so much about.

I am also grateful to other people who have read and/or commented on this book. They include Colin Barker, Fred Block, Julie Brook, Kurt Engelmann, John R. Hall, Daniel Myers, Sean Noonan, Katy Pickvance, Sabrina Ramet, John Walton, students in the Comparative Historical and Writing seminars in the Sociology Department at UC Davis, the editors at the Chinese Community Forum, as well as some of the participants at the conferences where I have presented my research.

It should go without saying that I am grateful to my parents, grandparents, and brother, my in-laws, and the rest of my family and friends, but it won't. They have helped me in innumerable ways, many of which they don't even know, and have always supported me so that I could more easily get through the hoops and over the hurdles of the learning, researching, and writing processes. The best of life is often captured in these types of intangibles that they provided and I truly appreciate being a part of these networks of love and support. Cheers to Mark Lettiere for helping me get into the Ph.D. program in Sociology at UC Davis, as well as more into the substance of sociology.

I also want to acknowledge the good guidance and insidious inspiration of some of my classroom teachers. At its best, teaching is a subversive activity, as Neil Postman and Charles Weingartner suggest. My teachers have been subversive in various wonderful ways, some of which I only came to appreciate later on. They include: Mrs. Guber (P.S. 247); Mrs. Wiesenberg (P.S. 236); Mr. Rubin (Roy H. Mann Junior High School); Eleanor Kahn, Paul Manson, Mollie Spiegel, and Susan Weliky (Edward R. Murrow High School); Cynthia Enloe, Bernie Kaplan, Sid Peck, Richard Peet, Bob Ross, Ann Seidman, Barbara Thomas-Slayter, and Kent Trachte (Clark University); Rufus Browning, Mina Caulfield, Angela Davis, Gerry Heather, Don Lowe, Kirk Mac Gugan, and Abdiel Oñate (San Francisco State University); Fred Block, David Boyd, Jack

Goldstone, Alex Groth, John Roemer, Joaquim Silvestre, and John Walton (University of California, Davis). Of course, I have had innumerable teachers *outside* the classroom as well. Teachers can and *do* come in many forms. It is often true that "when the student is ready, the teacher appears". To a very large extent, we are what we learn and it is to that extent that I owe a great debt to my teachers that I hope I can chronically repay to my students and others.

Special thanks also go to Linda Potoski, the Disability Resource Center, and Betty Hewitt for their fine and helpful work; to my brother Scott Brook for electronically storing versions of this manuscript in cyber-Massachusetts; to my brother(-in-law) Glenn Hammel for giving me a little red-and-purple piece of the Berlin Wall, which I keep near my computer; to Or Shalom Jewish Community in San Francisco for being a community; to Berkeley for its libraries, bookstores, and whimsy; to Brooklyn for being a great place to be born; to San Francisco for being a stimulating and enjoyable place to live, eat, and play; and to Jack Goldstone, the Sociology Department, and the Graduate Student Association at UC Davis for financial support to attend and present portions of this manuscript at professional conferences.

I wish I could thank a more progressive and generous welfare state and government, but unfortunately I cannot. True, my education has been publicly subsidized, yet neither nearly as much as it should be nor as much as many private corporations are. Public education through the secondary level was made free in the U.S. during the time of this country's continuing industrial growth period early in the twentieth century. It should be more than obvious that as we are now in a new political economic era dominated by electronics, services, information, and knowledge, based notably on computers and communications technologies, colleges and universities should also be made completely tuition-free with students and teachers being amply rewarded for their educational efforts. This remains one of our many national shames. Leaders who fail to underwrite and support education, impoverish and undermine society. It takes bread to create wisdom, as a Jewish proverb suggests, just as it takes wisdom to create bread. We should eagerly and enthusiastically nurture this dialectical relationship.

I would also like to note my deep appreciation for the natural and constructed beauty of our world, which continually keeps me humbly amazed, happily distracted, and relatively sane. Nature truly is "a constant miracle", one that I try to constantly recognize, celebrate, preserve, and enhance.

Vitally, I want to especially thank my wife Julie Hammel Brook for being, among many other wonderful things, my biggest fan, my harshest critic, and my best friend, and my son Zev Shalom Hammel Brook for giving me added perspective, his creative wisdom, tremendous joy, and the eternal hope for a better world and a just future. Words cannot adequately express my profound gratitude for and dedication to them.

The theme of this book is essentially about people struggling together for the right to be heard while protesting against governments that refuse to listen. This is an all too common occurrence throughout history, and the people who resist and rebel most often do so at tremendous risk, little material reward, but sometimes also great personal satisfaction. It is to these people—past, present, and future—that this book is dedicated. These radicals are the truly civic-minded, patriotic, and heroic members of society, though unfortunately they are too rarely recognized as such. I recognize them here and am highly confident that history will absolve them. The struggle continues...

Chapter I.

Introduction:

Modern Revolution in Perspective[1]

"You might not be interested in [revolution], but [revolution] is interested in you" — Leon Trotsky

---

[1] A much earlier and much different version of this book was presented as "The (Re)Production of Velvet: On the Dynamics of Czechoslovakia's Modern Revolution" at the *Second Annual Regional Conference on Russian, East European, and Central Asian Studies*, Seattle, Washington, 20 April 1996.

It was an historic line spoken during the rush of history when anything seemed possible and everybody seemed to realize it. Timothy Garton Ash, a British author, boasted to the dissident-playwright Václav Havel that "In Poland it took ten years, in Hungary ten months, [and] in East Germany ten weeks" to overthrow the Communist Party regimes. Ash added, jokingly, that "perhaps in Czechoslovakia it will take ten days".[2] Havel, who soon after became President of Czechoslovakia, enjoyed the joke but did not expect it to become reality. He retorted that "It would be fabulous, if it could be so...". In one sense, it did become true. The Czechoslovak people seemingly rose up in November 1989, demanded their freedom, and toppled the Communist Party from power. In another, and more fundamental, sense, however, the seeds of popular insurrection and revolution were sown at least as far back as the 1960s, perhaps as

---

[2] Timothy Garton Ash, *The Magic Lantern: The Revolution of '89 Witnessed in Warsaw, Budapest, Berlin, and Prague* (New York: Random House, 1990), p. 78 and Timothy Garton Ash, "The Revolution of the Magic Lantern", *New York Review of Books*, January 18, 1990. This quip was immediately repeated on videotape for the *samizdat Videojournál* and soon after shown, retold, reprinted, and cited very widely both inside and outside of Czechoslovakia. A political commentator later added that in Romania it only took ten hours. Will people say of China that it took ten decades?

I employ the term "Communist Party" as an adjective rather than "communist" purposely. I subscribe to the view that Communist Party governments and countries are/were not communist in any meaningful theoretical sense, just as these so-called people's democracies are/were not democracies (or workers' paradises) in any meaningful theoretical sense. The latter, it seems, is already taken for granted in (at least) the West; we must begin to concede the former. *Cf.* the discussion of "The 'Socialist' Countries" in Michael J. Kinnucan, "Political Economy and Militarism", *PS: Political Science & Politics*, September 1992, pp. 506-07; also see Ivan Szelenyi, Katherine Beckett, and Lawrence P. King, "The Socialist Economic System" in Neil J. Smelser and Richard Swedberg, eds., *The Handbook of Economic Sociology* (Princeton, NJ and New York: Princeton University Press and Russell Sage Foundation, 1994); and see Sharon L. Wolchik, *Czechoslovakia in Transition: Politics, Economics & Society* (London and New York: Pinter Publishers, 1991), p. 60: "From February 1948 until late 1989, Czechoslovakia's state structure was characterized by the parallel government and party hierarchies that typically have been found in communist states. Thus, while the government formally wielded supreme power within the country, it was actually the corresponding Communist Party body at each level that was the more effective or powerful body". Also see Ash, *The Magic Lantern*, p. 92.

early as October 1918 when Professor Tomás Garrigue Masaryk founded the Republic and became its first President after being granted a velvet independence.[3]

It is no doubt true, as Havel has said, that "this spectre [of dissent] has not appeared out of thin air".[4] The Velvet Revolution of 1989 (as it was quickly dubbed by Havel for its extraordinary peacefulness)[5] was a spectacular culmination and flowering of the roots of rebellion which were nourished by massive amounts of social, cultural, psychological, political, and economic discontent over a period of decades. Indeed, crisis, in the words of Georg Lukács, is simply the

---

[3] The term velvet is used in this paper to imply, as Havel does with the revolution, that a particular event and/or process, normally violent, is relatively peaceful and smooth with little or no bloodshed. Some analysts have also noted that Poland, for example, was symbolically founded by a soldier (Józef Pilsudski), whereas Czechoslovakia was founded by intellectuals (Tomás Masaryk and Eduard Benes). Havel nicely follows in this tradition of "philosopher-kings".

[4] Václav Havel, "The Power of the Powerless" in Václav Havel, *et al.*, *The Power of the Powerless: Citizens Against the State in Central Eastern Europe* (Armonk, NY: M.E. Sharpe, 1985), p. 23. *Cf.* Mostafa Rejai, "Survey Essay on the Study of Revolution", *Journal of Political and Military Sociology*, Fall 1973, p. 302: "revolutions do not occur haphazardly or purely spontaneously. A syndrome of variables coalesce before... revolutions take place. These variables consist of an array of observable economic, political, social, and psychological changes or occurrences".

[5] As Ash effectively states it, the revolution was "remarkable for [its] almost complete lack of violence.... No bastilles were stormed, no guillotines erected. Lamp posts were used only for street-lighting" (Ash, *The Magic Lantern*, p. 139 cited in Samuel P. Huntington, *The Third Wave: Democratization in the Late Twentieth Century* (Norman: University of Oklahoma Press, 1991). Huntington, no friend of democracy beyond occasional lip service (he elsewhere speaks of an "excess of democracy"), thankfully tries to keep his values detached from his otherwise insightful analyses "95 percent" of the time). The spirit of Frantz Fanon, busy in Romania, was conspicuously absent in Czechoslovakia. See Frantz Fanon, *The Wretched of the Earth* (New York: Grove Press, 1963 [1961]), esp. "Concerning Violence" [ch. 1] and Frantz Fanon, *Toward the African Revolution* (New York: Grove Press, 1967 [1964]). Havel's coining of the term Velvet Revolution also may have been inspired by the rock group Velvet Underground, which he admires, and whose record album be brought back to Prague from his trip to the U.S. in 1968.

"intensification of everyday life". To that extent, modern revolution, in the words of Rod Aya adapting von Clausewitz, is "merely the continuation of politics by other means". Yet crisis is also, as the Chinese character for the word suggests, danger plus opportunity.

It has been claimed by some that revolution is something best experienced vicariously. That clearly depends on which side you are on and your level of civic commitment. In either case, though, revolution *and* its study are fraught with danger plus opportunity. Scholars no less than participants differ with respect to their commitments, ideologies, theories, definitions, methodologies, and goals. As with all choices, there are gains and losses associated with one's decisions and non-decisions, what one includes and what one omits. It is, of course, no different with this book. All observers and analysts are biased. All one can do is admit to some of them, though few people do so.

In this book, I have constructed a certain definition of revolution so as to allow for maximal specificity rather than a maximum number of cases; and I have chosen the comparative historical method of analysis because I believe it is the most effective method—despite its limitations—for studying a few cases with many causal variables, such as modern revolution;[6] and I have decided to focus on Czechoslovakia (the heart of Europe) and China (the middle kingdom), both for these two countries' intrinsic interest and for the remarkable similarities and differences that they display, especially vis-à-vis the pivotal year of 1989, which allows us to glimpse a novel view of modern revolution. The most obvious similarity between Czechoslovakia and China is that, as Communist Party countries, they both experienced a major threat to the regime in 1989. The most salient difference, however, is that while Czechoslovakia experienced a (peaceful) revolution, China experienced a rebellion that was (violently) repressed.

It should be noted here that, in general, I side with the revolutionaries, throughout time and space, against the regimes that they oppose. The sheer energy, exuberance, hope, freedom, democracy, and liberation that revolutions give rise to during their surge to power—even if only temporarily—are worth the problems and pain that they engender, though the "victims" and others may not agree. As a radical democrat, I can plainly see the limitations and unfulfilled promises of revolutions and their leaders littered throughout history; yet these are still to be preferred

---

[6] Jack A. Goldstone, "Methodological Issues in Comparative Macrosociology", *Comparative Social Research*, Vol. 16 (1997)

to the limitations and unfulfilled promises of the governments that they replaced. Even when a revolutionary government becomes odious, it is usually less so than its predecessor.[7] Regardless, for at least moral and aesthetic reasons "we must rid ourselves temporarily of our compulsive concerns with causes and consequences to empathize properly with the phenomenon under consideration which is itself characterized by a suspension of these concerns".[8] Further, the historian Howard Zinn reminds us that the cries of the powerless are not always just, but if we ignore those cries we will never know what justice is.[9]

In this study of a particular recent revolution, and its analogues, an attempt is made both to analyze the causes of the 1989 Velvet Revolution in Czechoslovakia specifically and to generate hypotheses regarding the nature and long-term success of modern revolutions generally. I try to accomplish this by specifically analyzing the *causal convergence* that resulted in the Velvet Revolution. I also relate this particular case, whenever appropriate, with other relevant cases, both temporally (*e.g.* Czechoslovakia in 1968) and spatially (*e.g.* between the Czech Republic and Slovakia, and among other Communist Party countries, notably those in Eastern Europe and especially China in 1989), thereby constructing "plausible and illuminating analogies" which can clarify the past, present, and future of revolutionary situations.[10] In this way, a single country can provide multiple cases.

---

[7] But see, *e.g.*, Edmund Burke, *Reflections on the Revolution in France* [1789-90], J.G.A. Pocock, ed. (Indianapolis, IN and Cambridge: Hackett Publishing Co., 1987), pp. 52-54; and Jack A. Goldstone, *Revolution and Rebellion in the Early Modern World* (Berkeley and Los Angeles: University of California Press, 1991), p. 483. Burke counsels "infinite caution" before embarking on the revolutionary path, while Goldstone instructs that the association of revolution with democracy is a mere "illusion".

[8] Aristide R. Zolberg, "Moments of Madness", *Politics and Society*, Winter 1972, p. 186

[9] Howard Zinn, *A People's History of the United States* (New York: Harper & Row, 1980), p. 10

[10] William Sewell, "Assessing Structural Approaches to Comparative Revolution" cited in Jeremy D. Popkin, "Media and Revolutionary Crises" in Jeremy D. Popkin, ed., *Media and Revolution: Comparative Perspectives* (Lexington: University Press of Kentucky, 1995), p. 13

It is hoped that this study can shed further light on the subject of revolution generally, in addition to highlighting a new variant of revolution which we here call modern revolution.[11] Simultaneously, this book employs the comparative historical method and demonstrates its utility for macro-sociological studies. It is further hoped that the methods, analyses, explanations, and conclusions in this book will aid in the study of other revolutions, social movements, societal transitions, and other forms of collective behavior and social change, in addition to the study of modern dictatorships, especially in Communist Party-led countries.

Throughout the process of this study, in addition to an illumination of particular cases and how they relate to each other, the goal of a general theory of modern revolution is kept alive despite the probability that it can never be achieved. The quest for unattainable goals is no less important than the pursuit of smaller, more realizable goals. Indeed, it is even possible that while journeying towards potentially mythical lands on the seas of scientific uncertainty, one can discover many real and fruitful islands of knowledge that otherwise may have passed unnoticed, undiscovered, and unknown. In this way, the arduous and circuitous quest for general theory could paradoxically be the simplest and straightest path toward partial theories. Other scholars, ultimately, will have to make their own judgements.

---

[11] *Cf.* Jack A. Goldstone, Ted Robert Gurr, and Farrokh Moshiri, eds., *Revolutions of the Late Twentieth Century* (Boulder, CO: Westview Press, 1991) which introduces and discusses the term and concept of "contemporary revolution" as opposed to "traditional revolution" or "classic revolution". Also see Goldstone, "Revolutions in Modern Dictatorships" in Goldstone, ed., *Revolutions*, Second ed. for a discussion of similarly useful concepts; and Ted Robert Gurr and Jack A. Goldstone, "Comparisons and Policy Implications" in Nikki R. Keddie, ed., *Debating Revolutions* (New York and London: New York University Press, 1995), p. 325. The typology of modern revolution presented here is implicitly contrasted with another typology of revolution constructed by Samuel Huntington (*i.e.* Eastern and Western) and elaborated by Robert Dix (*i.e.* Latin American).

Chapter II.

Methodology, Etiology, and Dynamics[1]

"Thinking without comparisons is unthinkable. And, in the absence of comparisons, so is all scientific thought and all scientific research. No one should be surprised that comparisons, implicit and explicit, pervade the work of social scientists"

— Guy Swanson[2]

---

[1] A much earlier and different version of this section was presented as "Doing Social Research: Modern Revolution in Czechoslovakia and Beyond" at the 91st Annual Meetings of the American Sociological Association on *Social Change: Opportunities & Constraints*, New York, New York, 16-20 August 1996.

[2] Guy Swanson, "Frameworks for Comparative Research" in Ivan Vallier, ed., *Comparative Methods in Sociology* (Berkeley: University of California Press, (continued...)

"Sociological explanation is necessarily historical. Historical sociology is thus not some special kind of sociology; rather, it is the essence of the discipline"

— Philip Abrams[3]

Although it has been claimed that "Successful science does not depend on following an articulated methodology" and that "too much methodological self-consciousness [can be] an obstacle to good science", the methodology for this book nevertheless will be articulated here.[4] In their edited volume, Charles Ragin and Howard Becker ask, and the contributors attempt to answer, "What is a case?".[5] For this present study, we could be examining cases of Communist Party countries, or state breakdowns, or regime changes, or democratic transitions, or capitalist transitions, or revolutionary situations, or some other related phenomena. To some extent, we *are* examining all of these. Yet more specifically, I am presenting "cases" of modern revolution. Comparing Czechoslovakia in 1968 and Czechoslovakia in 1989, in addition to comparing the Czech Republic and Slovakia, as well as contrasting Czechoslovakia with China, may be as close to a "controlled experiment" as one can get in the social sciences, even though we know that "no comparison of real-world macrosocial cases can ever hope to be, even abstractly, a 'true' experiment".[6] As with Theda Skocpol (and Timothy Wickham-Crowley), "my 'cases' [a]re not simply countries; they [a]re *episodes* of societal-level

---

[2](...continued)
1971), p. 145. Swanson elsewhere states that the critical test for theory is its ability to explain social change.

[3] Philip Abrams, *Historical Sociology* (Ithaca, NY: Cornell University Press, 1982), p. 2

[4] Michael Burawoy, "Two Methods in Search of Science: Skocpol Versus Trotsky", *Theory and Society*, November 1989, p. 761

[5] Charles C. Ragin and Howard S. Becker, eds., *What is a Case?: Exploring the Foundations of Social Inquiry* (Cambridge and New York: Cambridge University Press, 1992)

[6] Goldstone, "Methodological Issues in Comparative Macrosociology"

sociopolitical conflict within the histories of certain kinds of regimes".[7] By defining and choosing cases to study, I am making hypotheses, both explicitly and implicitly.

Indeed, cases themselves, as John Walton suggests, "are *always* hypotheses".[8] Walton elaborates by stating that "The question of cases, their designation and reformulation, therefore, is a theoretical matter. The processes of coming to grips with a particular empirical instance, of reflecting on what it is a case of, and contrasting it with other case models, are all practical steps toward constructing theoretical interpretations".[9] Theory, in (dialectical) turn, names and frames the empirical phenomena that it is interpreting. Hence, just as one cannot realistically separate economic (causal) phenomena from the social realm,[10] one also

---

[7] Theda Skocpol, "Reflections on Recent Scholarship about Social Revolutions and How to Study Them" in Theda Skocpol, ed., *Social Revolutions in the Modern World* (Cambridge and New York: Cambridge University Press, 1994), p. 322, original emphasis

[8] John Walton, "Making the Theoretical Case" in Ragin and Becker, eds., *What is a Case?*, p. 122, emphasis added. *Cf.* Burawoy, "Two Methods in Search of Science", p. 773, original emphasis: "facts are already *interpretations*".

[9] *Ibid.*, p. 129

[10] See, *e.g.*, Karl Marx, "Wage Labor and Capital" [1847, 1849] in Robert C. Tucker, ed., *The Marx-Engels Reader*, Second Ed. (New York: W.W. Norton, 1978), p. 207, original emphasis: "A cotton-spinning jenny is a machine for spinning cotton. It becomes *capital* only in certain relations. Torn from these relationships it is no more capital than gold in itself is *money* or sugar the price of sugar"; Karl Polanyi, *The Great Transformation: The Political and Economic Origins of Our Time* (Boston: Beacon Press, 1957 [1944]), p. 46: "[our] economy, as a rule, is submerged in [our] social relationships"; Marshall Sahlins, *Stone Age Economics* (New York: Aldine Publishing, 1972), pp. 185-86: "A material transaction is usually a momentary episode in a continuous social relation"; Marshall Sahlins, *Culture and Practical Reason* (Chicago: University of Chicago Press, 1976), p. 205: "material aspects are not usefully separated from the social"; John Walton, *Reluctant Rebels: Comparative Studies of Revolution and Underdevelopment* (New York: Columbia University Press, 1984), p. 29: "economic grievances cannot be separated from the cultural forms in which they are experienced and understood, nor from the political forms in which they are expressed"; Mark Granovetter, "Economic Action and Social Structure: The (continued...)

cannot unhinge theoretical issues from methodological approaches without either doing a disservice to both and/or being intellectually dishonest. "In fact, by the time [people] begin to write about their research", according to Howard Becker, "they have made many seemingly unimportant choices of details that have foreclosed their choice of a theoretical approach".[11]

---

[10](...continued)
Problem of Embeddedness", *American Journal of Sociology*, November 1985, p. 505: "all market processes are amenable to sociological analysis and... such analysis reveals central, not peripheral, features of these processes"; Fred Block, *Postindustrial Possibilities: A Critique of Economic Discourse* (Berkeley and Los Angeles: University of California Press, 1990), p. 27: "when we recognize that the pursuit of economic self-interest is itself a cultural creation, then it is apparent that we, too, are ruled by deeply held, but unexamined, collective beliefs"; Fred Block, "The Roles of the State in the Economy" in Smelser and Swedberg, eds., *The Handbook of Economic Sociology*, p. 700: "market relations are social relations and, like all social relations, are bound up with the exercise of political power"; Neil J. Smelser and Richard Swedberg, "The Sociological Perspective on the Economy" in *Ibid.*, p. 19: "the cultural dimension---meaning historically constructed sets of group meaning and social 'scripts'---is present in all varieties of economic activity"; Paul DiMaggio, "Culture and Economy" in *Ibid.*, p. 27: "economic processes have an irreducible 'cultural' component"; Naila Kabeer, *Reversed Realities: Gender Hierarchies in Development Thought* (London and New York: Verso, 1994), p. 134: "the dichotomy between 'economic' and 'cultural' is one of methodological convenience rather than empirical accuracy. In practice, economic processes frequently work through cultural relations, and cultural 'rules' have concrete, material effects"; Richard Peet, "Cultural Production of Economic Forms in the New England Discursive Formation", unpublished manuscript: "economic forms are culturally created, economically maintained, and interact with subjective processes of identity formation". Similar arguments have been made regarding gender, as well (see, *e.g.*, Candace West and Don H. Zimmerman, "Doing Gender", *Gender and Society*, 1987 and Sarah Fenstermaker, Candace West, and Don H. Zimmerman, "Gender Inequality: New Conceptual Terrain" in Rae Lesser Blumberg, ed., *Gender, Family, and the Economy: The Triple Overlap* (Newbury Park, CA: Sage Publications, 1991)).

[11] Howard S. Becker, *Writing for Social Scientists* (Chicago and London: University of Chicago Press, 1986), p. 135. *Cf.* Daniel Little, *Varieties of Social Explanation* (Boulder: Westview Press, 1991), p. 236: "data [are] often or always theory-laden".

Methodology and theory inescapably and dialectically inform one other.[12]

One clear example of the necessary marriage of methodology and theory should enter the scene early in the study of revolutionary dramas. Just as we ask "what is a case?", one must then ask, and explicitly answer, "what is a modern revolution?". The answer implies both methodological and theoretical approaches, which will necessarily guide and constrain any conclusions that can be reasonably drawn from the study. This is inevitable. Therefore, one can define revolutions in the broadest possible sense by applying the term to all mass mobilizations, all regime changes, and, for that matter, all seemingly major changes and happenings in the social system. To define revolution in this way has the potential advantage of including the largest number of cases. However, in my opinion, the disadvantages of reducing, or perhaps eliminating, the meaning of those special and rare phenomena which Lenin described as "the festivals of the oppressed and the exploited" greatly outweigh any advantages. In the

---

[12] On a further methodological note, there is a problematic issue when the Velvet Revolution is viewed as a democratic transition. It is, at best, rough velvet. This raises the questions of "what is democracy?" and "democracy for whom?". While it is true that there are now free elections and other standard (bourgeois!) freedoms in Czechoslovakia and other countries of Eastern Europe, there are also new restrictions. First, the democratic transition is parallel to the capitalist transition. The mass media, therefore, is not necessarily free, but it does have new masters. A poignant example from Czechoslovakia is of an "American publisher [who] was ready to show his sympathy for censored authors in Communist countries, but only on the condition that they submit to his own commercial censorship" (Milan Kundera, "Author's Note" in Milan Kundera, *The Joke*, Definitive Vers. (New York: HarperPerennial, 1982, 1992 [1967]), p. viii). Additionally, there is also unemployment and homelessness for the first time. Second, there has been a backlash against women and ethnic minorities, including Jews and Romany (Gypsies). Whereas minorities have been verbally and physically assaulted in an organized way, women of all ethnicities have faced additional problems. Legally, reproductive rights, especially abortion, have been restricted or repealed. Economically, women *en masse* have been pulled out of employment and pushed back into the home (à la post-World War II America). Socially, the meteoric rise and pervasive distribution of pornography is another important issue facing women. Prostitution has also mushroomed. Third, pensioners and people with disabilities are also threatened with being the revolution's "collateral damage". All of these and other issues underscore the limits of a democratic political system, especially alongside a capitalist "free market" economy. *Cf.* Ted Robert Gurr, "Minorities in Revolution" in Goldstone, ed., *Revolutions*, Second ed.

study of revolutions, it is conceptually useful, and ultimately more fruitful, to separate the concepts of strikes, rallies and protests, demonstrations, social and political movements, separatist or secessionist movements, realigning elections, coups d'état, riots, vandalism, guerrilla warfare, banditry, insurrections and rebellions, martial law, regime changes, *etc.*, from those of revolutions, despite their family resemblance. Some of the former may precede, follow, or coincide with a revolution, but they are certainly not equivalent to one.

It is considerably better to have fewer "good" cases than a much larger number of conceptually muddled cases. "What would be gained in (sometimes spurious) generality", Tim McDaniel convincingly argues, "would be lost in analytical power".[13] To this end, *modern revolution is defined (narrowly) here as a process which includes, as its central event, an extra-constitutional, mass-based movement which successfully seizes state power from a one-party dictatorship in an industrialized society, dramatically and substantially altering the social, political, and economic symbols and structures of that country.*

Qualifying terms for revolution such as "social", "political", "radical", "mass", or "great" are dispensed with as they are definitionally redundant. I concur with Marx in his declaration that *every* revolution is social and political, in addition to being radical and great.[14] It is important to recognize that all revolutions are simultaneously social, political, economic, and great, both in their causes and in their effects. In contrast to the theories of Karl Marx and Friedrich Engels, Mao Zedong, Chalmers Johnson, Harry Eckstein, Samuel Huntington, Charles Tilly, Theda Skocpol, John Walton, Anthony Giddens, and various others, however, a revolution neither has to be violent, preceded or followed by internal or external war, led by a particular class, nor centered in the countryside.[15]

---

[13] Tim McDaniel, "Rejoinder to Goodwin", *Theory and Society*, December 1994, p. 791

[14] Karl Marx, "Critical Marginal Notes on the Article 'The King of Prussia and Social Reform'" [1844] in Tucker, ed., *The Marx-Engels Reader*, p. 132. *Cf.* Andrew Arato, "Interpreting 1989", *Social Research*, Fall 1993, p. 624

[15] Karl Marx and Friedrich Engels, *The Manifesto of the Communist Party* [1848] in *Ibid.*; Georges Sorel, *Reflections on Violence* (New York: Collier Books, 1961 [1950]); Chalmers Johnson, *Revolution and the Social System* (Stanford, (continued...)

Indeed, *modern* revolutions do not rely on any of these characteristics. In fact, modern revolutions tend to be relatively peaceful in tactics, multi-class in composition, and urban in location.[16]

Importantly, modern revolution also does not have to result in political repression, one-party rule, or a centralization of the state. The 1989 revolutions in Eastern Europe disproved all of these former "requirements". Some of these former requirements were already disproved in 1979 and thereafter. In 1979, both Iran and Nicaragua experienced revolutions. Nicaragua was a thriving multiparty democracy in the 1980s; and until 1989, Iran was unique in having experienced an

---

[15](...continued)
CA: Hoover Institution on War, Revolution, and Peace, 1964), pp. 6-10 and Chalmers Johnson, *Revolutionary Change* (Boston, MA and Toronto: Little, Brown, 1966), pp. 1-2; Harry Eckstein, "On the Etiology of Internal Wars", *History and Theory*, 1965; Régis Debray, *Revolution in the Revolution?*, trans. by Bobbye Ortiz (New York: Grove Press, 1967); Samuel P. Huntington, *Political Order in Changing Societies* (New Haven and London: Yale University Press, 1968), ch. 5; Dunn, *Modern Revolutions*, p. 12; Rejai, "Survey Essay on the Study of Revolution", pp. 301-02; Mark N. Hagopian, *The Phenomenon of Revolution* (New York: Dodd, Mead & Co., 1974), p. 170; Charles Tilly, *From Mobilization to Revolution* (Reading, MA: Addison-Wesley, 1978); Theda Skocpol, *States and Social Revolutions: A Comparative Analysis of France, Russia, and China* (Cambridge: Cambridge University Press, 1979), p. 4; Walton, *Reluctant Rebels*, p. 6; Theda Skocpol, "France, Russia, China: A Structural Analysis of Social Revolutions" in Jack A. Goldstone, ed., *Revolutions: Theoretical, Comparative, and Historical Studies* (San Diego, CA: Harcourt Brace Jovanovich, 1986), p. 69; Anthony Giddens, *Sociology* (Oxford: Polity Press, 1989), pp. 604-05; Peter Calvert, *Revolution and Counter-Revolution* (Minneapolis, MN: University of Minnesota Press, 1990), p. 17. For a focus on rural revolutions, see Barrington Moore, Jr., *Social Origins of Dictatorship and Democracy* (Boston, MA: Beacon Press, 1966); Eric Wolf, *Peasant Wars of the Twentieth Century* (New York: Harper & Row, 1969); and Jeffery M. Paige, *Agrarian Revolution* (New York: Free Press, 1975).

[16] *Cf.* Gurr and Goldstone, "Comparisons and Policy Implications" in Keddie, ed., *Debating Revolutions*, esp. p. 338: "The use of violence for political ends is central to most definitions of revolution, but the evidence... suggests that this is a misplaced emphasis."

urban-based revolution.[17] Ironically, whereas France in 1789 may have experienced the first revolution because it actively and dramatically changed, rather than merely restored, the *ancien régime*,[18] the Iranian Revolution of 1979 *could* have been the first modern revolution. However, the state structure of post-revolutionary Iran and the violent nature of the Iranian and Nicaraguan revolutions sets them apart from the Eastern European ones.

Additionally, the present definition of modern revolution excludes *coups d'état* and so-called "revolutions from above", also termed "elite revolutions" by Ellen Trimberger (*e.g.* Japan in 1868, Turkey in 1919, Egypt in 1952, and Peru in 1968), as these are viewed as state *reforms*, albeit major ones.[19] Also excluded are social situations, even

---

[17] It has been argued that the Nicaraguan Revolution was urban-based (see, *e.g.*, Farideh Farhi, *States and Urban-Based Revolutions: Iran and Nicaragua* (Urbana and Chicago: University of Illinois Press, 1990)), but this contention neglects the crucial role of the rural struggle alongside the urban one (see, *e.g.*, John A. Booth, *The End and the Beginning: The Nicaraguan Revolution* (Boulder, CO and London: Westview Press, 1985)).

[18] See, *e.g.*, Francois Furet, "From 1789 to 1917 & 1989: Looking Back at Revolutionary Traditions", *Encounter*, September 1990, p. 3

[19] Ellen Kay Trimberger, *Revolution from Above* (New Brunswick, NJ: Transaction Books, 1978). One might also add the U.S. during "Reconstruction" from 1865-1876, the fascification of Germany and Japan in the early twentieth century, the Stalinization of Russia beginning in 1928, and Portugal in 1974. For possibly the best, and certainly the most interesting, study of coups, see Edward Luttwak, *Coup d'État: A Practical Handbook* (Cambridge: Harvard University Press, 1968, 1979). Ash has coined the word *refolution* (also the less catchy word *revorm*) to describe some of the events of Eastern Europe in 1989, implying a mixture of reform and revolution. However, *all* revolutions involve reform, which makes them no less revolutionary. Ash merely highlights the evolutionary and reformist components of revolutions. *Cf.* Jeffery N. Wasserstrom, "Mass Media and Mass Actions in Urban China, 1919-1989" in Jeremy D. Popkin, ed., *Media and Revolution: Comparative Perspectives* (Lexington: University Press of Kentucky, 1995); Jack A. Goldstone, "Theories of Revolution, Elite Crisis, and the Transformation of the USSR", Paper prepared for a conference on *Elite Change and Regime Change*, Santa Maria del Paular, Spain, 8 May 1996, p. 40, fn. 1. For a further discussion of definitions and theories of revolution, see Jack A. Goldstone, "Theories of Revolution: The Third Generation", *World Politics*,

(continued...)

revolutionary ones, which result in regime changes, but which leave the fundamental structures of the state and society intact (*e.g.* Bolivia in 1952, the Dominican Republic in 1961, and both Haiti and the Philippines in February 1986). Similarly, the so-called Revolutions of 1848 that swept across Europe should be seen from this perspective as rebellions, some of which resulted in reforms or regime changes, as these rebellions largely engendered state repression. As Jack Goldstone notes, in none of these cases was there a collapse of the state.[20] Without a collapse of the state, there is clearly an absence of revolution. The events of May 1968 in Paris are analogous to those of 1848; the results were reform and repression, not revolution. On the contrary, the Paris Commune of 1871 is an example of a failed, or rather violently suppressed, revolution. All of the above discussion suggests, among other things, that certain social, political, and demographic dimensions "that so many theorists expect to find in revolutions are not necessarily universal after all.... [H]istory has not always followed the[ir] 'rules of revolution'".[21] As a new type of social phenomenon with new forms, new ways, and new content, therefore, modern revolutions are especially meaningful to analyze and understand.

In (re)constructing history, I also take a shorter view than many in determining a conception of what constitutes "modern". A longer sweep of history could characterize the world capitalist era since at least the fifteenth or sixteenth century as modern, and one could certainly classify as modern the time period from the eighteenth century on, beginning with the American and French Revolutions. However, in the present context, I (subjectively) employ the term "modern" to denote the period from the time of the Second World War, when the Cold War between the U.S. and

---

[19](...continued)
April 1980.

[20] Goldstone, "Theories of Revolution, Elite Crisis, and the Transformation of the USSR", p. 2

[21] Clifton B. Kroeber, "Theory and History of Revolution", *Journal of World History*, Spring 1996, pp. 26, 36. Also see Charles Tilly, *European Revolutions, 1492-1992* (Oxford and Cambridge, MA: Blackwell Publishers, 1993), p. 237.

the Soviet Union began to surface, to the present.[22]

It has been fruitfully argued that a revolutionary situation, however dramatic, "should be conceived of more as process than event",[23] should be read more as discourse than word or schema, and should be viewed more as movie picture than still photograph, both before and after the actual seizure of state power. "There is no such thing as the one dazzling insight that turns people into full-blown revolutionaries", the Ehrenreichs say, speaking of the student uprisings of the 1960s. "[M]any tiny confrontations preceded the mass rebellions... [a]uthoritarian institutions will not just collapse by themselves under the weight of their own contradictions. In confronting them, people make them unbelievable. As they become more unbelievable, they become more vulnerable to every assault".[24] Indeed, Clifton Kroeber posits that the "[p]rocesses involved in radical change are at the core of revolutions", despite their absence from

---

[22] For a discussion revolving around whether the revolutions of Eastern Europe were *post*modern, see Arato, "Interpreting 1989", pp. 624-30. In some ways, a better example of a postmodern revolutionary movement would be the EZLN, or Zapatistas, of Chiapas, Mexico, which erupted onto the world stage on New Year's Day 1994.

[23] Thomas H. Greene, *Comparative Revolutionary Movements: Search for Theory and Justice*, Second Ed. (Englewood Cliffs, N.J.: Prentice-Hall, 1984), p. 15. *Cf.* Goldstone, *Revolution and Rebellion in the Early Modern World*, p. 59, original emphasis: "The essence of historical explanation, even in the natural sciences, is relating events to each other through a *process*". Goldstone employs a "demographic/structural" approach to the study of rebellions and revolutions across Eurasia "in which what matters is the impact of demographic trends on economic, political, and social *institutions*" (p. xxvi, original emphasis). Also see Jack A. Goldstone, "An Analytical Framework" in Goldstone, Gurr, and Moshiri, eds., *Revolutions of the Late Twentieth Century*, esp. p. 37: "Revolution... is a complex process.... the causal trends... often span decades"; and V.I. Lenin, *What Is To Be Done?* [1902], p. 186: "revolution itself must not by any means be regarded as a single act... but as a series of more or less powerful outbreaks rapidly alternating with more or less intense calm". So too with groups and governments, classes and capitalism, praxis and patriarchy, dictatorship and democracy, states and social movements. Yet processes and events are sometimes one and the same, therefore needing a new conceptual amalgam such as event-process.

[24] Barbara and John Ehrenreich, *Long March, Short Spring* (New York and London: Monthly Review Press, 1969), p. 184

the core of many theories of revolution.[25] Yet these processual descriptions, or what Goldstone calls "process-tracing", still ignore a crucial dynamic.[26]

While clearly superior to past explanations which focused almost exclusively on the main event, purely processual interpretations of revolutions produce a similarly serious shortcoming. One can, and indeed must, focus on one aspect at a time for heuristic purposes, yet one should never forget that the essence of any dialectical relationship is reciprocity.[27] Continuous events, "big" and "small", colligate into a process, and a process itself can be an "Event". Furthermore, both events and processes can become cultural icons, which then become used in and for future

---

[25] Kroeber, "Theory and History of Revolution", p. 23. Also see Jaroslav Krejcí, *Great Revolutions Compared* (New York: St. Martin's Press, 1983), p. 17 cited in *Ibid.*: "the revolutionary process can be considered as concluded only when the main issues which caused the revolution have lost their acuteness and other issues have become matters of primary concern". For an interesting twist on this idea, see Franz Kafka, "Reflections on Sin, Pain, Hope, and the True Way" [#6] in *The Basic Kafka* (New York: Pocket Books, 1979), p. 237: "The decisive moment in human development is a continuous one. For this reason the revolutionary movements which declare everything before them to be null and void are in the right, for nothing yet has happened". Incidentally, Kafka was Czech as well as Jewish. Also see Clifford Geertz, "The Judging of Nations" cited in Robert W. Jackman, *Power Without Force: The Political Capacity of Nation-States* (Ann Arbor: University of Michigan Press, 1993), p. 73: "Like prophesies, revolutions restart time". It is partly due to this belief that revolutions can be considered to be the art of the impossible, though, in reality, they are usually an "incoherent amalgam of possible and impossible aspirations to change the world" (Zolberg, "Moments of Madness", p. 192).

[26] Goldstone, "Methodological Issues in Comparative Macrosociology". For the similar concept of "issue history", see Andrew Szasz, *EcoPopulism: Toxic Waste and the Movement for Environmental Justice* (Minneapolis: University of Minnesota Press, 1994) and my "Review", *Journal of Political Ecology*, 1994.

[27] N.B. Jack A. Goldstone, "The Comparative and Historical Study of Revolutions" in Goldstone, ed., *Revolutions*, Second Ed., p. 1: "Revolutions are complex events and originate in long and complicated causal processes." Also see Jack A. Goldstone, "An Analytic Framework" in Goldstone, Gurr, and Moshiri, eds., *Revolutions of the Late Twentieth Century.*

events and processes.[28] In this sense, a revolution is an iconographic event-process; therefore, Goldstone's comparative macrosociological procedure should be expanded to *event-process-tracing*.

Just as physicists have proven that light is both a particle and a wave, social scientists must demonstrate that revolutions (and other complex social phenomena) are simultaneously both an event and a process. The dichotomies typical in western thought, especially those deriving from Aristotelian philosophy, must be deconstructed; light is a particle-wave and a revolution is an event-process. Niels Bohr, the 1922 recipient of the Nobel Prize in Physics, eloquently raises this issue in his "theory of complementarity":

> Even if it is impossible to determine both the velocity and the position of an electron at the same time, nonetheless each (separately) is needed to gain a full picture of the atomic reality—just as both the "particle picture" and the "wave picture" are two complementary portrayals of the same reality, even if they can't be charted at the same time. In other words, despite one's *methods* being limited to either/or, one's *conception* can embrace both, and glimpse the whole.[29]

Revolutions, for heuristic purposes, sometimes can be best viewed analytically as events while at other times as processes.

---

[28] *Cf.* Zolberg, "Moments of Madness", p. 203: "historical events become encoded into culture as patterns of socialization".

[29] Cited in Robin Morgan, *The Anatomy of Freedom, Feminism, Physics, and Global Politics* (Garden City, NY: Anchor Books/Doubleday, 1984). *Cf.* Fritjof Capra, *The Tao of Physics* (New York: Bantam Books, 1975). Capra assesses the similarities between Western science and Eastern philosophy, especially in that they both transcend rigid dichotomous conceptions. Mystical Jews, called Kabalists, among others, have made similar points. Also see Pierre Bourdieu, "Viva la Crise!: For Heterodoxy in Social Science", *Theory and Society*, 1988-89.

Revolutions in actuality, however, are neither precisely because they are both. Therefore, revolutions are not only revolutionary, but are simultaneously evolutionary. In this sense, we can conceive of, pace Heisenberg and Einstein, a *Social* Uncertainty Principle analogous to the one in quantum mechanics. The revolutions we study are simultaneously events and processes; so are the social scientists who study them. Both the observed and the observers are caught up in a dialectical dance in which neither can stop moving long enough to get a highly accurate, let alone an objective, picture. Social reality is elusive because we are inside of it and, indeed, we *are* it. Hence the inherent uncertainty. Indeed, science is essentially about uncertainty and continual exploration and discovery, not certainty, which is the dogmatic realm closer to religion and ideology. As elusive and uncertain as it is, though, whether it is a sub-atomic particle or a super-societal revolution, it is not wholly unknowable. Quite the contrary, there is a great deal that is knowable, even while we must accept incompleteness, inconclusiveness, and indeterminacy.[30]

Interestingly, a revolution, as an event-process, is dialectical on various levels. On one level, there are continuously negotiated discourses, processes, and relationships, for example, amongst the ruling group, amongst the opposition(s), between rulers and citizens, between rhetoric/symbols and their many interpreters, among ideologies, among strategies, amongst the sexes and genders, among age cohorts, among ethnicities, and between the past and the present. On another level, revolutions are dialectical in that, on the one hand, structures both constrain and empower actors, while on the other hand, agency can both reinforce and subvert structures.[31] All of these dialectical phenomena are ubiquitous, continuous, and simultaneous.

One can also say that a "revolution is a way of defining reality

---

[30] Interestingly, the Japanese philosophy of *wabi-sabi* embraces and celebrates "a beauty of things imperfect, impermanent, and incomplete" (Leonard Koren, *Wabi-Sabi: For Artists, Designers, Poets & Philosophers* (Berkeley, CA: Stone Bridge Press, 1994), p. 7).

[31] *Cf.* Little, *Varieties of Social Explanation*, p. 104: "Social structures are enduring regulative systems that define opportunities and constraints that guide, limit, and inspire individual [and collective] action"; Anthony Giddens, *The Constitution of Societies* (Cambridge: Polity Press, 1984).

[and] changing reality",[32] a way for society to re-write its autobiography (or more accurately, a way for certain segments of society to re-write their society's (auto)biography). It can be said that the etiology of the Velvet Revolution in Czechoslovakia, and indeed all revolutions, is of a wide scope and long duration, despite the fact that the revolutionary *moment* itself, *i.e.* the central event, may be relatively fast-paced and short-lived.

With the definition of "modern revolution" in mind, and making neither *specific* predictions nor postdictions, but only engaging in more general "retrodiction",[33] this study primarily will seek to illuminate, analyze, and explain some of the major causes of the genesis and success of the Velvet Revolution in Czechoslovakia, with cross-temporal and cross-national comparative cases, especially that of the 1968 Prague Spring and the 1989 Democracy Movement in China. To these cases, I apply a primarily inductive method which infers causal explanations and interpretations from comparable social phenomena.[34] While it is true that neither historical facts nor their observers are "out there" in any value-

---

[32] C. Wright Mills, *Listen, Yankee: The Revolution in Cuba* (New York: Ballantine Books, 1960), p. 114

[33] *Cf.* Paul Veyne, *Writing History: Essay on Epistemology*, trans. Mina Moore-Rinvolucri (Middletown, CT: Wesleyan University Press, 1984 [1971]), ch. 8, esp pp. 146-47: "we know very well that, whatever effort we make, we can never specify with certainty what definite circumstances would make the lessons valid or invalid.... [we must admit] our inability to prophesy the future and to explain the past. So we always keep a margin of haziness and also of uncertainty: causality is always accompanied by mental reservation". Retrodiction, therefore, allows for *generalized* prediction and postdiction à la seismology, meteorology, and geology. Goldstone, in "The Comparative and Historical Study of Revolutions" (p. 17) and in *Revolution and Rebellion in the Early Modern World* (pp. 35, 148-49, 175), submits the analogy of earthquakes; while in "Analyzing Revolutions and Rebellions" in Keddie, ed., *Debating Revolutions*, pp. 178-79, Goldstone makes the geological case; and Tilly, in *European Revolutions* (pp. 7, 11), adds the study of traffic to this category; while Sharon Welch submits the apt metaphor of jazz: "Think about the logic of jazz. Jazz emerges from the inner play of structure and improvisation, of individuality and collectivity, tradition and innovation.... The final element of good jazz: when all of this comes together, it swings" (Sharon Welch, "Populism and the 1996 Elections", *Tikkun*, September/October 1996, pp. 35-36).

[34] Burawoy, "Two Methods in Search of Science"

neutral position, social scientists should not—and indeed cannot—abandon either those "facts" that they "discover" or their observation points from which they are able to glimpse their subjects via their physical, social, cultural, psychological, ideological, and other lenses. Even in our highly imperfect and extremely complex world, we should continue to strive for explanatory perfection (as an unobtainable goal); yet never be disillusioned when we fail to attain that perfection.

Choosing to analyze the case(s) of Czechoslovakia within the category of modern revolutions, even with definitional clarity, still does not resolve all of the methodological (and therefore theoretical) issues. Some sort of framework for an approach to this topic needs to be constructed. I prefer to work in that ambiguous terrain between single-shot historical case studies and wide-ranging comparative sociology. "Sociological analyses of revolutions tend to emphasize the primacy of some single cause of revolutions, systematically subordinating other causes to the chosen explanatory factor", William Sewell, Jr. argues, and "historical analyses typically attempt to recount the course of a revolution in some semblance of its original complexity... [thereby allowing] crucial causal processes... to get lost in a muddle of narrative detail".[35] Each of these methods alone—the sociological or the historical—is too simplistic for comparing complex cases over time. That ambiguous terrain where history and sociology meet appears to be comparative historical sociology.[36] Indeed, as Goldstone rightfully suggests, "good comparative

---

[35] William H. Sewell, Jr., "Three Temporalities: Toward an Eventful Sociology" in Terrence J. McDonald, ed., *The Historic Turn in the Human Sciences* (Ann Arbor: University of Michigan Press, 1996). *Cf.* David Collier, "The Comparative Method" in Ada W. Finifter, ed., *Political Science: The State of the Discipline II* (Washington, D.C.: American Political Science Association, 1993).

[36] In general, "comparative researchers are more explicitly concerned with causation and causal complexity than are most [other] researchers" (Charles C. Ragin, *Constructing Social Research: The Unity and Diversity of Method* (Thousand Oaks, CA: Pine Forge Press [Sage], 1994), p. 112). *Cf.* Dunn, *Modern Revolutions*, p. xiii: "in the study of politics, history and sociology are activities which are rendered absurd by being separated".

history illuminates *both* similarities and differences".[37] This book on modern revolution attempts to do no less.

Of course, "There are no infallible research approaches!", as Skocpol declares, but the comparative historical "approach is better than the alternatives" for the study of revolutions.[38] Skocpol claims that "Whatever the source(s) of theoretical inspiration, comparative histor[ical sociology] succeeds only if it convincingly fulfills th[e] goal [of "the actual illumination of causal regularities across sets of historical cases"]. And when it *is* successfully employed, comparative historical [sociological] analysis is an ideal strategy for mediating between theory and history".[39] Moreover, Ragin asserts that "qualitative comparison allows examination of constellations, configurations, and conjunctures. It is especially well suited for addressing questions about outcomes resulting from multiple and conjunctural causes—where different conditions combine in different and sometimes contradictory ways to produce the same or similar outcomes".[40] Skocpol also states that "Comparative historical analysis is distinctively appropriate for developing explanations of macro-historical phenomena of which there are inherently only a few cases.... Comparative historical analysis is, in fact, the mode of multivariate analysis to which one resorts when there are too many

---

[37] Goldstone, "Analyzing Revolutions and Rebellions", in Keddie, ed., *Debating Revolutions*, p. 179

[38] Skocpol, "Reflections on Recent Scholarship about Social Revolutions and How to Study Them" in Skocpol, ed., *Social Revolutions in the Modern World*, p. 321

[39] Skocpol, *States and Social Revolutions*, pp. 39-40. *Cf.* Theda Skocpol, "Emerging Agendas and Recurrent Strategies in Historical Sociology" in Theda Skocpol, ed., *Vision and Method in Historical Sociology* (Cambridge: Cambridge University Press, 1984), p. 4: "historical sociology is... a continuing ever-renewed tradition of research devoted to understanding the nature and effects of large-scale structures and fundamental processes of change".

[40] Charles C. Ragin, *The Comparative Method: Moving Beyond Qualitative and Quantitative Strategies* (Berkeley and Los Angeles: University of California Press, 1987), p. x

variables and not enough cases".[41] But as with all strategies, even so-called "ideal" ones, there is dissent. Sewell argues, for example, that because cases are invariably neither independent nor equivalent, comparative historical sociological analysis is futile, as mutual influences always exist. This appears to be true in Czechoslovakia, and in the rest of Eastern Europe and China. It is likely also to be true in *all* comparative analyses in the social world. To some extent, of course, all social phenomena are unique. James Scott, for example, goes so far as to say that, in some ways, each individual, family, village, city, and region, let alone country, may have its own unique revolution.[42] Yet as social scientists, we search for patterns amongst the complexity and seeming chaos of the social world.

As Goldstone persuasively argues, "the causes of revolutions are numerous, and no two revolutions are exactly alike; yet certain patterns of events and causal relationships do consistently recur".[43] In order to ascertain these "patterns of events and causal relationships" when there are relatively many variables and relatively few cases, the comparative historical method is most appropriate. The pragmatic compromise appears to be in using heuristic devices, while jettisoning philosophical purity, and admitting all relevant biases. Causes need to be separated analytically to show how they connect all the more. To do otherwise, as Wickham-Crowley suggests, "is to exit from all social-science theorizing".[44] Sewell and Scott may be correct philosophically, but Skocpol and Wickham-

---

[41] Skocpol, *States and Social Revolutions*, p. 36. *Cf.* Skocpol, "Emerging Agendas and Recurrent Strategies in Historical Sociology" in Skocpol, ed., *Vision and Method in Historical Sociology*

[42] James C. Scott, "Foreword" in Gilbert M. Joseph and Daniel Nugent, eds., *Everyday Forms of State Formation: Revolution and the Negotiation of Rule in Modern Mexico* (Durham and London: Duke University Press, 1994), p. viii. Also see the discussion in Andrew E. Newman, "Escape from Flatland: Is Comparative-Historical Research Acontextual?", *Comparative & Historical Sociology*, Winter 1995, pp. 1, 3, 5.

[43] Jack A. Goldstone, "Revolution, Theories of" in David Miller, ed., *The Blackwell Encyclopaedia of Political Thought* (Oxford and New York: Basil Blackwell, 1987), p. 437. *Cf.* Eckstein, "On the Etiology of Internal Wars"

[44] Timothy Wickham-Crowley, "Structural Theories of Revolution", unpublished manuscript

Crowley are more useful sociologically.[45] As always in social science, and much else, there has to be a balance between depth and breadth.

A purely quantitative study might conduct a superficial survey of many cases, whereas a purely qualitative study might carry out an in-depth investigation of only one (unique) case. Both of these methodologies have their advantages and their disadvantages. The tactic chosen here, closer to the qualitative approach, is the comparative method applied to two major cases (*i.e.* Czechoslovakia and China) with allusions to various other cases (*e.g.* other countries in Eastern Europe and some of these countries at different time periods). The historical component of this method is another form of comparison as, in many ways, "the past is another country", with its "memories" and "mis-memories" which are consequently "shaping and misshaping" the "myths" of the past, present, and future.[46] Indeed, "The making of cross-cultural, cross-temporal assumptions is enough to send every well-trained Western academic into catatonia, but there is no avoiding it".[47] For better or worse, making comparisons, along with engaging in historical analysis, are the essence of social science, and indeed, humanity.

It is true that social scientists and others were almost universally unable to specifically predict the revolutions of 1989 (just as they were unable to predict the Soviet domination of Eastern Europe and the Soviet Union's subsequent invasions of Hungary in 1956 and Czechoslovakia in 1968, in addition to most other major historical events of this century).[48]

---

[45] *Cf.* the symposium of Charles Tilly, "Macrosociology, Past and Future", Mustafa Emirbayer, "Symbols, Positions, and Objects: Toward a New Relational Strategy of Historical Analysis", and Jeff Goodwin, "A Case for Big Case Comparison" in *Comparative & Historical Sociology*, Fall/Winter 1995.

[46] Tony Judt, "The Past is Another Country: Myth and Memory in Postwar Europe", *Daedalus*, Fall 1992

[47] Michael Dorris, "Indians on the Shelf" in Calvin Martin, ed., *The American Indian and the Problem of History* (New York and Oxford: Oxford University Press, 1987), p. 104

[48] *Cf.* Paul Hollander, "The Mystery of the Transformation of Communist Systems" in Louis Kriesberg and David R. Segal, eds., *Research in Social Movements, Conflicts and Change*, Vol. 14: The Transformation of European (continued...)

[48](...continued)
Communist Societies (Greenwich, CT and London: JAI Press, 1992), esp. pp. 13-15; Randall Collins and David Waller, "What Theories Predicted the State Breakdowns and Revolutions of the Soviet Bloc?" in *Ibid.*, esp. p. 44: "Most social science perspectives on the Soviet bloc missed seeing in advance that there was any possibility, let alone a likelihood, of the collapse of Soviet power". Also see, *e.g.*, Samuel P. Huntington, *Political Science Quarterly*, Summer 1984: "the likelihood of democratic development in Eastern Europe is virtually nil". Even Lenin and Havel were pessimistic about the chances of revolution within a year of them becoming leaders. Some pre-revolutionary leaders were doubtful of revolution as well. On 14 July 1789, the day the Bastille was stormed, King Louis XVI entered one word in his diary: "Nothing". That same year he also quipped that "The French people are incapable of regicide". The Shah of Iran, Mohammed Reza Pahlavi, was equally wrong when he declared in 1978 that "Nobody can overthrow me. I have the support of 700,000 troops, all the workers, and most of the people. I have the power". He was overthrown the following year. The Russian Revolution was similarly unanticipated (except perhaps by Trotsky). Based on this, Kuran argues that surprise is integral to revolution, and that we will likely be surprised repeatedly, citing that 76 percent of East Germans admitted in early 1990 to having been completely surprised by the revolution (and one would guess that this is probably an underestimate); only 5 percent of those surveyed claimed they saw it coming so soon (which is probably an overestimate) (Timur Kuran, "Now Out of Never: The Element of Surprise in the East European Revolution of 1989", *World Politics*, October 1991. *Cf.* Timur Kuran, "Sparks and Prairie Fires: A Theory of Unanticipated Political Revolution", *Public Choice*, April 1989 and Timur Kuran, "The East European Revolution of 1989: Is It Surprising That We Were Surprised?", *American Economic Review*, May 1991; also see Nikki R. Keddie, "Can Revolutions Be Predicted; Can Their Causes Be Understood?", *Contention*, Winter 1992; and Baruch Fischhoff and Ruth Beyth, "'I Knew It Would Happen': Remembered Probabilities of Once-Future Things", *Organizational Behavior and Human Performance*, February 1975). But see Jack A. Goldstone, "Predicting Revolutions: Why We Could (and Should) Have Foreseen the Revolutions of 1989-1991 in the USSR and Eastern Europe", *Contention*, Winter 1993, esp. pp. 127-29; and Goldstone, "Theories of Revolution, Elite Crisis, and the Transformation of the USSR", pp. 3-4: "States can present strong facades, buoyed up only by history and habit, long after their real foundations have rotted.... the essential surprise... was not that people in Eastern Europe rose up, but that the Soviet regime thoroughly broke down." Also see some of the above articles with responses and replies by Keddie and Goldstone, as well as others essays, in Keddie, ed., *Debating Revolutions*.

Although Dahrendorf jokes that "At least no one will ever say that the (continued...)

Ivo Banac passively remarks that the Eastern European revolutions' "timing was resistant to prediction".[49] Other scholars pessimistically declare that "Searching for the causes of democracy [in Eastern Europe] from probabilistic associations with economic, social, cultural, psychological or international factors has not so far yielded any general law of democratization, nor is it likely to do so in the near future, despite the recent proliferation of cases".[50] Indeed, "Social science", Adam Przeworski concedes, "is not very good at sorting out underlying causes and precipitating conditions".[51] This may be due to the social analog of

---

[48](...continued)
revolution in Europe was a CIA conspiracy", conspiracy theorists have in fact claimed that, in East Germany, the *stasi* itself fomented the revolution through its vast network of "informal collaborators" (Ralf Dahrendorf, *Reflections on the Revolution in Europe* (New York: Times Books, 1990), p. 153). Some scholars did make some vague predictions regarding change in Russia and Eastern Europe, while other scholars have retrospectively claimed to have made accurate predictions. I remain highly skeptical of most of these claims. The Oracle of Delphi, too, was famous for being correct so often precisely because it hedged its predictions so well with ambiguous statements that easily could be interpreted in various ways to suit various possibilities and outcomes. Also see Thomas M. Franck and Edward Weisband, *Word Politics: Verbal Strategy Among the Superpowers* (New York: Oxford University Press, 1972), p. 11: "Once an event has occurred, it is almost impossible to remember that it had once been virtually unthinkable."; and John Feffer, *Shock Waves: Eastern Europe After the Revolutions* (Boston, MA: South End Press, 1992), p. 1: "In retrospect, historical outcomes always seem inevitable".

[49] Ivo Banac, ed., *Eastern Europe in Revolution* (Ithaca, NY and London: Cornell University Press, 1992), p. ix

[50] Terry Lynn Karl and Philippe C. Schmitter, "Modes of Transition in Latin America, Southern and Eastern Europe", *International Social Science Journal*, May 1991, p. 270

[51] Adam Przeworski, *Democracy and the Market: Political and Economic Reforms in Eastern Europe and Latin America* (Cambridge: Cambridge University Press, 1991), p. 1. *Cf.* Little, *Varieties of Social Explanation*, p. 197, original emphasis: "In the social sciences... we often do *not* find the strong types of regularities and laws that would make us confident in the causal connectedness of social phenomena. Instead, we find laws of tendency and exception-laden
(continued...)

Chaos Theory, which, for the natural world, states in part that even very small changes in the beginning of a causal sequence can result in extremely different and dramatic effects. In a social system, moreover, these effects potentially may be even more pronounced.

Timur Kuran makes the best case for why we *should* have been surprised.[52] He argues that most people were "united in amazement" regarding the events of 1989 due to the epistemological phenomenon of "preference falsification". This approach implies that even while *private* political preferences are shifting towards oppositional and potentially revolutionary politics, *public* opposition may remain relatively constant. This may be true in all societies, but it is especially salient in authoritarian ones where dissenting opinions and oppositional activity are harshly repressed. Given such a psycho-cultural situation, Kuran asserts that a "latent bandwagon" effect is established whereby, following the Social Uncertainty Principle, any of various decisions or events can act as a catalyst to precipitate a dramatic increase in public oppositional activity as "long-repressed grievances burst to the surface". In the case of Eastern Europe in 1989, Kuran maintains that there were millions of people prepared to oppose Communist Party rule whenever it was safe to do so. Several events made it safer to do so, but Kuran cites only a few: Gorbachev's reforms in the Soviet Union and then his statements of political and especially military non-interference in the affairs of other countries; and the decision of some East German officials to cancel Erich Honecker's order to fire on the peaceful demonstrators in Leipzig. Due to these and other events, including the rhetoric and actions of dissidents and government leaders, "fear changed sides: where people had been afraid to oppose the regime, they came to fear being caught defending it". These were, of course, contingent events. Kuran therefore suggests that we will likely be repeatedly surprised by revolutions based on "inescapable

---

[51](...continued)
regularities". On a much more cynical note, see Kenneth Hoover and Todd Donovan, *The Elements of Social Scientific Thinking*, Sixth ed. (New York: St. Martin's Press, 1995), esp. p. 25: "Science is a slightly elevated form of muddling".

[52] Kuran, "The East European Revolution of 1989: Is It Surprising that We Were Surprised?", pp. 121-25. *Cf.* Timothy Garton Ash, "Czechoslovakia Under Ice" [February 1984] in Timothy Garton Ash, *The Uses of Adversity* (New York: Random House, 1983-89), p. 70

unpredictability". He offers consolation, however, in the epistemological belief that "establishing the limits of knowledge is itself a contribution to the pool of useful knowledge".

However, there is also dissent to the dissent! Barrington Moore, Jr.'s *Social Origins of Dictatorship and Democracy*, Dietrich Rueschemeyer, Evelyne Stephens, and John Stephens' *Capitalist Development & Democracy*, and Timothy Wickham-Crowley's *Guerrillas & Revolution in Latin America* (employing Ragin's method of Boolean algebra[53]) are all fine examples and strong evidence that work in this area can be fruitfully accomplished. All three of these exemplary books sort out "underlying causes" of revolution and democracy. As Skocpol reminds us, besides Marx, Weber, and Durkheim, many other social scientists have produced outstanding studies employing the comparative historical method, including Marc Bloch, Karl Polanyi, S.N. Eisenstadt, Reinhard Bendix, Perry Anderson, E.P. Thompson, Charles Tilly, Immanuel Wallerstein, Barrington Moore, Daniel Chirot, and Lynn Hunt, to name a few.[54]

As with many "answers" in the social sciences, though, this one also leads to new questions. The most pressing of these is, "what is a *cause*?". A cause, in the sense of this study, is technically a sub-cause; all of the factors may have been collectively necessary and none of the causes is individually sufficient (as is always the case). The (sub)causes must be interactive and synergistic or they do not become causes at all. This perspective, first articulated by Aristotle over 2,300 years ago, has been characterized as "causal pluralism" (by Max Weber), as "configurations of conditions" (by Theda Skocpol), as "revolutionary conjuncture" or as a "conjunctural model" (by Jack Goldstone), as "multiple conjunctural causation" (by Charles Ragin), or as a "simultaneity" of factors by others; I prefer to employ the phrase *causal convergence*. The term causal

---

[53] Ragin, *The Comparative Method: Moving Beyond Qualitative and Quantitative Strategies*, ch. 6-8. Also see Ragin, *Constructing Social Research*, ch. 5.

[54] Skocpol, ed., *Vision and Method in Historical Sociology*. Needless to say, many others have also done so, including Fernand Braudel, Brian Downing, Cynthia Enloe, Peter Evans, Michel Foucault, Jack Goldstone, Samuel Huntington, Michael Mann, Tim McDaniel, Philip McMichael, Joel Migdal, Sheila Rowbotham, William Sewell, Barbara Tuchman, John Walton, Timothy Wickham-Crowley, and of course Theda Skocpol herself.

convergence is particularly useful for our cases of modern revolution as it clearly implies that the reasons for and causes of revolution are necessarily multiple and synergistic.

In interpreting the causes of revolution and their convergence, one cannot simply analyze either agents or structures alone. To do so is naive; all social phenomena involve both agents and structures with the mediating links of culture (*e.g.* myths and memories, ideologies and religious beliefs, language(s) and the arts, signs and symbols, rituals and traditions, national heroes and anniversaries, *etc.*). This is the necessary dialectical interplay of micro and macro social forces inherent in all complex processual phenomena. Marx states, for example, that people "make their own history, but they do not make it just as they please; they do not make it under circumstances chosen by themselves, but under circumstances directly found, given and transmitted from the past".[55] More specifically, Wickham-Crowley adds that "Powerful revolutionary movements [do] indeed 'make' revolutions... but only because they faced regimes that exhibited structural weaknesses in the face of an increasingly national opposition".[56] Skocpol's "structural analysis" appears largely to neglect the other part of this crucial dialectic, namely agency and culture.

Culture, admittedly, is like air; it is real, it is necessary and life-sustaining, it is in and around us, and yet it is also amorphous, intangible, and highly elusive. Culture is "beyond us, yet ourselves".[57] Therefore, "Each researcher who writes about culture employs it differently"; yet

---

[55] Karl Marx, "The Eighteenth Brumaire of Louis Bonaparte" [1852] in Tucker, ed., *The Marx-Engels Reader*, p. 595. *Cf.* Kathy McAfee, "Environment", *In Brief* [Oxfam America], 1992, p. 1: "Individuals can make a difference—but only if a climate for change supports their efforts".

[56] Timothy P. Wickham-Crowley, *Guerrillas & Revolution in Latin America: A Comparative Study of Insurgents and Regimes Since 1956* (Princeton, NJ: Princeton University Press, 1992), p. 7

[57] Wallace Stevens, "The Man with the Blue Guitar" cited in Wendy Griswold, *Cultures and Societies in a Changing World* (Thousand Oaks, CA: Pine Forge Press, 1994), p. 18

paradoxically, "This might be one of its advantages".[58] Perhaps this should not be surprising, for culture itself is paradoxical; and it is paradoxical (and playful) largely because it is multifarious, eclectic, and heterogeneous. Tilly contends that "'Social change' is not a general process, but a catchall name for very different processes varying greatly in their connection to each other".[59] The same could be said for culture. Cultural processes, in their manifold forms, almost invariably get theoretically conflated and conceptually equalized, when in fact they are separate phenomena, having different effects across time and space. Unfortunately, structuralists, rational choice practitioners, resource mobilization and political process theorists, and others do not partake of the potential advantages of culture in whatever forms or functions in which it manifests and mediates. These theorists, inadvertently (for the most part), tend to demographically norm their abstract social actors. Who are these people that make the revolutions they study?

Culture, in this schema, is a standing condition, or as Clifford Geertz puts it, "culture is not a power... it is a context", or setting.[60] In the view of Granovetter, "culture is not a once-for-all influence but an ongoing process, continually constructed and reconstructed during interaction. It not only shapes its members but also is shaped by them, in part for their own strategic reasons".[61] This is the ongoing and ubiquitous dialectic of culture and action.

---

[58] Eileen M. Otis, "Gender and the Politics of Chinese Nationalism", unpublished manuscript. For debates over the (mis)uses of the culture concept, see Robert Brightman, "Forget Culture: Replacement, Transcendence, Relexification", *Cultural Anthropology*, November 1995.

[59] Charles Tilly, *Big Structures Large Processes Huge Comparisons* (New York: Russell Sage Foundation, 1984), p. 12. This constitutes the third of "eight Pernicious Postulates of twentieth-century social thought" (p. 11; also see pp. 33-40).

[60] Clifford Geertz, *The Interpretation of Cultures* (New York: Basic Books, 1993 [1973]), p. 14. *Cf.* Bourdieu, "Viva la Crise!: For Heterodoxy in Social Science"

[61] Granovetter, "Economic Action and Social Structure", p. 486. *Cf.* Richard G. Fox, *Lions of the Punjab: Culture in the Making* (Berkeley and Los Angeles: University of California Press, 1985), p. 13: "Culture always 'is', but it has always just become so".

Culture is simply, as Daniel Chirot notes, "the store of knowledge any society possesses".[62] Yet culture is not monolithic nor homogenous. There is not one Culture in a given society, just as there is neither one History, one Truth, nor one National Interest.[63] Culture is never total or totalizing. Culture is, in actuality, a myriad of variegated and polychromatic cultures, and none of these cultures or subcultures is an all-encompassing web that totally ensnares its members. Especially during times of change and crisis, though in eras of "normalcy" as well, culture is as contradictory as it is coherent and as disposable as it is durable. There is always a sizeable range of choice amongst all of the "given" cultural possibilities for people to strategically or inadvertently choose from.

Culture is subjective and selective, as are those who employ it, whether knowingly or not. It is in this way that political entrepreneurs package pieces of culture, both inherited and invented, and market them to the public. Culture is inherently social and collective, not individual; yet individuals can and do peddle their wares in attempts to get their sub-cultural (and sometimes counter-cultural) perspectives into the mainstream of cultural discourse and social action. "This kind of self-conscious production, marketing, and distribution system", Wendy Griswold maintains, "applies to ideas as much as it does to tangible cultural objects".[64]

"Culture influences action", according to Ann Swidler, "not by providing the ultimate values toward which action is oriented, but by shaping a repertoire or 'tool kit' of habits, skills, and styles from which

---

[62] Daniel Chirot, *How Societies Change* (Thousand Oaks, CA: Pine Forge Press, 1994), p. 4

[63] *Cf.* Goldstone, "Methodological Issues in Comparative Macrosociology". Also see Arato, "Interpreting 1989", p. 628: There are a "variety of available traditions in each national history, all of which are open to interpretation".

[64] Griswold, *Cultures and Societies in a Changing World*, p. 70. Following Bourdieu, Griswold also argues that "Like economic capital, cultural capital can be accumulated and invested; moreover, it can be converted into economic capital" (*Ibid.*, p. 82).

people construct 'strategies of action'".[65] Extending Chirot's metaphor of the store of knowledge, we can imagine a gigantic, multi-level cultural supermarket in which members of society can and do select objects, icons, images, ideas, characters, signs, symbols, people, beliefs, jokes, folk tales, words, songs, slogans, proverbs, clichés, languages, rituals, traditions, past events, myths, and memories for their baskets to take and use as they please. These cultural items then can become the "weapons of criticism" which are employed in the struggle for social change. Certain cultural items will, of course, be more popular and resonant with their fellow shoppers; some sub-cultures are stronger than others, just as some cultures are stronger than others.[66] It is precisely in this way that the metaphor of social change as velvet enters the Czech theatre of operations.

If, as Walton (and others, including Sewell) suggests, "history

---

[65] Ann Swidler, "Culture in Action: Symbols and Strategies", *American Sociological Review*, April 1986, p. 273. *Cf.* E.F. Schumacher, *Small Is Beautiful: A Study of Economics as if People Mattered* (London: Abacus, 1973), p. 70: "What matters is the tool-box of ideas with which, by which, through which, we experience and interpret the world"; Griswold, *Cultures and Societies in a Changing World*, p. 21: "culture provides orientation... and directs behavior toward certain lines of action and away from others". George Konrad refers to a "democratic tool-box" and its use by dissident East Europeans. Also see Max Weber, "The Social Psychology of the World Religions" in H.H. Gerth and C. Wright Mills, eds., *From Max Weber: Essays in Sociology* (New York: Oxford University Press, 1946), p. 280: "Not ideas, but material and ideal interests, directly govern [people's] conduct. Yet very frequently the 'world images' that have been created by 'ideas' have, like switch[es], determined the tracks along which action has been pushed by the dynamic of interest"; Peter L. Berger and Thomas Luckmann, *The Social Construction of Reality* (New York: Anchor Books, 1966); for the notion of *habitus*, Pierre Bourdieu, *The Logic of Practice* (Stanford, CA: Stanford University Press, 1990); Roger Friedland and Robert Alford, "Bringing Society Back In: Symbols, Practices, and Institutional Contradictions" in Walter W. Powell and Paul J. DiMaggio, eds., *The New Institutionalism in Organizational Analysis* (Chicago: University of Chicago Press, 1991). It is also worth noting that Harrison White has commented that "culture is intensely saturated with emotion", while Kathleen M. Carley postulates that "culture and structure co-evolve".

[66] *Cf.* Chirot, *How Societies Change*

made at one time becomes one of the conditions of action at another",[67] conditions of action made culturally relevant through the social transformer of ideology, then we can apply this "path determinacy" framework to Czechoslovakia. History may not repeat itself, as Trotsky suggests, though it often does channel subsequent events into repetitively similar pathways and cycles.

Czechoslovakia was granted a velvet independence in 1918, had a velvet Communist Party *coup* in 1948, launched a top-down velvet socio-political restructuring in 1968, formed a velvet opposition in 1977, experienced a velvet general strike and a velvet revolution in 1989, went through a velvet election and a further velvet transfer of power in 1990, initiated a velvet foreign policy when it prohibited the export of arms and a velvet domestic policy when it abolished the death penalty that same year, and even had a velvet divorce in 1993 when the federation split into

---

[67] John Walton, *Western Times and Water Wars: State, Culture, and Rebellion in California* (Berkeley and Los Angeles: University of California Press, 1992), p. 10. *Cf.* Robert Park, "The City: Suggestions for the Investigation of Human Behavior in the Urban Environment", *American Journal of Sociology*, 1916: "the past imposes itself upon the present"; Debray, *Revolution in the Revolution?*, p. 19: "We see the past superimposed on the present, even when the present is a revolution"; Sewell, "Three Temporalities" in McDonald, ed., *The Historic Turn in the Human Sciences*; Skocpol, *States and Social Revolutions*, pp. 23-24; Walter LaFeber, *Inevitable Revolutions* (New York and London: W.W. Norton, 1983, 1984), pp. 284-93; Jerzy Jedlicki, "The Revolution of 1989: The Unbearable Burden of History", *Problems of Communism*, July-August 1990; and Robert D. Kaplan, "3 Views of the Atrocities of Bosnia—And Our Role", *San Francisco Examiner*, 8 March 1995, p. C-5: "while the past certainly *helps* determine the future, rather than be fatalistic we should see the past as a challenge, not as a foregone conclusion". For much stronger versions of "path determinacy", what is often referred to as "path dependency", see Michael Harrington, *Taking Sides* (New York: Holt, Rinehart and Winston, 1985): "We never discard the past, no matter how radically we break from it"; and especially Walter Mead, "In the Shadow of History", *Worth*, September 1994, p. 52: "The lesson of Eastern Europe is sad but important: The future is rooted in the past. No economic reforms and no paper constitutions can cancel out the effects of centuries of conflict, culture, and tradition". But see Maya Angelou, "On the Pulse of the Morning", Poem read at the U.S. Presidential Inauguration, 20 January 1993: "History, despite its wrenching pain,/ Cannot be unlived, but if faced/ With courage, need not be lived again".

the Czech Republic and Slovakia.[68] Moreover, inasmuch as "political life and political culture during the communist period continued to be determined to some degree by Czechoslovakia's pre-communist history, culture, and level of economic development.... The legacy of communist rule is also reflected in many of the political issues that face the current government".[69]

It is no doubt true to some extent, as Ronald Inglehart argues, that choosing which factor is of primary importance in determining a particular outcome is to pose a false alternative.[70] It is perhaps valid, albeit unknown, that *all* of the factors were necessary and therefore each was of "primary" importance. At the very least, *none* of the factors was individually sufficient (as is always the case). "We do not have", as has been noted, "a parsimonious explanation for 1989".[71]

In any case, I believe that it is still possible heuristically to isolate and to discuss what appear to be the several *major* factors which cumulatively contribute to the realization of revolutionary ideas, action,

---

[68] *Cf.* Carol Skalnik Leff, "Could This Marriage Be Saved?: The Czechoslovak Divorce", *Current History*, March 1996, p. 130: On 25 November 1992, the Federal Assembly approved the dissolution of the Czechoslovak federation "without a military battle, without a referendum, without a clear secession, and without even a widespread independence movement in either republic".

[69] Wolchik, *Czechoslovakia in Transition*, p. 60. *Cf.* Karl Marx, "The Possibility of Non-Violent Revolution" [8 September 1872] in Tucker, ed., *The Marx-Engels Reader*, p. 523: "[W]e have not asserted that the ways to achieve that goal [of revolution] are everywhere the same. You know that the institutions, mores, and traditions of various countries must be taken into consideration, and we do not deny that there are countries... where the [people] can attain their goal by peaceful means."

[70] Ronald Inglehart, *Culture Shift in Advanced Industrial Society* (Princeton, NJ: Princeton University Press, 1990), pp. 3-14. Inglehart focuses on post-materialist values and generational replacement. Post-materialist values, which tend to arise in younger cohorts with a level of material security, include such issues as greater freedom and participation, peace, health and safety, the environment, leisure, *etc.*

[71] Daniel N. Nelson and Samuel Bentley, "The Comparative Politics of Eastern Europe", *PS: Political Science & Politics*, March 1994, p. 49

and success. Some of the major factors that interactively contributed to the Velvet Revolution were distinctive to Czechoslovakia, while others were common to the Communist Party countries of Eastern Europe and China in 1989. In this book, there is an attempt to unravel the historical narratives and to place the causal factors in rough chronological order, even though, of course, they inherently intersect, intertwine, and interact with each other.[72] By analytically separating the causal factors of revolution from each other, one can more clearly assess and comprehend the causal convergence that may lead to modern revolution.

Before doing so, however, it is necessary to very briefly review the standard accounts of the Eastern European revolutions of 1989. In short, these popular and conventional views generally posit some vague "causes" of revolution that are powerful only in the sense that they are simple and partially correct. Just as President Eisenhower employed the metaphor of dominoes to represent his fear of Communist Party takeovers in Southeast Asia, both policy makers and policy analysts now (unimaginatively) use the same metaphor to "explain" the ouster of the Communist Party from power in the countries of Eastern Europe.

In this vein, it has been said, more journalistically than social scientifically, that the Eastern European revolutions were the result of a so-called "domino effect" of subjugated countries full of repressed citizens seeking "freedom", which were initially tipped by the then recently less dogmatic Kremlin. The loosening grip of the Kremlin, due to Mikhail Gorbachev's programs of *Perestroika* (Restructuring) and *Glasnost* (Openness), in addition to his policies of democratization and "new thinking" in foreign policy, tipped the first domino of Poland (with waves of strikes leading to negotiated discussions and elections), which knocked down the domino of Hungary (first opening its border with Austria and then with the reburial and rehabilitation of Imre Nagy and the commemoration and legitimation of the 1956 Uprising, again leading to negotiations and elections), then East Germany (with the availability of the "exit" option and the seductiveness and support of West Germany), then Bulgaria (with its environmentally-led dissident movement, Eco-Glasnost), then Czechoslovakia (with the charismatic leadership of Havel), and finally Romania (with the pent up anger at the Ceausescu family). China, which did not experience a revolution in 1989, is of course completely omitted or left largely unexplained.

---

[72] Goldstone, "Methodological Issues in Comparative Macrosociology"

Przeworski, for example, puts all of his causal eggs into one theoretical basket regarding this issue. He states: "What happened in Romania was caused by what had occurred in Czechoslovakia, what ensued in Czechoslovakia resulted from the breakdown in East Germany, what stimulated masses of people to fill the streets in East Germany followed the political changes in Hungary, what showed Hungarians a way out was the success of the negotiations in Poland"; and "The entire event was one single snowball [and] once hundreds of thousands of people had flooded the streets of Leipzig, Dresden, and Berlin, once the wall had fallen, the pressure on Czechoslovakia was irresistible".[73] This domino theory analysis, though seductive, seems rather facile. The Prague Spring, for example, was neither the consequence of a Berlin Spring nor the cause of a Warsaw Spring. Causes need to be analytically explained, not simply assumed and asserted. The conventional view is misleading not because it is wrong, but precisely because it is simple and contains an element of truth, but just an element; it is grossly incomplete. Unfortunately, and all too often, both the conventional wisdom and the academic theories regarding revolution assume continuity, linearity, and inevitability.[74] Teleological assumptions are easy, but generally incorrect; "chaotic" hypotheses are more complex and difficult, but are often empirically more accurate.

It is absolutely crucial to remember that individual dissidents, opposition organizations, the governments, and the militaries of all these countries each made *choices* (that perhaps could have been different), albeit based on the pressures (both constraining and empowering) of their respective histories, cultures, and organizations, in addition to the then-present social, cultural, political, and economic possibilities and opportunities. Again, it is the comparative historical method that can best assess these actors, their choices, and the opportunities available to them

---

[73] Adam Przeworski, "The 'East' Becomes the 'South'?: The 'Autumn of the People' and the Future of Eastern Europe", *PS: Political Science & Politics*, March 1991, p.21. Przeworski claims that "Henry Kissinger's 'domino theory' triumphed; all he missed was the direction in which the dominoes would fall" (*Ibid.*); Przeworski, *Democracy and the Market*, pp. 3, 4-5

[74] *Cf.* Maureen Hallinan, "The Sociological Study of Social Change", Presidential Address to the 91st Annual Meetings of the American Sociological Association conference on *Social Change: Opportunities & Constraints*, New York, New York, 17 August 1996

within the social, cultural, political, and economic contexts over the time and space in which they operated. "Along with temporal processes and contexts", according to Skocpol,

> social and cultural differences are intrinsically of interest to historically oriented sociologists. For them, the world's past is not seen as a unified developmental story or as a set of standardized sequences. Instead, it is understood that groups or organizations have chosen, or stumbled into, varying paths in the past. Earlier "choices", in turn, both limit and open up alternative possibilities for further change, leading toward no predetermined end.[75]

Skocpol's points are no less true with regard to modern revolution and rebellion in Czechoslovakia and China, respectively. Social change in Czechoslovakia and China, both because of and in spite of cultural continuity, was and is still not inevitable, but neither were and are the event-processes in these countries random occurrences.

---

[75] Theda Skocpol, "Sociology's Historical Imagination" in Skocpol, ed., *Vision and Method in Historical Sociology*, pp. 1-2

Chapter III.

Histories of Democracy

"The self-confidence of the human being, freedom, has first of all to be aroused again in the hearts of these people.... Only this feeling can again transform society into a community of human beings united for the highest aims, into a democratic state"
— Karl Marx[1]

One standing factor, or what Robert Merton calls a "latent" aspect, in the revolutionary causal convergence that is important to Czechoslovakia is that its citizens have "the memory of a stable

---

[1] Karl Marx, Letter to Arnold Ruge, 1843 cited in Colin Barker, "'The Mass Strike' and 'The Cycle of Protest'", unpublished manuscript

democratic past".[2] Such a memory—even a living memory—does not of course cause revolution. However, it does give dissidents and revolutionaries a powerful, and potentially unifying, symbolic and collective political tradition to draw upon, and it additionally may give support to the success of a post-revolutionary democratic government and a strong civil society, while enhancing their socio-political stability. The experiences of the Czech Republic and Slovakia (now called the Slovak Republic) appear to support this hypothesis.

Between World Wars I and II, Czechoslovakia maintained a thriving political democracy, the only one in Eastern Europe. After having resisted the Nazis (especially on the Czech side of the country) during the German occupation, while simultaneously maintaining a government-in-exile in London, Czechoslovakia reverted to its system of multiparty parliamentary democracy following the war. However, in hopes of bringing down the government in early 1948, the non-Communist Party government ministers resigned in protest over the activities of the Communist Party ministers and their control, use, and politicization of the police forces. Having polled a plurality of 38 percent support in the free and fair elections of 1946, and no longer needing to call new elections, the Czechoslovak Communist Party in February 1948 mobilized its supporters for mass demonstrations and then seized power in what can be called a *velvet coup d'état*. Thereafter, political democracy was suspended and, in the following years of Stalinist repression and terror, many opponents of the Communist Party and others caught up in this maelstrom of history were imprisoned, "re-educated", and/or executed. Czechoslovakia had been the only remaining country in Eastern Europe not taken over and ruled by the political party proxies of the Soviet Communist Party. The

---

[2] Pietro Grilli di Cortona, "From Communism to Democracy: Rethinking Regime Change in Hungary and Czechoslovakia", *International Social Science Journal*, May 1991, p. 325. This is what Emile Durkheim would refer to as a democratic "collective conscience". *Cf.* Ash, "Czechoslovakia Under Ice", p. 67: "The Czechs are intensely proud of their interwar democracy, which they justly claim was unique in Central and Eastern Europe". Also see Miriam Golden, "Historical Memory and Ideological Orientations in the Italian Workers' Movement", *Politics & Society*, March 1988.

hope of resuming political democracy in the near future quickly faded.[3]

[3] Janusz Bugajski, *Czechoslovakia: Charter 77's Decade of Dissent* (Westport, CT: Praeger, 1987), p. 3; James de Candole, *Czechoslovakia: Too Velvet a Revolution?* (London: Institute for European Defense and Strategic Studies, 1991), p. 7. It is interesting to note that Jürgen Habermas regards the transition to socialism "as depending more upon processes of democratization than upon changes in the mode of production" (cited in Tom Bottomore, *The Frankfurt School* (London and New York: Tavistock Publications, 1984), p. 66). Moreover, what Marx would later describe as socialism, he earlier refers to as democracy.

A.

Prague Spring as Prelude

"[A]ll great, world-historical facts and personages occur, as it were, twice... the first time as tragedy, the second as farce"
— Karl Marx, 1852[1]

It would take a full twenty years for significant social change to occur in Czechoslovakia. After growing opposition to the leadership, including that of some senior Party officials, Antonin Novotny was replaced as First Secretary of the Communist Party by Alexander Dubcek in a *velvet succession* in 1968.

A group of Prague students demonstrated against the absence of

[1] Karl Marx, "The Eighteenth Brumaire of Louis Bonaparte" in Tucker, ed., *The Marx-Engels Reader*, p. 594

electricity in their dormitories in late 1967. The students marched in the streets, some holding banners which simply read: "Give us Light". The Communist Party Central Committee, which was meeting nearby at that time, understood the word "light" as a metaphor for freedom, openness, and liberty (whether due to past experience or their guilty conscience is unknown). Based on their (understandable) misinterpretation, the Communist Party sent in the police to violently suppress the demonstration. The shock and disgust at the unnecessary and disproportionate violence used by the government helped to lead the way for the hardline Novotny to be replaced by the reformist Dubcek.[2]

In 1956, the Soviet Party Congress had recognized the right of each Communist Party to take its own path toward socialism. Avoiding the major pitfalls of the Hungarian Uprising of October 1956 that appeared to most frighten and anger the Kremlin—especially the withdrawal from the Warsaw Pact and Comecon, and a declaration of neutrality—Dubcek and the other Reform Communists in Czechoslovakia believed that they could carry out their bold experiment without foreign interference, particularly without military intervention from the Soviet Union.[3]

In April 1968, under the leadership of Dubcek, the Communist Party launched a *velvet rebellion*. They criticized the previous twenty years of Stalinism and began an "action program" of "reform communism", which they informally called "socialism with a human face". Dubcek's idea was to allow freedom of expression, to encourage democratic participation *within* the Party, and to introduce *some* market principles into the economy. Dubcek intended to liberalize society, to invigorate the economy, *and* to strengthen the Communist Party. He was forging a new Czechoslovak path toward socialism, namely some form of democratic market socialism.

People were open and free in discussing and writing about politics and culture, while the media and the arts flourished in their regained freedom. The role of the mass media during the Prague Spring was a notable departure from recent totalitarian practice in Czechoslovakia. The leading reformers in the movement, along with the ideas they were heralding, were being regularly broadcast in print and on

---

[2] Mark Frankland, *The Patriots' Revolution: How East Europe Won Its Freedom* (London: Sinclair-Stevenson, 1990), pp. 278-79

[3] Bernard Wheaton and Zdenek Kavan, *The Velvet Revolution: Czechoslovakia, 1988-1991* (Boulder: Westview Press, 1992), p. 14

radio and television.[4] The newly independent labor unions even donated "Days for Dubcek" by voluntarily working overtime to help grow the economy. Czechoslovakia was energized and enthusiastic.

The Reform Communists, however, miscalculated the reaction of the Soviet Union. The Warsaw Pact countries—led by the Soviet Red Army—invaded Czechoslovakia with half a million troops and thousands of tanks on 21 August 1968 stifling the Prague Spring.[5] The leaders of the reform movement were kidnapped and flown to the Soviet Union where they were forced to sign the "Moscow Protocols". This "agreement" accepted the invasion as legitimate, allowed Soviet troops to remain in Czechoslovakia, rescinded reform legislation, and required most of the leadership's resignations.

There was little armed resistance against the invasion, and no mass demonstrations or strikes; however, there were numerous incidents of symbolic and passive resistance. People argued with and chastised the invading Warsaw Pact soldiers, while denying them provisions such as food and water. Signs and graffiti denouncing the enemies of reform, as well as pictures of Dubcek, appeared on walls and nearly everywhere else. This may have led to Dubcek being able to remain in office until the next year. Franck and Weisband report that the Soviet Politburo was deeply divided regarding a response to the Prague Spring. They argue that the invasion was launched only after a "series of procrastinations", and that had the predicted costs been assessed at a higher level by the Kremlin, the narrow majority "might have tilted the other way and the invasion might never have taken place".[6] This is yet another reminder that what may appear to some as an inevitable political economic and historical necessity is simply another circumscribed contingency that went one way and not another.

The next month, the "Brezhnev Doctrine" was published in

---

[4] Owen V. Johnson, "Mass Media and the Velvet Revolution" in Popkin, ed., *Media and Revolution*, p. 223

[5] Yugoslavia never joined the Warsaw Pact, Romania denounced and refused to take part in the invasion while remaining a member of the organization, and Albania quit the Warsaw Pact in protest over the invasion of Czechoslovakia. China also condemned the invasion.

[6] Franck and Weisband, *Word Politics*, p. 12; also see their ch. 2 for a more detailed and lively account of the invasion.

Pravda, justifying the recent invasion and establishing a direct sphere of influence for the Soviet Union in Eastern Europe to facilitate and rationalize future intervention, military and otherwise.[7] The new leadership of the so-called "normalization" regime (originally called the "consolidation" regime and what Ash refers to as to "regime of forgetting") in Czechoslovakia, was comprised of hard-line Communists loyal to the Soviet Union and maintained little legitimacy amongst the people. What "legitimacy" did exist rested on the interactive use of ideology and power by the Communist Party.[8] The Prague Spring was completely extinguished the following year when Dubcek was replaced in April 1969 and censorship of the media and arts was re-established the following September. The new Czechoslovak government could have chosen a more reformist path—as did Hungary following the 1956 Soviet invasion which crushed a popular rebellion—but this "Kádárist" path was not taken by the hard-line Husak regime. "Eastern European regimes had a choice of political strategies", according to Judy Batt, "and their choices were conditioned as much by the preferences of the particular local party leaderships and by domestic conditions as by specific Soviet directives".[9]

---

[7] Tim D. Whipple, ed., *After the Velvet Revolution: Václav Havel and the New Leaders of Czechoslovakia Speak Out* (New York: Freedom House, 1991), p. 5. *Cf.* Franck and Weisband, *Word Politics*, ch. 3

[8] Mark Wright, "Ideology and Power in the Czechoslovak Political System" in Paul G. Lewis, ed., *Eastern Europe: Political Crisis and Legitimation* (London and Sydney: Croom Helm, 1984), pp. 111-53. *Cf.* Jean-Jacques Rousseau, *On the Social Contract* [1762], Bk. I, Ch. III: "The strongest [are] never strong enough to be master all the time, unless [they] transform force into right and obedience into duty."; Antonio Gramsci, *Selections from the Prison Notebooks* [1929-35], trans. by Quintin Hoare and Geoffrey Nowell Smith (New York: International Publishers, 1971); Jackman, *Power Without Force*, p. 99: "Legitimacy... simply requires a degree of acquiescence, an acceptance of the political order as generally reasonable, given the known or feasible alternatives.... Unlike domination, which involves physical coercion by the state, hegemony requires persuasion and manipulation to generate consent. While the former, with its use of force, may be common to political crises, hegemony is the 'normal' mechanism by which compliance is induced. Moreover, compliance is likely to be passive rather than active".

[9] Judy Batt, "East-Central Europe: From Reform to Transformation" in Gilbert Rozman *et al.*, eds., *Dismantling Communism: Common Causes and Regional*

(continued...)

For most, "normalization" meant a reactionary turn back to the abnormality and harshness of a totalitarian system.

The seeds of rebellion, though, had already been sown in the hearts and minds of the people. Daniel Chirot argues that "Whatever potential [reform communism] may have had in the Prague Spring of 1968, the way in which it was crushed... brought to an end the period in which intellectuals could continue to hope about the future of communism".[10] Cracks in the system of control started to reappear just a few years later. A Soviet joke tells of a man distributing leaflets in Red Square. Stopped by a police officer, it is discovered that the leaflets are blank. "What information are you spreading?", the officer asks, declaring in confusion that "Nothing is written!". "Why write?", the man responds, "Everybody already knows...".

The Czechoslovak equivalent to Leonid Brezhnev's "little deal" started to break down in the late 1970s.[11] The "little deal" (or "little tradition") refers to the unspoken social contract under which the citizens and the government agreed that the government would supply its citizens with a certain level of material well-being, both officially (*e.g.* jobs, security) and unofficially (*e.g.* tacit acceptance of the black market), in return for the citizens' political support, or, at the very least, their public conformity and political apathy. Czechoslovak citizens did not necessarily have to believe in the system, as Havel notes, but they did have to act *as if* they believed in the system. As with so many other social phenomena in totalitarian countries, civil society was turned on its head. Pierre Bourdieu

---

[9](...continued)
Variations (Washington, D.C. & Baltimore and London: Woodrow Wilson Center Press & Johns Hopkins University Press, 1992), pp. 255-56

[10] Daniel Chirot, "The East European Revolutions of 1989" in Goldstone, ed., *Revolutions*, Second Ed., pp. 171-72. Oft-quoted, Abba Eban once quipped that the Palestinians "never miss an opportunity to miss an opportunity"; perhaps this is true of the Communists as well.

[11] James R. Millar, "The Little Deal: Brezhnev's Contribution to Acquisitive Socialism", *Slavic Review*, Winter 1985. *Cf.* Przeworski, "The 'East' Becomes the 'South'?, p.20

describes this type of phenomenon as one of "euphemization".[12] Euphemization is the driving public myth of totalitarian societies. Ash neatly concretizes this phenomenon in his usual literary way:

> *Forgetting* is the key... In effect, the regime has said to people: Forget 1968. Forget your democratic traditions. Forget that you were once citizens with rights and duties. Forget politics. In return we will give you a comfortable, safe life. There'll be plenty of food in the shops and cheap beer in the pubs. You may afford a car and even a little country cottage—and you won't have to work competitively. We don't ask you to believe in us or our fatuous idcology. By all means listen to the Voice of America and watch Austrian television. All we ask is that you will outwardly and publicly conform: join in the ritual "elections", vote the prescribed way in the "trade union" meetings, enroll your children in the "socialist" youth organization. Keep your mind to yourself.[13]

---

[12] Pierre Bourdieu, *Outline of a Theory of Practice*, trans. by Richard Nice (Cambridge: Cambridge University Press, 1977 [1972]), p. 191. *Cf.* Serge Schmemann, "In Hope and Dismay, Lenin's Heirs Speak" in Bernard Gwertzman and Michael T. Kaufman, eds., *The Collapse of Communism* [an anthology of *New York Times* articles] (New York: Times Books, 1990), p. 8, emphasis added: "what matters is that you *profess* belief in Marx, and it doesn't matter what Marx you believe in". Also see Ivan Volgyes, "Political Socialization in Eastern Europe: A Comparative Framework", *Journal of Political and Military Sociology*, Fall 1973; and Ekiert, "Democratic Processes in East Central Europe", p. 302.

[13] Ash, "Czechoslovakia Under Ice", p. 62

Based on his analyses of these so-called public myths and societal euphemizations, Scott ably discusses and harshly critiques Marx's concept of "false consciousness" and Antonio Gramsci's concept of "hegemony".[14] Scott, however, is not just *critical* of Marx and Gramsci on this issue, but indeed argues quite the opposite. He declares that "If there is a social phenomenon to be explained here, it is the reverse of what theories of hegemony and false consciousness purport to account for. How is it that subordinate groups... so often believed and acted as if their situations were not inevitable when a more judicious historical reading would have concluded that it was?... We require instead", Scott continues, "an understanding of a *misreading* by subordinate groups that seems to exaggerate their own power, the possibilities for emancipation, and to underestimate the power arrayed against them".[15]

Although "close readings of historical and archival evidence tend to favor a hegemonic account of power relations", Scott marshals volumes of evidence to convincingly demonstrate that even when subordinates voice support for a directive publicly, they may speak and act differently in private and, indeed, "the more menacing the power, the thicker the mask".[16] In East Germany, for example, "minor", "limited", and "factual" criticisms were offered *within* state-sponsored institutional forums, but these criticisms "remained veiled and local... When people raised direct criticism or opposition they always carefully wrapped it in rhetoric beyond reproach. A preferred method was reporting subversive opinions held by others, often 'women and non-Party members' [!]. In this way participants distanced themselves from the disreputable beliefs, but still raised the

---

[14] James C. Scott, *The Moral Economy of the Peasant* (New Haven, CT and London: Yale University Press, 1976), pp. 225-40; James C. Scott, *Weapons of the Weak: Everyday Forms of Peasant Resistance* (New Haven and London: Yale University Press, 1985), pp. 40-41, 314-50; and especially James C. Scott, *Domination and the Arts of Resistance: Hidden Transcripts* (New Haven and London: Yale University Press, 1990), *passim*. What was required of citizens was not "orthodoxy" but "orthopraxy" (J.F. Staal, "Sanskrit and Sanskritization", *Journal of Asian Studies*, May 1963, cited in *Ibid.*, p. 117).

[15] *Ibid.*, p. 79, original emphasis

[16] *Ibid.*, pp. xii, 3

concerns".[17] Other forms of "deliberate ambiguity" were also used to "voice" criticisms and denunciations in a passive, non-confrontational way, thereby leaving room for plausible denial and therefore political and sometimes physical survival. Furthermore, even the public rhetoric and actions of relatively powerless subordinates often dispel the ideas of false consciousness and hegemony if the viewer is willing to pierce the veils of euphemisms, jokes, songs, folktales, proverbs, rituals, hyper-politeness, playing dumb, plausible denial, and other coded behaviors and technologies of disguise and resistance. In fact, some have argued that "In the Communist world, the underground joke is often the best index of conditions".[18] Humor and deceit, Scott illustrates, can have both substantial and substantive implications. There is a "crucial distinction", he argues, "between a *practical failure* to comply and a *declared refusal* to comply. The former does not necessarily breach the normative order of domination; the latter almost always does".[19] One method may appear accomodationist (*i.e. de facto*), while the other one is confrontational (*i.e. de jure*); yet, importantly, both are clearly forms of resistance (on a vast continuum).

As Michel Foucault points out, power and resistance imply each other dialectically and are ubiquitous in all societies.[20] For every appeal by the Communist Party élite to *noblesse oblige*, there may have been a corresponding use of *travailleurs obligent* by the people. This is partially

---

[17] E. Pierre Deess, "Social Change in the German Democratic Republic: The Role of Institutional Pre-Mobilization Practices (IPPs)", Paper presented at the 91st Annual Meetings of the American Sociological Association, New York, New York, 16-20 August 1996, pp. 6-7. People also applied the larger Soviet debates over *Perestroika* and *Glasnost* to their local problems, thereby, in a Millsian way, using their "sociological imagination" to construct new levels of criticism and solidarity.

[18] Schmemann, "In Hope and Dismay, Lenin's Heirs Speak" in Gwertzman and Kaufman, eds., *The Collapse of Communism*, p. 3. In this way, "culture [is] to some extent a substitute for politics" (Wolchik, *Czechoslovakia in Transition*, p. 293).

[19] Scott, *Domination and the Arts of Resistance*, p. 203, original emphasis

[20] See, *e.g.*, Michel Foucault, *Discipline and Punish* (New York: Vintage Books, 1995 [1975]); Anthony Giddens, *Profiles and Critiques in Social Theory* (London: Macmillan, 1982), esp. pp. 198-99.

corroborated by the saying that circulated in the Soviet Union and Eastern Europe which joked that "they pretend to pay us and we pretend to work". This was all part of a *political economy of deception* that operated in Czechoslovakia and elsewhere. It is not surprising, then, that

> In Czechoslovakia, as in other communist countries, the actual political beliefs, attitudes, and values of the population, *i.e.* the country's political culture, differed considerably from the official ideology.... [and] the success of the leadership in harnessing culture to political ends was largely illusory. As in other communist countries, many intellectuals in Czechoslovakia remained alienated from the political system. Many of those who formed part of the official cultural world tried to increase their autonomy and gain greater freedom of action whenever political circumstances allowed.[21]

The Prague Spring was, up until that time, the most dramatic proof of this truism. The artists and intellectuals who were actively involved in the Prague Spring in the 1960s also later became the nuclei of the various dissident cells and organizations which surfaced in the late 1970s and 1980s.

It could be argued that the progressive Prague Spring and the reactionary events of that summer sealed the fate of the Communist Party,

---

[21] Wolchik, *Czechoslovakia in Transition*, pp. 108, 286. *Cf.* Stanley Meisler, "'...All They Are Saying Is Give Prague a Chance'", *Smithsonian*, June 1993, p. 72: Meisler quotes "Vladimir Vodicka, the... former director of the Theater of the Balustrade, where Havel got his start" as claiming that Czech society 'lost the Jewish intellectuals in World War II, and Prague culture was based 40 to 50 percent on them'. One can only wonder how world history would have turned out differently were it not for the massive tragedy of World War II and the accompanying Holocaust.

in particular, and Czechoslovakia, in general. In that sense, the Velvet Revolution was a delayed, and more radicalized, result of the Prague Spring. However, the realization of revolution after the repressive period of "normalization" required certain changes in the Czechoslovak theatre of operations.[22]

Despite the Prague Spring, the Velvet Revolution was neither automatic nor inevitable; the dialectical development of institutional structures and human agency, with their many cultural mediators, are *always* partners in social change. The success of the Velvet Revolution involved both structural changes and human initiative—domestically, regionally, *and* internationally—which were built upon politico-historical experiences, especially the interwar years of parliamentary democracy and the Prague Spring, which were themselves built upon politico-historical experiences, including the imperial era, Czechoslovakia's independence and first republic led by Masaryk, and the country's experiences surrounding World War II. Especially since 1968, dissidents in Czechoslovakia "carried on an uninterrupted, now hidden, now open fight" against their totalitarian system, including the people and policies that sustained it.[23]

The Prague Spring, further, was in essence an undemocratic approach to democratic change. The Prague Spring entailed a top-down change in policy, albeit one which acquired some autonomy amongst civil society. In contrast, the Velvet Revolution, twenty-one years later, was more radical and more democratic not only in its demands and tactics, but also in its nature and demographic composition. The Velvet Revolution was a successful effort by the masses, despite leadership by the intelligentsia and some former leaders of the Prague Spring, in a thoroughly bottom-up phenomenon.

As to the future, the Czechoslovak history of democracy and support of equality, tolerance, and liberalism will likely bode well for the Czech Republic's future as a stable, democratic nation. Slovakia, however, with a less "civic culture", may not fare as well, in terms of democratic

---

[22] A theatre of operations, in this context, is employed analogously to an ecosystemic approach. It encompasses the entire country, though there might be emphases on certain parts, yet also includes relevant interactions with, and among, neighboring countries, regional power blocs, and the superpowers.

[23] Marx and Engels, *Manifesto of the Communist Party* in Tucker, ed., *The Marx-Engels Reader*, p. 474

stability.[24] It is important to remember that the Czechs and Slovaks each entered (in 1918) and left (in 1993) the Czechoslovak state "with very different levels of economic development, political experiences, national traditions, and histories. The cultural heritages of these two peoples who speak mutually intelligible languages also differed substantially".[25] Slovakia was and is less politically and economically developed, less urbanized, and less literate. There is also more unemployment in Slovakia and this trend is likely to continue. During the imperial era, the Czechs were ruled by Vienna, which allowed them (limited) political participation, save from 1871 to 1879, in the *Diets*, or Parliaments, of Bohemia and Moravia, in addition to the Parliament in Vienna. The Slovaks, in contradistinction, ruled by Hungary, were wholly restricted from political participation. During the 1930s, furthermore, Slovakia was much harder hit than the Czech Lands by the Depression, thereby exacerbating already desperate conditions.

For at least the last century or two, segments within the now Czech Republic have been aligned more with the liberal and democratic traditions of Western Europe than has Slovakia, which has been more socially, culturally, and politically in sync with Albania, Bulgaria, Romania, the former Yugoslavia (especially Serbia, Montenegro, and Kosovo), and Russia (and some of the former Soviet Republics). Indeed, while one can now confidently say that the Czech Republic and Hungary are political democracies, one can just as confidently declare that Slovakia

---

[24] See Gabriel A. Almond and Sidney Verba, *The Civic Culture* (Newbury Park, CA: Sage Publications, 1989 [1963]). Almond and Verba specifically study "five democracies": the U.S., Great Britain, Germany, Italy, and Mexico. But see Robert A. Dahl, *A Preface to Economic Democracy* (Berkeley and Los Angeles: University of California Press, 1985), p. 49: "Like manners and mores, political culture is an elusive quality; probably in no area of comparative political analysis is good evidence so skimpy. The essential characteristics of a democratic culture, like those of a 'democratic personality', remain uncertain and sharply debated". *Cf.* Margaret R. Somers, "What's Political or Cultural about Political Culture and the Public Sphere? Toward an Historical Sociology of Concept Formation", *Sociological Theory*, July 1995 and Margaret R. Somers, "Narrating and Naturalizing Civil Society and Citizenship Theory: The Place of Political Culture and the Public Sphere", *Sociological Theory*, November 1995.

[25] Wolchik, *Czechoslovakia in Transition*, p. 7

and Romania are not even democratizing.[26]

This split has been further institutionalized in December 1995, when the Czech Republic became the first post-communist state admitted to the Organization for Economic Cooperation and Development [OECD], followed by Hungary in May 1996, Poland in November 1996, and Slovakia in December 2000. In the 1990s, one could see that the Czech Republic had both the highest GNP per capita and life expectancy at birth, while having the lowest under-five mortality, inflation, and unemployment rates in all of Eastern Europe.[27] The differences with Slovakia in this regard are striking and, in some sense, make all the difference.

---

[26] Sabrina P. Ramet, "Eastern Europe's Painful Transition", *Current History*, March 1996, p. 99. Gwertzman and Kaufman refer to "democratization" as a "half measure" of democracy (Gwertzman and Kaufman, eds., *The Collapse of Communism*, p. 25).

[27] York W. Bradshaw and Michael Wallace, *Global Inequalities* (Thousand Oaks, CA, London, and New Delhi: Pine Forge Press, 1996), p. 123

Chapter IV.

The Power of Human Rights

"Revolutions come with panhuman ideals, not trivial regional ones"
— Barrington Moore[1]

In the mid-1970s, the issue of human rights was being placed on the global agenda. On 1 August 1975, Czechoslovakia signed the Helsinki Final Act of the Conference on Security and Cooperation in Europe, which then automatically became Czechoslovak law. Under the Act, nearly three dozen countries agreed to various international human rights provisions, encompassing the "promotion of tourism" and "travel for personal or professional reasons", "reunification of families", "improvement of the circulation of, access to, and exchange of information", "refraining from the threat or use of force", and notably the "respect for human rights and fundamental freedoms, including the freedom of thought, conscience,

[1] Moore, *Social Origins of Dictatorship and Democracy*, p. 385

religion or belief", and "equal rights and self-determination of peoples".[2] Although the Eastern European countries initially fought to keep human rights off the agenda—and then fought the wording once it was on the agenda—they eventually regarded the Act as a foreign policy victory, despite being a potential diplomatic nuisance. Communist Party newspapers throughout Eastern Europe trumpeted the Act, proudly reprinting it for their citizens to read, which many did. By the end of August 1975, various people in Eastern Europe and the Soviet Union sensed that there was a new political opportunity and began demanding that their governments comply with the newly signed international agreement. Some of these dissidents also made contacts abroad—especially in Helsinki, London, and New York—thereby constructing a "transnational network to monitor compliance with Helsinki [Act] norms".[3]

At around the same time, the U.S. Council on Foreign Relations made human rights one of its top priorities for the second half of the 1970s. The United States' supportive stance regarding human rights was solidified, however, with the successful candidacy of Jimmy Carter for President. Inspired by these phenomena, a few dissidents, including Havel, established the *velvet opposition* group Charter 77 on 1 January 1977.[4]

---

[2] Conference on Security and Co-Operation in Europe, Final Act, Helsinki, 1 August 1975, http://www.hri.org/docs/Helsinki75.htm. The signatories are Austria, Belgium, Bulgaria, Canada, Cyprus, Czechoslovakia, Denmark, East Germany, France, Greece, Hungary, Iceland, Ireland, Italy, Liechtenstein, Luxembourg, Malta, Monaco, the Netherlands, Norway, Poland, Portugal, Romania, San Marino, Spain, Sweden, Switzerland, Turkey, the USSR, the United Kingdom, the United States, the Vatican, West Germany, and Yugoslavia.

[3] Daniel C. Thomas, "Social Movements and the Strategic Use of Human Rights Norms: A Comparison of East European Cases", 9 November 1994, http://hdc-www.harvard.edu/cfia/pnscs/f94thoma.htm, p. 5. *Cf.* William H. Luers, "Czechoslovakia: Road to Revolution", *Foreign Affairs*, Spring 1990, pp. 86, 92. Luers is a former U.S. Ambassador to Czechoslovakia.

[4] Whipple, ed., *After the Velvet Revolution*, p. 7. Two months later in March, one of the three founding members, the philosopher Jan Patocka, died after police interrogation. The third founding member and spokesperson was Professor Jirí Hájek, Dubcek's foreign minister. Claiming to be too old for politics himself, Hájek told a crowd in November 1989 that he supported their "every move" (continued...)

The Charter 77 Declaration was first published in West Germany on 6 January 1977 and then immediately reprinted in newspapers and magazines throughout the world. The Charter then continued to spread through *samizdat*—underground media, most notable of these in Czechoslovakia being The Padlock Press, the journal *Critical Review*, and *Videojournál*.

Interestingly, the issue of human rights—rights that are considered inherent in being human but were also recognized by governments and others—created social and political opportunities for citizens of Eastern Europe to dissent and mobilize around an issue with international, governmental, and popular legitimacy. Seizing these opportunities, dissident individuals and "small vanguard" groups spontaneously and simultaneously emerged in the Soviet Union and

---

[4](...continued)
(Amos Elon, "Prague Autumn", *New Yorker*, 22 January 1990, p. 127). "Although men outnumbered women as signatories of Charter 77... women accounted for a substantial proportion of those who signed the Charter.... [and] one of the three designated Charter spokespersons was generally a woman" (Wolchik, *Czechoslovakia in Transition*, pp. 200-01. Women activists also played a large role in the mass demonstrations of 1989, as leaders and as participants, yet no feminist movement has emerged in Czechoslovakia, as it had in the Soviet Union, Poland, and Yugoslavia (see, *e.g.*, Barbara Einhorn, "Where Have All the Women Gone?: Women and the Women's Movement in East Central Europe", *Feminist Review*, Winter 1991). Unfortunately, it was Havel who allegedly referred to feminism as a calling "for bored housewives and dissatisfied mistresses" (cited in Peggy Watson, "Eastern Europe's Silent Revolution: Gender", *Sociology*, August 1993, p. 477). Signatories of the Charter 77 declaration often faced "interrogation, house arrest, loss of jobs, forced exile, imprisonment, and other forms of harassment [which] kept the price of open identification with the Charter and other dissident groups high and restricted their activities" (*Ibid.*, p. 155). It has been noted by Julio Godoy, though, that 'while the Moscow-imposed government in Prague would degrade and humiliate reformers, the Washington-made government in Guatemala would kill them. It still does, in a virtual genocide'. Likewise, a Salvadoran Jesuit journal commented that "in their country Václav Havel... wouldn't have been put in jail—he might well have been hacked to pieces and left by the side of the road somewhere" (cited in Noam Chomsky, *What Uncle Sam Really Wants* (Berkeley, CA: Odonian Press, 1992), pp. 49-50, 70).

various Eastern European countries, including Czechoslovakia.[5] With these "early risers", civil society was re-emerging and melding with political society, as well as reminding everyone that the Communist Party did not in fact have a monopoly on socio-political thought and action. This "small motor" of dissident ideas, organization, and personal action facilitated the "large motor" of resistance, rebellion, and revolution.[6] Individuals like Havel and groups like Charter 77 were the social infrastructure that supported the socio-political structures of oppositional activity. The totalitarian wall had been breached, leading to what Havel refers to as post-totalitarianism.

The activists in groups such as Charter 77 always believed that ideas could be powerful weapons. "An idea may be so strong, so appealing, so illuminating", according to Chirot, "that it acquires a power of its own. Once it spreads, it will change societies, sometimes even overriding their material interests".[7] The specific concept of human rights is one of these ideas, as is democracy more generally, and it became a social issue of wide appeal in Czechoslovakia. The power of the human rights issue united a broad coalition of dissidents and other citizens across class, ethnicity, religion, occupation, interests, and ideology, including: Reform Communists, radical socialists, liberals, peace activists, Greens, the "unofficial" Catholic Church, nationalists, artists, actors, teachers, and students around a "master frame" through which they could organize and channel their claims against the Communist Party élite and the state. Importantly, "the transfer of the allegiance of the intellectuals" to the opposition had begun.[8]

---

[5] Sidney Tarrow, "'Aiming at a Moving Target': Social Science and the Recent Rebellions in Eastern Europe", *PS: Political Science & Politics*, March 1991

[6] Debray, *Revolution in the Revolution?*

[7] Chirot, *How Societies Change*, p. 75. *Cf.* Max Weber, *The Protestant Ethic and the Spirit of Capitalism* [1904-05], trans. by Talcott Parsons(London: Unwin Paperbacks, 1987).

[8] Lyford P. Edwards, *The Natural History of Revolution* (Chicago, 1927) cited in Crane Brinton, *The Anatomy of Revolution*, Revised and Expanded Ed. (New York: Vintage Books, 1965 [1938]), p. 42. For an interesting twist, see Huntington, *Political Order in Changing Societies*, p. 290: "[I]ntellectuals cannot (continued...)

The non-violent and non-partisan nature of human rights advocacy as a technology of resistance to the Communist Party regime in Czechoslovakia had numerous advantages. First, it extended the scope and strengthened the unity of the people who opposed the regime. The Czechoslovak opposition was not solely a "negative revolutionary coalition", as most revolutionary movements are.[9] The coalition *was* negatively united against the government, but it was also positively united around human rights, freedom, democracy, and social justice, even if these terms were rarely defined.[10]

Second, using Czechoslovak laws and governmental promises regarding human rights, the opposition was effectively able to contrast the rhetoric and reality of the regime from a Czechoslovak perspective. Charter 77 specifically cited clauses and articles of the Czechoslovak Constitution, covenants and treaties signed and ratified by Czechoslovakia, and Czechoslovak laws in support of their struggle for human and civil rights. Charter 77 also insisted that they were not a group or independent party (which would have been illegal), but rather a collection of individuals with a shared interest in human rights, thereby acting within the letter of the law. The opposition could not easily, therefore, be accused of breaking the law, importing foreign ideologies, supporting *bourgeois* democracy, or of being counter-revolutionary pawns.

Third, the issue of human rights was clearly recognizable and highly respectable, allowing its proponents to maintain the high moral ground against the government; it is not very difficult for people to feel sympathy towards human rights appeals, especially ones that are codified

---

[8](...continued)
desert the existing order because they have never been a part of it. They are born to opposition, and it is their appearance on the scene rather than any transfer of allegiance which is responsible for their potentially revolutionary role." On the role of ideas, values, and meaning in politics and social movements, see, *e.g.*, Neil J. Smelser, *Theory of Collective Behavior* (New York: Free Press, 1962); and Michael Lerner, *The Politics of Meaning* (Reading, MA: Addison-Wesley, 1996).

[9] Robert Dix, "Why Revolutions Succeed and Fail", *Polity*, Spring 1984. *Cf.* Goldstone, "Revolutions in Modern Dictatorships" in Goldstone, ed., *Revolutions*, Second ed., pp. 70-77

[10] *Cf.* Gurr and Goldstone, "Comparisons and Policy Implications" in Keddie, ed., *Debating Revolutions*, pp. 336-37

in both national and international law.

Fourth, the issue of human rights was also known to be (at least nominally) supported by the United States, the European Community, the United Nations, and later, the Soviet Union under Gorbachev. Importantly, human rights were also supported by many individuals and non-governmental organizations in these and other countries, including Amnesty International and Human Rights Watch, and various personal and institutional relationships and networks were forged across national borders.

J. Craig Jenkins and Charles Perrow suggest, based on their resource mobilization approach, that in order for a successful outcome to obtain, "movements by the 'powerless' require strong and sustained outside support".[11] However, this does not appear to be the case empirically, especially with regard to China, Cuba, and Nicaragua. Although material support is often preferable, symbolic support and solidarity is also important and should not be underestimated or discounted, perhaps especially in the Cold War era. Neither, though, is absolutely necessary nor certainly sufficient in itself.

Fifth, advocacy of human rights is an issue of dissidence which is secular and relatively non-political in that it does not seek the attainment of institutionalized power, as does a conventional political party, but only rights that supposedly already exist and are inherent in both citizenship and being human. The Charter 77 Declaration, for example, states that

---

[11] J. Craig Jenkins and Charles Perrow, "Insurgency of the Powerless: Farm Worker Movements (1946-1972)", *American Sociological Review*, April 1977, p. 251. Theda Skocpol, Susan Eckstein, resource mobilization theorists, and others have made similar points about the necessary role of external phenomena in support of revolutionary movements. However, the Chinese Revolution, for example, seems anomalous in this regard. Indeed, Mao Zedong declares that "We stand for self-reliance. We hope for foreign aid but cannot be dependent on it; we depend on our own efforts [and] creative power" (Mao Tse-tung [Mao Zedong], "We Must Learn to Do Economic Work" [10 January 1945] in *Quotations from Chairman Mao Tse-tung* (Peking [Beijing]: Foreign Languages Press, 1966), pp. 194-95). Other than media attention, Castro's forces did not receive any foreign support against Batista until the last year of the Batista regime in 1958. The Sandinistas also received very little external material support until 1978-79, less than a year before they overthrew Somoza and took power in Nicaragua. The foreign aid was late, limited, and small; therefore, it was hardly decisive in these (and other) cases. *Cf.* Wickham-Crowley, *Guerrillas & Revolution in Latin America*, esp. ch. 5, 8, 12

"Charter 77 is not an organization; it has no rules, permanent bodies or formal membership.... It does not form the basis for any oppositional political activity.... Charter 77 is a loose, informal and open association of people of various shades of opinions, faiths and professions united by the will to strive individually and collectively for the respecting of civil and human rights in our own country and throughout the world".[12] The dissidents were, in effect, (re)constructing and (re)defining a "moral economy" of civil and political subsistence.[13]

Scott invokes the phenomenological concept of a minimum range of justice below which people are susceptible to resistance and rebellion

---

[12] See the Appendix on Charter 77 below.

[13] *Cf.* E.P. Thompson, "The Moral Economy of the English Crowd in the Eighteenth Century", *Past and Present*, February 1971; and Scott, *The Moral Economy of the Peasant.* Also see Barrington Moore, Jr., *Injustice: The Social Bases of Obedience and Revolt* (White Plains, NY: M.E. Sharpe, 1978). For an illustration from antiquity, see Howard Fast, *The Jews: Story of a People* (New York: Dell Publishing, 1968), p. 106:

> During the Temple period, Jews always resented taxation fiercely. They knew the wealth of Jerusalem, and since they were constantly rendering tithes in both money and kind to the Temple, they saw no reason why they should be taxed in addition. There was a reason, however; the Seleucids were on the path of conquest, and there was no other way for them to function except with mercenary armies. Antiochus IV probably kept a hundred thousand men in the field—at times twice that many, and the core were heavily armed Macedonians. Such troops cost money, a vast amount of money. The Jewish farmers were being squeezed to death; but it took the gestures against their religion to move this people of peace into action.

For similar themes of resistance and rebellion against marketization and control over the food supply, see Polanyi, *The Great Transformation*, esp. Part Two (and my "The Great Transformation—Its Relevance Continues", *American Journal of Economics and Sociology*, October 1994); and Charles Tilly, "Food Supply and Public Order in Modern Europe" [ch. 6] in Charles Tilly, ed., *The Formation of Nation States in Western Europe* (Princeton, NJ: Princeton University Press, 1975).

until their socially constructed conception of "justice" is restored.[14] Justice, as with subsistence and the state itself, however, is historical and moral, social and relative, collective and continuous. "Human rights", and a broad conception of democracy, became the core values and "master frame" animating the moral economy of citizenship and resistance in Czechoslovakia.

The focus on human rights allowed for an opposition that was not too oppositional, *i.e.* confrontational—a powerful example of Havel's non-violent "anti-political politics" in practice. This did not mean that the opposition was *a*political; it was not. Rather, the opposition did not (originally) seek either to be a political party or to assume political power; however, it did pursue social change and political reforms, though primarily within the framework of the Czechoslovak Constitution and laws.[15] Human rights advocacy, in effect, created a *velvet opposition.*

The concept and advocacy of human rights, at least on its face, does not challenge the fundamental structures of a society. However, in a Kafkaesque (post)totalitarian society such as Czechoslovakia, *any* public opposition to the regime and its legitimacy is ultimately a fundamental challenge to the entire socio-political economic system. The Czechoslovak dissidents, therefore, often tried to portray their political opposition as palatably as possible. This is the nature of "constructive deviance", as Martin Bútora puts it. Dissidents were forced to develop "softwares", *i.e.* "alternative methods and solutions to problems that went around the

---

[14] *Cf.* Foucault, *Discipline and Punish*, pp. 82-83: "The least-favored strata of the population did not have, in principle, any privileges: but they benefitted, within the margins of what was imposed on them by law and custom, from a space of tolerance, gained by force or obstinacy; and this space was for them so indispensable a condition of existence that they were often ready to rise up to defend it; the attempts that were made periodically to reduce it, by reviving old laws or by approving the methods of apprehending, provoked popular disturbances, just as attempts to reduce certain privileges disturbed the nobility, the clergy and the bourgeoisie". Also see Tilly, *From Mobilization to Revolution*, esp. p. 135. Additionally, the anarchist Michael Bakunin romantically, and sometimes lyrically, spoke of a "sacred instinct of revolt".

[15] *Cf.* Jean Cohen and Andrew Arato, *Civil Society and Political Theory* (Cambridge, MA: MIT Press, 1992)

system".[16] In this sense, as in others, these "excellent dissidents" were truly "reluctant rebels".[17] Forced into opposition by a regime and a system which regulated and restricted most forms of social and political behavior, the dissidents reluctantly, though dutifully, assumed their roles as active citizens, rebels, and democrats.

Following the signing of the Helsinki Final Act in 1975, the Communist Party's acceptance of independent socio-political activities substantially increased, and mobilization around human rights became relatively high in Czechoslovakia. "[I]nternational human rights norms clearly promoted societal mobilization against authoritarian regimes in Eastern Europe which previously had tolerated no independent political initiatives", according to Daniel Thomas. He concludes that "societal groups used international norms to restructure the domestic political environment in a manner conducive to greater social autonomy and eventually to regime change".[18] This is yet another fine example of how agents and structures both constrain and empower each other in powerful and dialectical ways.

Even modern revolutionaries are "primitive rebels" in the sense that they are defensive and yearn for a particular (and almost invariably

---

[16] Cited in Wolchik, *Czechoslovakia in Transition*, pp. 154-55

[17] Gwertzman and Kaufman, eds., *The Collapse of Communism*, p. 36: "They had been excellent dissidents, which meant standing up, telling the truth and if necessary, going to jail"; Walton, *Reluctant Rebels*. The Chinese students, in the first paragraph of their 12 May 1989 "Hunger Strike Announcement", even referred to themselves as "reluctant": "In this bright sunny month of May, we are on a hunger strike. In this best moment of our youth, we have no choice but to leave behind us everything beautiful about life. But how reluctant, how unwilling we are!" [see the Appendix on the Chinese Students' Hunger Strike Announcement below]. Likewise, Chai Ling, a woman graduate student in Beijing at the time, had been described as a "reluctant commander" of the student movement in Tiananmen Square. For these reasons, Melanie Manion describes the students as "reluctant duelists", borrowing the term from Daniel Ellsberg (Melanie Manion, "Introduction: Reluctant Duelists: The Logic of the 1989 Protests and Massacre" in Michel Oksenberg, Lawrence R. Sullivan, and Marc Lambert, eds., *Beijing Spring, 1989: Confrontation and Conflict: The Basic Documents* (Armonk, NY and London: M.E. Sharpe, 1990)).

[18] Thomas, "Social Movements and the Strategic Use of Human Rights Norms", p. 7

mythologized) past, and consequently a particular (and almost invariably utopian) future; these rebels want to (re)create an invented culture and invented traditions.[19] Indeed, political entrepreneurs often (re)use, (re)enact, (re)interpret, and (re)invent tradition and culture through myth production and mass distribution, while simultaneously exploring new avenues of opportunity to add to their collective cultural repertoire of political action.[20]

This is certainly true of Charter 77 and other dissident groups. In the years from the founding of Charter 77 to its dissolution after the Velvet Revolution, for example, the organization radicalized its demands and actions from originally urging mere respect for human rights, to later getting involved in economic, ecological, religious, and peace issues. Charter 77 eventually demanded and demonstrated for the resignation of the government to be followed by free and fair elections.[21] From its inception, though more dramatically in 1989, Charter 77 was creating a

---

[19] E.J. Hobsbawm, *Primitive Rebels: Studies in Archaic Forms of Social Movement in the 19th and 20th Centuries* (New York: W.W. Norton & Co., 1959). *Cf.* Calvert, *Revolution and Counter-Revolution*, p. 31: "Time and again it seems that at moments of great social and political change people can only visualize the future in terms of an idealized past to which they must return"; Jedlicki, "The Revolution of 1989", pp. 39-40: "all revolutions arouse historical consciousness. A revolution implies a reevaluation of a nation's history.... the bigger the leap forward, the more anxiously we look backward"; Burawoy, "Two Methods in Search of Science", p. 790: "The reconstruction of history becomes a vehicle for understanding ways out of a continually changing present".

[20] *Cf.* Marx, "The Eighteenth Brumaire of Louis Bonaparte" in Tucker, ed., *The Marx-Engels Reader*, p. 595: "The tradition of all the dead generations weighs like a nightmare on the brain of the living. And just when they seem engaged in revolutionising themselves and things, in creating something entirely new, precisely in such epochs of revolutionary crisis they anxiously conjure up the spirits of the past to their service and borrow from them names, battle slogans and costumes in order to present the new scene of world history in this time-honoured disguise and this borrowed language." Also see Eric Hobsbawm and Terence Ranger, eds., *The Invention of Tradition* (Cambridge: Cambridge University Press, 1983).

[21] Grilli di Cortona, "From Communism to Democracy", p. 318

"parallel polis", challenging the government without direct confrontation.[22]

As Václav Benda suggests, creating "parallel structures... need not lead to a direct conflict with the regime, yet it harbors no illusions that 'cosmetic changes' can make any difference. Moreover, it leaves open the key question of the system's viability".[23] These qualities are emblematic of the "anti-political politics" that were practiced in Czechoslovakia. Benda further discusses other "parallel structures", such as a "parallel economy", a "parallel culture", a "parallel educational system", a "parallel information network", "parallel political structures" including a "parallel foreign policy", and "parallel civic activities". One can even discern "parallel languages" and "parallel behaviors", both of which are forms of political code switching.[24] Extending the position of Henry David Thoreau, Charter 77 essentially opted out of the state, yet without going into the self-exile of social—and political—isolation. Instead of escaping to an apolitical Walden Pond in rural Czechoslovakia for personal and spiritual betterment, these modern revolutionaries *organized* in downtown Prague for social, political, and collective change.

In discussing the dialectics of governmental legitimacy, Marx notes that "one man [*sic*] is king only because other [people] stand in the relation of subjects to him. They, on the other hand, imagine that they are subjects because he is king".[25] Members of Charter 77, and others in Czechoslovakia, deconstructed this power relation. This type of social and political activism was much less common in Slovakia, though, where open dissent, when it occurred at all, tended to be religiously based. Dissidence against the Communist Party regime in Czechoslovakia was, like most

---

[22] Václav Benda, "The Parallel 'Polis'" [originally distributed in *samizdat* form, May 1978] in H. Gordon Skilling and Paul Wilson, eds., *Civic Freedom in Central Europe: Voices from Czechoslovakia* (New York: St. Martin's Press, 1991), pp. 35-41

[23] *Ibid.*, p. 37

[24] *Cf.* Richard Rodriguez, *Hunger of Memory* (Boston: David Godine, 1982); Scott, *Domination and the Arts of Resistance*; E. Perry Link, *Evening Chats in Beijing: Probing China's Predicament* (New York: W.W. Norton, 1992)

[25] Karl Marx, *Capital*, Vol. One [1867], trans. by Ben Fowkes (New York: Vintage Books, 1977), p. 149, fn. 22. *Cf.* Gramsci, *Selections from the Prison Notebooks*

other political activity throughout the country's history, centered in the political and cultural center of Prague.

Historically, political entrepreneurs in Czechoslovakia have (re)produced *velvet political actions*. Consciously or not, the metaphor of social change as velvet has been employed by both rulers and dissidents, and consequently has channeled political rhetoric and collective action.[26]

Whereas French insurgents use their cultural repertoire of erecting barricades and hurling cobblestones to demand and effect social change, and Chinese rebels engage in hyper-patriotism and political theatre,[27] the Czechs employ their culture of soft social change—based on the implicit and cultural *velvet metaphor*—through petitions, peaceful rallies, and symbolic strikes. The protestors in Prague chose to ring their own keychains rather than wring the Party leaders' necks.[28] As Ash noticed while witnessing the Revolution in Prague, the protestors wanted to make the revolution "like the Czechs, that is, gently, tolerantly, without

---

[26] *Cf.* George Lakoff and Mark Johnson, *Metaphors We Live By* (Chicago and London: University of Chicago Press, 1980). Also see George Lakoff, "Bringing the Mind Into Intellectual Discourse", Paper presented at the conference honoring Pierre Bourdieu on *Fin-De-Siecle Intellectuals: Looking Back and Looking Forward*, Berkeley, California, 5 April 1996; George Lakoff, *Moral Politics*, 2nd ed. (Chicago: University of Chicago Press, 2002); and George Lakoff, *Don't Think Of An Elephant* (White River Jct., VT: Chelsea Green Publishing, 2004). Furthermore, "Words [and metaphors, and language generally,] d[o] not just reflect social and political reality; they [a]re instruments for transforming reality" (Lynn Hunt, "Introduction: History, Culture, and Text" in Lynn Hunt, ed., *The New Cultural History* (Berkeley and Los Angeles: University of California Press, 1989), p. 17).

[27] "If South Korean university students are at the militant extreme, totally rejecting the Government and battering lines of police with firebombs and wooden staves, then Chinese demonstrators are at the peaceful extreme. They sometimes go out of their way to say nice things about the Communist Party... and they overwhelm the police as much with courtesy as with force" (Nicholas D. Kristof, "A Chinese Lesson in Polite Protest" in Gwertzman and Kaufman, eds., *The Collapse of Communism*, p. 45). In this way, Chinese protestors have practiced the politics of "rhetoric above reproach".

[28] Many Czech fairy tales conclude with the line, "And the bell rang and that's the end of the story". The potent and almost primeval symbolism of ringing bells, honking horns, and rattling keys during general strikes and political demonstrations against the government was well understood in Czechoslovakia.

hatred and revenge".[29] Indeed, "such modes of collective action become part and parcel of popular culture, and [collective action] becomes something like a scenario... enacted by a large repertory company whose members know the basic plot and can step into the available roles".[30] Hence the opportunities and constraints, indeed the cultural continuity, inherent in the making of social change. The grammar of the Velvet Revolution had already largely been constructed by the time of Czechoslovakia's modern history. Grammars and languages, like states and cultures, *do* change, but only very slowly. Revolutionary times, or other times of crisis such as war or depression, can "telescope" this process, though the magnifying effects of such a lens will still be limited, and, importantly, may create distortion.

---

[29] Ash, *The Magic Lantern*, p. 121. Ash continues to comment that "it would be difficult to imagine a better revolution than the one Czechoslovakia had: swift, almost entirely non-violent, joyful and funny" (p. 129). Here are just a few illustrations of this: "Poster after poster warned against violence... Signs warned people not to write difficult-to-erase slogans with aerosol cans... Posters that were out of date were taken down and the wall from which they had been removed cleaned.... The Journalism Faculty [even] founded a Committee for a more Joyous General Strike". Civic Forum also distributed its "Eight Rules of Dialogue", with Rule One stating that an opponent is not an enemy but rather 'a partner in the search for truth' and with Rule Six counseling people not to offend 'the other' (Frankland, *The Patriots' Revolution*, pp. 284-85).

[30] Scott, *Domination and the Arts of Resistance*, p. 151. *Cf.* Swidler, "Culture in Action"

Chapter V.

The Quiddity of the Economy

"[W]hen we want to comfort ourselves... can we hopefully repeat that these economics are fortunately so contrary to human nature that they cannot finance either missionaries or armies and will surely end in defeat?"

— John Maynard Keynes[1]

Also beginning in the late 1970s, though especially during the 1980s, the economy declined, causing real wages ("lower by about 2 percent in 1983 compared to 1978") and living standards to stagnate and

---

[1] John Maynard Keynes, "A Short View of Russia" [1925], *Daedalus*, Spring 1992

fall. Shortages also became more frequent.[2] Sharon Wolchik states that "by the late 1980s, popular dissatisfaction with the stagnation in living standards and economic inefficiency was matched by official recognition of the need for more fundamental economic reform".[3] Indeed, public opinion polls in 1990 found that most people favored "a conversion to a market economy", though a mixed one with social services and safety nets.[4]

In the 1930s, Czechoslovakia "ranked 10th in the league of economically developed nations",[5] yet by 1980, the government not only declared a decline in gross national product [GNP, now called Gross Domestic Product, or GDP] for the first time, but also announced that only 2 percent of Czechoslovak products were equivalent in terms of quality to

---

[2] Bugajski, *Czechoslovakia*, p. 6. It should be noted that despite some economic problems in Czechoslovakia, inflation (whether official, repressed, or hidden) was relatively slight during the 1980s. Official inflation refers to the reported nominal increase in prices, which was trivial in the late 1980s. Repressed (or suppressed) inflation alludes to lines, product substitution, and forced savings which are estimated to have been less than 5 percent per year for the decade preceding the Revolution. Hidden inflation is associated with covert decreases in product quality which is estimated to have been between 0.5 and 3 percent per year (Zdenek Drabek, Kamil Janacek, and Zdenek Tuma, "Inflation in Czechoslovakia, 1985-91", World Bank Paper 1135, April 1993, http://www.worldbank.org; and Andrew Feltenstein and Jiming Ha, "An Analysis of Repressed Inflation in Three Transitional Economies", World Bank Paper 1132, April 1993, http://www.worldbank.org).

[3] Sharon L. Wolchik, "Czechoslovakia's 'Velvet Revolution'", *Current History*, December 1990, p. 413

[4] *Ibid.*, p. 435. Interestingly, though, "only 3 percent of citizens questioned in late November 1989 and early December 1989 wanted to see Czechoslovakia choose a [purely] capitalist path of development.... There was a similarly high degree of reluctance to accept privatization of the economy" (Wolchik, *Czechoslovakia in Transition*, p. 118).

[5] John F.N. Bradley, *Czechoslovakia's Velvet Revolution: A Political Analysis* (New York: Columbia University Press, 1992), p. xiii

those in the developed countries.[6] Furthermore, there was "a decline in the growth of output per worker in Eastern Europe from 5.5 per cent in the 70s to 2.2 per cent in the 80s".[7]

Moreover, by 1986, according to Bernard Wheaton and Zdenek Kavan, "public opinion polls indicated that a large proportion of the population" disagreed with the Party's ideology or policies.[8] Corruption and dishonesty played no small part in this. As Wheaton and Kavan maintain, "the fundamental challenge to the regime in the 1980s arguably lay in the oft-delayed solutions to structural economic problems that could no longer be put aside".[9] Czechoslovak leaders worried about the unsatisfactory economic performance of the late 1980s, while the planned targets for 1985-90, though modest, later had to be revised downward. Yet, in spite of this, Czechoslovakia achieved "a record harvest in 1984, and was nearly self-sufficient in grain in 1987 and 1988". There was even a further agricultural increase in 1989.[10]

Economic legitimacy began to fall nearly as low as political legitimacy. The "little deal", and with it the entire rigid system of "new class" bureaucracy and élitism, was crumbling.[11] Importantly, though, "the

---

[6] Whipple, ed., *After the Velvet Revolution*, p. 8

[7] Ramnath Narayanswamy, "Causes and Consequences of the East European Revolutions of 1989", *Economic and Political Weekly*, 15 February 1992, p. 367

[8] Wheaton and Kavan, *The Velvet Revolution*, p. 24. Public opinion research in Czechoslovakia dates back to 1946 (Wolchik, *Czechoslovakia in Transition*, p. 147). There are, of course, a multitude of potential problems with public polling, from the methodology to the form to the content. Nevertheless, I believe it is sometimes possible to use polls as provisional indicators, though never as conclusive results.

[9] Wheaton and Kavan, *The Velvet Revolution*, p. 13

[10] Wolchik, *Czechoslovakia in Transition*, pp. 227, 231-31

[11] *Cf.* James O'Connor, *The Fiscal Crisis of the State* (New York: St. Martin's Press, 1973) and Jürgen Habermas, *Legitimation Crisis*, trans. by Thomas McCarthy (Boston: Beacon Press, 1975). For an interesting synthesis of these two threads, see Alan Wolfe, *The Limits of Legitimacy* (New York: The Free Press, 1977). Also see Oskar Lange, "On the Theory of Economic Socialism" in

(continued...)

fundamental problem of socialism was not economic but political. On purely economic grounds socialism might have survived.... It was more difficult for socialist governments to develop democratic institutions than to implement economic reforms that produced sufficient economic growth".[12] China is a classic example of this phenomenon.

Economic phenomena are in actuality never separated from cultural factors, political concerns, social relations, and the environmental context; although it is possible to do so for heuristic purposes. Indeed, economic phenomena are always "embedded" within the social realm.[13] "Although the revolution of 1989 was not based primarily on economic grievances", according to Wolchik, "poor economic performance helped to erode popular support for or toleration of the [C]ommunist [Party]

---

[11](...continued)
Benjamin Lippincott, ed., *On the Economic Theory of Socialism* (Minneapolis: University of Minnesota Press, 1938) and Milovan Djilas, *The New Class: An Analysis of the Communist System* (New York: Praeger, 1957). Djilas' specific focus is on Yugoslavia, however his analysis applies equally well to all Communist Party countries. Bakunin launched similar prophesies and criticisms in his debates with Marx. *Cf.* Leon Trotsky, *The Revolution Betrayed* (London: Faber & Faber, 1937); R.W. Davies, "Gorbachev's Socialism in Historical Perspective", *New Left Review*, January-February 1990; and Chirot, *How Societies Change*, p. 97

[12] Szelenyi, Beckett, and King, "The Socialist Economic System" in Smelser and Swedberg, eds., *The Handbook of Economic Sociology*, p. 247. Oskar Lange, who coined the term "market socialism", believed that political bureaucratization poses a larger threat to socialism than does economic inefficiency.

[13] Polanyi, *The Great Transformation*; Karl Polanyi, Conrad Arensberg, and Harry Pearson, eds., *Trade and Market in the Early Empires: Economies in History and Theory* (Chicago: Henry Regnery Co., 1971 [1957]), p. 250: "The human economy... is embedded and enmeshed in institutions, economic and noneconomic. The inclusion of the noneconomic is vital. For religion or government may be as important to the structure and functioning of the economy as monetary institutions or the availability of tools and machines themselves"; Granovetter, "Economic Action and Social Structure: The Problem of Embeddedness". Also see Tsuyoshi Hasegawa, "The Connection Between Political and Economic Reform in Communist Regimes" in Rozman *et al.*, eds., *Dismantling Communism*.

during the last years of communist rule".[14] Ultimately, though, none of the mass popular protests of the revolutionary situations of 1989 were motivated by strictly economic factors. Economic factors, therefore, interacted indirectly, though synergistically, with other social, political, and cultural long-standing conditions.

To be quidditous is to be essential, trivial, or somehow both. The Czechoslovak economy was precisely that.

---

[14] Wolchik, *Czechoslovakia in Transition*, p. 224

Chapter VI.

The Gorbachev Phenomenon

"For me, Marxism is what Newton's physics is for a mathematician. Maybe Gorbachev with his changes is a kind of Einstein"
— Jiri Hajek[1]

The rise to power of Mikhail Gorbachev in March 1985 also spurred on the anti-authoritarian movement in Eastern Europe by increasing what has been called a "permissive international context" or "world-systemic opening".[2] Gorbachev's introduction of the policies of

---

[1] Cited in James M. Markham, "Across a Divided Europe, An Ideology Under Siege", *New York Times*, 23 January 1989, p. A11

[2] Walter Goldfrank, "Theories of Revolution and Revolution Without Theory: The Case of Mexico", *Theory and Society*, January-March 1979; John Foran and (continued...)

Glasnost and *Perestroika* into the Soviet Union in 1986 raised hopes and expectations throughout that country, in addition to raising hopes across Eastern Europe and in China, as well. Gorbachev, in contradistinction to all previous Soviet leaders, urged the leaders in Eastern Europe to reform the Communist parties and their centralized economies, so as to be more responsive to the masses in both the political and economic realms.

Gorbachev not only permitted popular social movements to develop in Eastern Europe, he even encouraged them. In yet another unprecedented historical move, Gorbachev apologized for the Soviet Union's past interference and use of violence in the affairs of other countries.[3] Gorbachev thereby effectively repealed the "Brezhnev Doctrine" and introduced what Karl and Schmitter have humorously termed the "Sinatra Doctrine"—"you can do it your own way".[4] On 25 October 1989, Gorbachev's Foreign Ministry spokesperson, Gennady Gerasimov, was asked whether the Brezhnev Doctrine was still the policy of the Soviet Union. He spontaneously (?) responded that "Sinatra had a song, 'I did it my way...'. So every country decides in its own way which road to take".[5] And so they did.

---

[2](...continued)
Jeff Goodwin, "Revolutionary Outcomes in Iran and Nicaragua: Coalition Fragmentation, War, and the Limits of Social Transformation", *Theory and Society*, 1993. More generally, this concept has been referred to as a social or political opportunity.

[3] Chomsky, *What Uncle Sam Really Wants*, pp. 69-71. No other superpower has ever done this. Interestingly, Chomsky notes, "The one country in Eastern Europe where there was extensive violence as the tyrannies collapsed was the very one where the Soviets had the least amount of influence and where [the U.S.] had the most: Romania.... Elsewhere in Eastern Europe, the uprisings were remarkably peaceful. There was some repression, but historically, 1989 was unique". Likewise with Yugoslavia. Romania and Yugoslavia also experienced the least amount of democratic social change in Eastern Europe.

[4] Karl and Schmitter, "Modes of Transition in Latin America, Southern and Eastern Europe", p. 274

[5] Cited in Dahrendorf, *Reflections on the Revolution in Europe*, p. 16. It is important to note that although this remark preceded the revolution in Czechoslovakia, it did not precede the revolutionary movement in that country or (continued...)

For Gorbachev, this idea of non-interference in the affairs of other countries was not an abstract concept; he practiced it, especially in 1989. Gorbachev recalled the last of the Soviet Red Army troops from Afghanistan on 15 February after over nine years of direct intervention, allowed the freest elections in Russian history on 26 March, visited China and gave moral support to the protesting students of Beijing in mid-May, and encouraged Cuba to withdraw its troops from Angola, and Vietnam to do the same with regard to Cambodia. In various speeches, moreover, Gorbachev stated that the military—or even the *threat* of force—should not, and *would* not, be used as a weapon of foreign policy. this was monumental and cannot be underestimated.

It is a strange but interesting fact that all Soviet soldiers returning from Afghanistan were given wristwatches by the Defense Ministry. Perhaps the Soviet military sensed that time was running out for the Communist Party and for its empire. Once again in the twentieth century, Soviet political economy and history were affecting Eastern European (and other) societies and biographies in a deeply profound way. "Indeed, superpower influence can be fatal to neopatrimonial regimes", Goldstone points out, "when superpower policy swings between contradictory goals, undermining the basis for such regimes".[6]

Ironically, Gorbachev's plans of *Glasnost* and *Perestroika* for the Soviet Union in the mid-to-late 1980s were not substantially dissimilar from those of Dubcek and the other Reform Communists for Czechoslovakia in 1968 (and from the path of Imre Nagy for Hungary in 1956). For this reason, Gorbachev's reforms may have had an additional psychic and cultural effect on the people of Czechoslovakia (and Hungary).[7]

Gorbachev first legitimated the Prague Spring in effect, and then eventually did so in word and deed, as well, thereby giving moral support to the forces of change in the late 1980s. Indeed, support for the Prague

---

[5](...continued)
any other country in Eastern Europe. In that sense, the remark was made *post facto*.

[6] Goldstone, "Revolutions in Modern Dictatorships" in Goldstone, ed., *Revolutions*, Second ed., p. 77. Also see Gurr and Goldstone, "Comparisons and Policy Implications" in Keddie, ed., *Debating Revolutions*, esp. pp. 332-33

[7] Bradley, *Czechoslovakia's Velvet Revolution*, p. 29

Spring of 1968 had become a metaphorical vehicle, and therefore a powerful and effective organizing tool, for support of revolutionary change in 1989. In this way, history itself was newly re-packaged as a symbol of hope and as an icon of rebellion. The events of '89, were for many, those of '68 turned upside down, both literally and figuratively, as many Czech protestors delighted in pointing out.

Perhaps it was not ironic, though, that Gorbachev's *Perestroika* and *Glasnost* were similar to Dubcek's reform communism. Gorbachev resurrected many people from Khrushchev's "reform generation" who worked in Prague during the 1960s and early 1970s on *The World Marxist Review*. Known as the "Prague Club" in Moscow, many of them became advisors to Gorbachev and the architects of Soviet reform policies in the late 1980s.[8]

Gorbachev's support for change and his unwillingness to intervene militarily was a necessary condition for the success of the Revolution, and especially for its velvet nature. Adam Przeworski is particularly blunt on this point:

> The Gorbachev revolution [*sic*] in the Soviet Union obviously played a crucial role in unleashing the events in Eastern Europe. It was the single precipitating event... The threat of Soviet intervention... was the constraint on internal developments in Eastern Europe. But it was only that: the constraint... The change in the Soviet Union did not propel transformations... what it did was to remove the crucial factor that had been blocking them. *The constraint was external, but the impetus was internal.*[9]

In short, Gorbachev created a political opening and opportunity that

---

[8] Luers, "Czechoslovakia: Road to Revolution", pp. 79-80

[9] Przeworski, *Democracy and the Market*, p. 5, emphasis added

dissidents in Czechoslovakia (and elsewhere in Eastern Europe) could take advantage of and that leaders had to respond to.

Goldstone appropriately makes the analogy between Gorbachev's *Glasnost* in 1989 and Louis XVI's calling of the Estates-General in 1789. Both were intended as major reforms, both symbolic and substantive, to stave off and coopt revolutionary processes already at work; yet both also opened up a political Pandora's Box. By encouraging their citizens to meet, raise, discuss, and debate the problems of the nation, both Louis XVI and Gorbachev could no longer control the forces of change that they had unleashed. The popular upsurges that followed were quick to materialize, irresistible, massive, and ultimately overwhelming.[10]

Gorbachev's policies were not just a cause of political economic changes, but also a result of earlier ones. Indeed, Gorbachev's reforms were a response to growing political and economic costs associated with empire. This was largely due to the Soviet bloc's sagging economies, its increasing dissidence and political independence, widespread social frustration, ethnic assertion, and other internal constraints and contradictions. At the same time, the possible military and other benefits of maintaining the Soviet empire were, to say the least, increasingly less obvious.

Pietro Grilli di Cortona refers to the upheavals in Eastern Europe, based on the Gorbachev phenomenon, as "a bundle of strictly inter-connected events".[11] Karl and Schmitter likewise consider the events of 1989 to be "part of the same process in that each successive one ha[d] contributed to the likelihood of the next".[12] Nevertheless, inasmuch as these events may have been linked in certain important ways, like siblings each one was also a unique phenomenon. To suggest otherwise is to ignore the variety of cultural histories, revolutionary trajectories, and socio-political economic outcomes in Eastern Europe and China, and indeed in the universe of Communist Party countries. Close comparisons of Czechoslovakia with, for example, Yugoslavia, let alone Cuba and Nicaragua; China and North Korea; Vietnam, Laos, and Cambodia; and

---

[10] Goldstone, "Theories of Revolution, Elite Crisis, and the Transformation of the USSR", p. 25

[11] Grilli di Cortona, "From Communism to Democracy", p. 324

[12] Karl and Schmitter, "Modes of Transition in Latin America, Southern and Eastern Europe", p. 280

Angola and Mozambique, would be rather difficult, though of course possible. Similarities and patterns may still exist, however, at higher levels of abstraction and causality.

Chapter VII.

Mass Media, Meaning, and Mobilization

"...the mobilization of information and knowledge may be as important as the mobilization of people..."
— Bernadette Barker-Plummer[1]

In addition to, and in conjunction with, Gorbachev's major reforms, the Czechoslovak people were also substantially influenced by the mass media, through which they learned about Gorbachev's proposals and other information of interest, which their own government neglected. News reports regarding events both inside and out of Czechoslovakia from the BBC, Radio Free Europe, and television stations from West Germany,

[1] Bernadette Barker-Plummer, "The Dialogic of Media and Social Movements", *Peace Review*, March 1996, p. 27

Austria, and Hungary, in addition to the Czechoslovak mass media were quite significant. The people were able to realize that their individual personal problems were also collective political issues, and ones that potentially could be addressed and resolved.

Connections between the mass media and revolutionary situations have been noted by both participants and observers for hundreds of years across a wide variety of countries and movements, from Thomas Paine to New York printshop workers, from Napoleon to Lenin, and from Khomeini to the student rebels in Tiananmen Square, to name just a few. Indeed, the first thing Lenin did, in 1901, to foment revolution in Russia was to publish and edit a newspaper which he appropriately called *The Spark*.[2] Newspapers and pamphlets may still be important for various functions, and they do have a role in revolutions; however, they clearly have been eclipsed by the much more powerful and graphic medium of television, especially during the revolutionary moment itself.

"The crucial medium was", Ash says of the Velvet Revolution in Czechoslovakia, "television, and to a lesser extent, radio. As in Poland and Hungary, the battle for access to and fair coverage on television and radio was one of the two or three most important political issues".[3] Most especially, the mass media coverage of radical upheavals occurring in the other countries of Eastern Europe and China, and the protest demonstrations within their own country being suppressed by state violence, were powerful influences on Czechoslovak citizens. Like nothing else, televised (and videotaped) depictions of symbols and icons were able to show graphically the past, present, and future of the Communist Party State and were very effectively able to contrast perceptions of what *is* with what *ought to be* and what *can be*. As Dahrendorf suggests, moreover, television especially changes the "time scale" of revolutionary situations

---

[2] Popkin, "Media and Revolutionary Crises" in Popkin, ed., *Media and Revolution*, p. 13. Lenin states that "a newspaper is not only a collective propagandist and a collective agitator; it is also a collective organizer" (cited in *Ibid.*).

[3] Ash, *The Magic Lantern*, p. 91; also see pp. 15, 22. *Cf.* "Romanian TV Becomes Soul of Revolution", *San Francisco Chronicle*, 27 December 1989, pp. A1+. But also see Johnson, "Mass Media and the Velvet Revolution" in Popkin, ed., *Media and Revolution*, esp. p. 220.

by quickening the pace between actions and reactions.[4] There's no doubt that, in 1989, revolutionary situations were moving quite rapidly in country after country.

"The world is now enmeshed in webs of telecommunication networks", according to Havel, "consisting of millions of tiny threads or capillaries that not only transmit information of all kinds at lightning speed, but also convey *integrated models of social, political, and economic behavior*. They are conduits for legal norms, as well.... More than that", he continues to assert, "the capillaries that have so radically integrated this civilization also convey information about certain modes of human coexistence that have proven their worth, like democracy [and] respect for human rights".[5] In the phrase of Edward Herman and Noam Chomsky, the mass media engage in "manufacturing consent"; in Czechoslovakia, and throughout Eastern Europe and China, it was in support of democratic dissidence and direct action.

Being western and corporate, the mass media biases were against Communism and totalitarianism, and towards capitalism and democracy—at least in the formal sense if not the substantive.[6] The mass

---

[4] Cited in Tyler Marshall, "TV a Star Player on the World's Political Stage", *Los Angeles Times*, 20 October 1992

[5] Václav Havel, 1995 Harvard University Commencement Address, http://world.std.com/~awolpert/gtr19.html, emphasis added. Corroboration is found in a leaked Hungarian Communist Party [Hungarian Socialist Workers Party] policy document— labeled strictly confidential—which states that *samizdat* publishers need to be suppressed and that the Communist Party's main concern was with the connections between the opposition and "Western propaganda centres" (Misha Glenny, "Hungary Opposition 'has links to West'", *Guardian*, 4 May 1987).

[6] Edward S. Herman and Noam Chomsky, *Manufacturing Consent: The Political Economy of the Mass Media* (New York: Pantheon, 1988). For an earlier study employing the same concept with regard to corporations and the labor process, see Michael Burawoy, *Manufacturing Consent: Changes in the Labor Process Under Monopoly Capitalism* (Chicago: University of Chicago Press, 1979). Further, E.E. Schattschneider in *The Semi-Sovereign People* (New York: Holt, Rinehart and Winston, 1960) discusses a "mobilization of bias", while Ralph Miliband refers to an "engineering of consent". Also see Ethan Huang, "Disinformation in Democratic Society", *Chinese Community Forum*, 23 October 1996.

(continued...)

media fueled, as William Gamson indicates in a different context, the symbolic struggle over meaning and interpretation and, indeed, "The sheer existence of a symbolic contest is evidence of the breakdown of hegemony and [is] a major accomplishment for a challenger".[7]

"Historically, the empowered elite have always sought to suppress the wider distribution of ideas, wealth, rights and, most of all, knowledge".[8] The Communist Party followed this pattern closely, obsessively suppressing information about the ideas, organizations, and activities of dissidents. However, the Communist Party's use of the mass media was a double-edged sword. Prior to 1989, the mass media were also extraordinarily effective in nationalizing (and internationalizing) both the opposition generally and the opposition leaders, such as Havel, in particular. As his work was banned in Czechoslovakia, his words were only known through the distribution of *samizdat*, and with that, still mostly in Prague. However, through news of both his awards and his arrests, the mass media, Western and Czechoslovak, helped to make Havel a *national*

---

[6](...continued)

Had the revolutionary movements in Eastern Europe and China been explicitly socialist, as well as (substantively) democratic, the biases and role of the mass media might have been different. Todd Gitlin seems to neglect the subtlety of this "suppressed historical alternative". Gitlin's argument that the mass media will "marginalize" or "incorporate" dissident voices and movements may apply even less so when the media are covering different, especially adversarial, social systems. *Cf.* Barker-Plummer, "The Dialogic of Media and Social Movements", p. 31: "the general tendency of routine media practices to work against serious representation of social change organizations, is simply that—a tendency". Unfortunately, a comparative analysis of the mass media during revolutionary moments is beyond the scope of this book, though necessary for a holistic study of revolutionary situations.

[7] William A. Gamson, "The Social Psychology of Collective Action" in Aldon D. Morris & Carol McClurg Mueller, eds., *Frontiers in Social Movement Theory* (New Haven, CT and London: Yale University Press, 1992), p. 68

[8] John Lippman, "Tuning in the Global Village: How TV is Transforming World Culture and Politics", *Los Angeles Times*, 20 October 1992, p. 2. "Marshall McLuhan coined the phrase 'global village' to describe how the electronics revolution [is] shrinking the world and shortening the time between thought and action".

leader for the first time.[9] Indeed, William Brinton argues that "the revolution from below that had elected him president... was based to a significant degree on the use of... television".[10] "To discredit Havel once and for all", in 1989, according to John Bradley, the Communist Party's "official press gave the playwright nationwide coverage not realizing that they were creating a charismatic opposition leader".[11]

In this way, the mass media, especially television, literally mediated the revolution by providing a graphic link between and among events and people. Havel himself has referred to "the media's double-edged power", as opposed to a Gramscian hegemonic conception. "Quickly, suggestively, and to an unprecedented degree", Havel elaborates, the media "can disseminate the spirit of understanding, humanity, human solidarity, and spirituality, or it can stupefy whole nations and continents".[12] What once appeared to be a strong weapon in the Communist Party's arsenal, quickly and quietly transformed itself into another weapon employed against the Party. In a form of cultural and political jujitsu, the power of the media, which the Communist Party once used so notoriously, was now being used *against* the Communist Party

---

[9] *Cf.* Tim McDaniel, *Autocracy, Modernization, and Revolution in Russia and Iran* (Princeton, NJ: Princeton University Press, 1991), p. 220: "The critical event [in Iran] was the vicious attack on Khomeini in a government-related newspaper in January 1978... The following day religious students in Qom demonstrated against the government, which reacted violently... From this time forward the religious forces never relinquished their leadership in the movement".

[10] William M. Brinton, "The Role of Media in a Telerevolution" in William M. Brinton and Alan Rinzler, eds., *Without Force or Lies: Voices from the Revolution of Central Europe in 1989-90* (San Francisco, CA: Mercury House, 1990), p. 460

[11] Bradley, *Czechoslovakia's Velvet Revolution*, p. 49. *Cf.* Foucault, *Discipline and Punish*, p. 67: "The condemned man found himself transformed into a hero by the sheer extent of his widely advertised crimes... [H]e appeared to have waged a struggle with which one all too easily identified. The proclamations of these crimes blew up to epic proportions the tiny struggle that passed unperceived in everyday life".

[12] Havel, 1995 Harvard University Commencement Address

regime itself.[13]

The attempted demonization of Havel and Charter 77, perhaps more than anything else, helped, to paraphrase Thomas Kuhn, shift the cultural paradigm and thereby create the basis for achieving a situation in which there was a viable alternative ideology, organization, and leader, as opposed to the government or state, to which people could—and did—give their allegiance and support. This is what Leon Trotsky calls "dual power" and what Charles Tilly refers to as "multiple sovereignty", but what in Czechoslovakia is known as "the parallel polis".[14]

When Czechoslovak citizens saw iconographic images of state security forces beating peaceful protestors, the people of Czechoslovakia simultaneously saw the past lashing out against the future in a desperate death spasm. As a result, people were increasingly mobilized and they enthusiastically joined the growing numbers of active dissidents.

A large, but peaceful, protest march on 17 November 1989 was violently suppressed by the state security forces. This event marks a highly significant point in the process of the revolution in Czechoslovakia. Approximately 15,000 people gathered in Prague on the evening of the

---

[13] *Cf.* Johnson, "Mass Media and the Velvet Revolution", in Popkin, ed., *Media and Revolution*, p. 229

[14] Thomas S. Kuhn, *The Structure of Scientific Revolutions*, Enlarged Second Ed. (Chicago: University of Chicago Press, 1970 [1962]); Leon Trotsky, *The History of the Russian Revolution* [1932], trans. by Max Eastman (Ann Arbor: University of Michigan Press, 1957); Tilly, *From Mobilization to Revolution*; Benda, "The Parallel 'Polis'" in Skilling and Wilson, eds., *Civic Freedom in Central Europe*.

It is interesting to note that a situation of dual power / multiple sovereignty exists between the People's Republic of China and the Republic of China (Taiwan), as the government of each political entity officially lays claim to the other, while both recognize Taiwan as a province of the mainland. As a province, and a relatively rich one at that, Taiwan certainly comprises a substantial part of (greater) China with a significant constituency, just as Beijing or Shanghai does. Despite this situation since 1949, though, a revolutionary situation does not exist, even though Beijing refers to Taiwan as a "rebellious province". The situation may at times be diplomatically tense, with the *potential* for military action ever present, but it is hardly revolutionary; discussions, meetings, tourism, trade, and investment still occur without difficulty. If anything, this situation can be characterized as a cold civil war. Perhaps the facts of geographical separation and of *de facto* independence for Taiwan make this case an anomaly; perhaps the theories of Trotsky and Tilly need to be rethought and revised regarding this issue.

17th to commemorate the fiftieth anniversary of the death of Jan Opletal, a dissident student killed by the Nazis after they closed the Czech universities in 1939. The demonstrators proceeded to the cemetery where Opletal is buried, at least doubling their size along the way. After the graveside speeches, some of which were directly critical of the government and the Party, some students led a large, and mostly young, contingent of protestors to the river and downtown toward Wenceslas Square. Many marchers called for various democratic freedoms, while being waved to and applauded from doorways, windows, and sidewalks.

On one street before Wenceslas Square, riot police suddenly appeared and blocked the marchers' way; more riot police came down a sidestreet and blocked a possible retreat. Many of the protestors sat down, placing lighted candles in the street, while others were trying to decorate some of the riot shields. The two groups of riot police moved towards each other, thereby squeezing the crowd and causing many to panic. Worse yet, the Ministry of Interior's Division for Special Purposes arrived in military uniforms and red berets, some of whom seem to have been hiding behind scaffolding. The police and soldiers violently attacked, arresting and wounding hundreds of people. A student named Martin Smid was (erroneously) rumored to have been killed.[15] The analogies to Jan Opletal were quickly, easily, and damningly made.

Some of the events of that fateful day and night were filmed and, within days, 2,000 videotapes were being seen throughout the country, especially in the Czech regions. A television in the window of the Magic Lantern Theatre showed one of these tapes almost continuously. Someone also placed a handwritten poster on the statue of St. Wenceslas which

---

[15] Frankland, *The Patriots' Revolution*, pp. 275-76, 280-83. The information came out in the spring of 1990, after an official inquiry, that two young State Security agents were involved in the violent suppression of the marchers in Prague on 17 November. One supposedly led the protestors into the police trap and then pretended to be dead, while another agent, Drahomira Drazska, told Petr Uhl, a distributor of dissident *samizdat*, that her boyfriend Martin Smid had been killed. Two days after the "massacre", *two* students named Martin Smid "were shown live on television and Petr Uhl was arrested for spreading false information about a death that had not taken place". It remains unclear why the security forces did this. One possibility would be to discredit the popular movement, while another possibility would be to covertly support the revolutionary movement. Open warfare never broke out between different branches of the government in Czechoslovakia, as it did in Romania (and later in Russia), however there were some *serious* disagreements on policy and tactics.

read: "Parents, come with us. We are your children". Many of them did. From that point on, continuous mass protest demonstrations crowded downtown Prague day after day without *any* further incidents of state repression or police violence. As a member of Charter 77 poignantly commented, "Sometimes there are days that are more important than years". Undoubtedly, the 17th of November 1989 was one of those days.

During the revolutionary situation, an Asian man, possibly Japanese or Chinese, dropped off "a valise full of brand-new and unmarked 2400-baud Taiwanese modems", which of course were illegal, with some physics and engineering students.[16] "The students immediately used these... modems to circulate manifestos, declarations of solidarity, rumors, and riot news" with other students using toaster-sized 300-baud modems.[17] Other narrow cast media, in addition to the internet, such as graffiti, handbills, posters, photographs, and pamphlets, were also employed to help mobilize dissent and rebellion.

The mass media, and also the mass mobilization, were much more pronounced in Prague and on the Czech side of Czechoslovakia as opposed to Bratislava and the Slovak side. On both sides of Czechoslovakia, however, it was a far cry ahead of the Prague Spring of twenty-one years earlier when communications networks were significantly less dense in the capital, the country, the region, and the world.

The mass media in 1989 were able to disperse symbolic power and actual legitimacy from the government to the opposition, especially Charter 77, and later the Czech opposition coalition, Civic Forum, and its Slovak counterpart, Public Against Violence. On 23 November, a Czech newspaper even advised its readers to talk with their fellow citizens and not be misled by the mass media. By 27 November, a television anchorperson declared support for the general strike of that day and showed pictures of huge crowds in the streets of Prague around Wenceslas Square. This is probably why Napoleon stated: "I fear the Cologne Gazette

---

[16] Bruce Sterling, "Triumph of the Plastic People", *Wired*, January 1995, http://www.hotwired.com/wired/3.01/features/prague.html, p. 2

[17] *Ibid.*

more than 10,000 bayonets".[18] Napoleon's fear was not misplaced.

As Sidney Tarrow argues, "in 1989, the spread of the democratic movement in Eastern Europe—not to mention its tragic echo in China—left little doubt that collective action can spread by global communication".[19] Indeed, it is interesting to note that when Lech Walesa was asked what he thought caused the ouster of the Communist Party regime, he didn't point to his organization, Solidarity, rather he pointed to a television set and said: "It all came from there".[20] Largely due to these phenomena, Ash claims that "at the end of the twentieth century all revolutions are telerevolutions".[21] The mass media is inescapable.

---

[18] Cited in Wickham-Crowley, *Guerrillas & Revolution in Latin America*, p. 174

[19] Sidney Tarrow, *Power in Movement: Social Movements, Collective Action and Politics* (Cambridge and New York: Cambridge University Press, 1994), p. 194

[20] Cited in Lippman, "Tuning in the Global Village", p. 1

[21] Ash, *The Magic Lantern*, p. 94

Chapter VIII.

The Role of Relative Deprivation

"Although Eastern Europe is much more developed than the Third World, it is much less developed than Western Europe"
— York Bradshaw & Michael Wallace[1]

Recalling a better past and desiring a better future, the stagnation and misery of the present augmented discontent and feelings of "relative deprivation". According to Ted Gurr, relative deprivation is defined as "a perceived discrepancy between [people's] value expectations and [their] value capabilities", *i.e.* a situation when people are not getting what they

[1] Bradshaw and Wallace, *Global Inequalities*, p. 122

reasonably feel that they deserve.[2] While it may be true that there is always

---

[2] Ted Robert Gurr, *Why Men Rebel* (Princeton, NJ: Princeton University Press, 1970). *Cf.* Marx, "Wage Labor and Capital" in Tucker, ed., *The Marx-Engels Reader*, p. 211: "If capital is growing rapidly, wages may rise; the profit of capital rises incomparably more rapidly. The material position of the worker has improved, but at the cost of his social position. The social gulf that divides [the worker] from the capitalist has widened"; Émile Durkheim, *Socialism and Saint-Simon* [1928] cited in Irving M. Zeitlin, *Ideology and the Development of Sociological Theory*, Second ed. (Englewood Cliffs, NJ: Prentice-Hall, 1981), pp. 255-56: "What is needed if social order is to reign... is that the mass of [people] be content with their lot. But what is needed for them to be content, is not that they have more or less but that they be convinced they have no right to more"; W.E.B. Du Bois, "The Revelation of Saint Orgne the Damned" [commencement speech at Fisk University in 1938] in Philip S. Foner, ed., *W.E.B. Du Bois Speaks* (New York: Pathfinder, 1970), p. 107 cited in James Jennings, *Understanding the Nature of Poverty in Urban America* (Westport, CT: Praeger, 1994), p. 79: the "most distressing fact in the present world is poverty; not absolute poverty... not poverty as great as some lands and other historical ages have known; but poverty more poignant and discouraging because it comes after a dream of wealth; of riotous, wasteful and even vulgar accumulation of individual riches"; Albert O. Hirschman, *Shifting Involvements: Private Interest and Public Action* (Princeton, NJ: Princeton University Press, 1982); Walton, *Reluctant Rebels*, p. 152: "immediately prior to the revolutionary outbreak [in the Philippines, Colombia, and Kenya] there was a redoubling of economic and political deprivation (absolutely, not to mention relatively)"; Mary Crow Dog, *Lakota Woman* (New York: HarperPerennial, 1990), p. 26: "To be angry, poverty has to rub shoulders with wealth"; Block, *Postindustrial Possibilities*, p. 180: "Although most people [in the U.S.] were better off at the end of the 1970s than at the beginning, the improvement was far smaller than what people imagined they were due [partly because of high inflation]... The result was a sense of disappointment". (On the following page, Block cites a 1987 *New York Times* article entitled "Feeling Poor on $600,000 a Year" [!] which details how some bankers feel relatively deprived because they do not feel that they have attained the level of status that they desire.); Tarrow, *Power in Movement*, p. 165: "Like many other protest cycles, the 1848 [Rebellions] left the most bitter memories where the hopes it had generated were highest".

Gurr's typology of relative deprivation includes decremental, aspirational, and progressive. Others have added "accelerated" (Hagopian, *The Phenomenon of Revolution*, pp. 174-75). But see Goldstone, "Theories of Revolution: The Third Generation", esp. pp. 427-28; also see David Snyder and Charles Tilly, "Hardship and Collective Violence in France, 1830 to 1960", *American Sociological Review*, October 1972, p. 526: "The theories of a linkage (continued...)

a certain level of expectations, frustration, and relative deprivation,[3] relative deprivation is *itself* relative, and is therefore amenable to an increase (or decrease) at certain times.

It is when relative deprivation *increases* that people are much more likely to resist and rebel.[4] And that is precisely what the people of Czechoslovakia, especially the Czechs, did. Teodor Shanin notes that

> Social scientists often miss a centrepiece of any revolutionary struggle—the fervour and anger that drives revolutionaries and makes them into what they are. Academic training and bourgeois convention deaden its appreciation. The "phenomenon" cannot be easily "operationalized" into factors, tables and figures.... At the very centre of revolution lies an emotional upheaval of moral indignation, revulsion and fury with the powers-that-be, such that one cannot remain

---

[2](...continued)
between relative deprivation and collective violence [collective action?] propounded by... Gurr and many others can safely be rejected... The alternative theories which we favor treat collective violence as a by-product of struggles for political power.... Collective violence, then, tends to occur when one group lays claim to a set of resources, and at least one other group resists that claim." Snyder and Tilly seem to be mischaracterizing Gurr's conception and neglecting the varieties in his typology, however.

For earlier uses of the concept of relative deprivation, see S.A. Stouffer *et al.*, *The American Soldier*, Vol. 1 (Princeton, NJ: Princeton University Press, 1949); Robert K. Merton, *Social Theory and Social Structure* (New York: Free Press, 1957); and James C. Davies, "Toward a Theory of Revolution", *American Sociological Review*, February 1962.

[3] See, *e.g.*, Tilly, *Big Structures Large Processes Huge Comparisons*, p. 104

[4] See, *e.g.*, Davies, "Toward a Theory of Revolution"; Gurr, *Why Men Rebel.*

> silent, whatever the cost.[5]

This does not imply, as Gurr suggests, that relative deprivation is uni-causal, deterministic, or teleological in any way, or that the socio-political responses to relative deprivation necessarily result in violence. Nor should relative deprivation only imply individual psychological responses.

Relative deprivation, by definition of course, does not arise in isolation and, besides being psychological, must be understood within a broad social, cultural, political, and economic context. Relative deprivation is inherently social, moral, historical, and relational. Additionally, people's responses to relative deprivation do not necessarily have to be aggressive or violent, but rather more likely will result in "cognitive liberation", "political consciousness", "undirected anger", or general "frustration", unless it is effectively organized. The role of the political entrepreneur is to channel this new (private) energy toward social and collective (*i.e.*, public) goals.

Paul Hollander asserts that one of the "distinctive attributes" of Communist Party systems is their capacity to inspire frustration and discontent. This is due to the epidemic awareness of the significant rift

> between theory and practice, propaganda and reality, political promise and material fulfillment. In every society social ideals diverge from daily practices but communist systems magnify and intensify awareness of this divergence by the flagrant and routinized denials of reality... these systems implanted historically unparalleled levels of cynicism, dissatisfaction, sense of deprivation and disgust with the

[5] Teodor Shanin, *The Roots of Otherness: Russia's Turn of the Century*, Vol. 2: *Russia, 1905-1907, Revolution as a Moment of Truth* (New Haven and London: Yale University Press, 1986), p. 30 cited in John Foran, "Revolutionizing Theory / Theorizing Revolutions", *Contention*, Winter 1993, p. 86

[ruling élite].[6]

These feelings of "deprivation and disgust", ubiquitously felt, generally remained private—and therefore invisible—in Eastern Europe.

Relative deprivation in 1989 was probably higher than at any other time in Czechoslovak history, with the possible exception of the immediate post-Prague Spring era. The normalization regime which replaced Dubcek, however, did not allow the widespread feelings of relative deprivation to be translated into any collective action. Individual beliefs were tolerated to the extent that they were socially and publicly invisible. The ideological and coercive powers of the state repressed nearly all outward and public manifestations of frustration with a variety of harsh measures designed simultaneously to punish the individual perpetrator and to terrorize the general populace. With certain notable exceptions, it seemed to be a remarkably successful strategy. Yet this success, too, was more appearance than reality. In 1989, the political stewpot in Czechoslovakia, along with those in the rest of Eastern Europe and China, began to boil over again; however, this time the causal convergence gave rise to certain social and political opportunities which allowed for more collective and public manifestations of frustration.

Being smaller and poorer, the Slovak section had gained more vis-à-vis the Czech section, both politically and economically, under Communist Party rule in Czechoslovakia. Therefore, both the Prague (not Bratislava!) Spring and the Velvet Revolution were "very much... Czech affair[s]".[7] Indeed, "Since 1968 greater efforts ha[d] been made to raise the Slovaks' economic level [and political standing vis-à-vis the Czechs'], and so their sense of relative deprivation may [have been] less acute than that of the Czechs".[8] This is further illustrated by surveys from 1991 that report up to "80 percent of Slovaks... opposed to a market economy" and 87 percent dissatisfied with post-revolutionary socio-economic

---

[6] Hollander, "The Mystery of the Transformation of Communist Systems", p. 21

[7] Otto Ulc, "The Bumpy Road of Czechoslovakia's Velvet Revolution", *Problems of Communism*, May-June 1992, p. 29

[8] Zvi Gitelman, "The Politics of Socialist Restoration in Hungary and Czechoslovakia" in Goldstone, ed., *Revolutions*, p. 278

conditions.[9] With the Czech Lands' liberal traditions and democratic history, and its considerably lesser gains under Communist Party rule vis-à-vis Bratislava and Slovakia, in addition to Prague being a node of networks for the arts and philosophy, relative deprivation was more pervasive there.

It was especially in Prague where artistic and intellectual networks clearly perceived, and increasingly communicated, the chasm between Communist Party rhetoric and Czech reality to other civil society networks. Prague and Budapest, for example, may have been materially better off than, say, Bratislava, Warsaw, Sofia, Tirana, Bucharest, and Minsk, let alone Banska Bystrica, Kielce, Stara Zagora, Timisoara, and hundreds of other cities throughout Eastern Europe. However, it is not absolute conditions that matter, but *relative* ones; likewise, it is not objective "reality" that is determinate, but *subjective perceptions.*

The Czechs felt deprived relative to the Western European nations (what Czechs referred to simply as "Europe"). The Czechs, especially due to their geographical location and a sense of their perceived "European" history and culture, viewed (and continue to view) Western Europe as their reference point. This is precisely why so many Czechs consider themselves "Central Europeans", caught somewhere between the democratic western bloc of "Europe" and the historically authoritarian eastern bloc of Russia and Eastern Europe.[10] Slovaks are much more likely to look eastward when they seek to orient themselves.

"Frustrated hope", Michael Harrington asserts, "is a potent but not always rational force".[11] Relative deprivation was widespread due to, among other reasons, intellectuals being forced to do manual labor, declining incomes and standards of living, declining national prestige, the discrepancies between the government's rhetoric and the reality of everyday life, and the evidence of viable and desirable political economic alternatives. The working class, created so effectively by the Communist Party, created for itself rising expectations of an increasing standard of living *ad infinitum*. As with the other countries of Eastern Europe, though,

---

[9] Ulc, "The Bumpy Road of Czechoslovakia's Velvet Revolution", p. 29

[10] *Cf.* Tony Judt, "Nineteen Eighty-Nine: The End of *Which* European Era?", *Daedalus*, Summer 1994

[11] Michael Harrington, *The New American Poverty* (New York: Penguin Books, 1984), p. 24

the Czechoslovak system "did not produce hungry people. Poverty or hunger seemed not to be a revolutionary issue in [the Autumn of] 1989. Rather, it was the *social deprivation* of an entire nation", indeed an entire multi-national region, that felt left out from the course of history, and wanted back in.[12] Zvi Gitelman further asserts that "East Europeans were... increasingly aware of the gap between their standards of living and that of their Western neighbors as a result of the diffusion of videos and personal computers and via increased tourism in both directions".[13] The moral economy of civil subsistence was dangerously damaged in Eastern Europe. By November of 1989, the Czechoslovaks had seen the authoritarian regimes in Poland and Hungary fall with the one in East Germany quickly crumbling. The Czech people believed in *what could be*, but were still stuck in *what was*.

While the East Germans were able to choose the "exit" option in 1989, people in Czechoslovakia could only "choose" the more dangerous alternative of "voice" as a public method of dissent and disloyalty toward the government.[14] Albert Hirschman describes "exit" and "voice" as

> two contrasting responses of consumers or members of organizations to what they sense as deterioration in the quality of the goods they buy or the services and benefits they receive. Exit is the act of simply leaving, generally because

---

[12] Dinu Pietraru, "The Significance of a Classic Revolution. Romania 1989", Paper presented at the *91st Annual Meetings of the American Sociological Association*, New York, New York, 16-20 August 1996, p. 11, fn. 11, emphasis added

[13] Zvi Gitelman, "The Roots of Eastern Europe's Revolution", *Problems of Communism*, May-June 1990, p. 90

[14] Albert O. Hirschman, *Exit, Voice, and Loyalty: Responses to Decline in Firms, Organizations, and States* (Cambridge: Harvard University Press, 1970) and Albert O. Hirschman, "Exit, Voice, and the Fate of the GDR: An Essay in Conceptual History", *World Politics*, January 1993. But, again, see Scott, *Weapons of the Weak*; and Forrest Colburn, ed., *Everyday Forms of Peasant Resistance* (Armonk, NY: M.E. Sharpe, 1989) for covert, and even subconscious, methods of resistance.

> a better good or service or benefit is believed to be provided by another firm or organization... Voice is the act of complaining or of organizing to complain or to protest.[15]

The (post)totalitarian systems of Eastern Europe allowed—as much as was possible—neither exit nor voice in the social, cultural, political and economic spheres. Loyalty to the government, party, and system, whether feigned or sincere, was generally the only public "option" available. Such a bleak situation left these "closed" systems without any social mechanism that could ameliorate their problems. Like China in the nineteenth and early twentieth centuries, Czechoslovakia and the other Communist Party countries in the late twentieth century staved off liberalization and social change until it was too late for smaller and more gradual state reforms.

In 1989, Czechoslovakia was caught between the contrast of a semi-mythical past of idealized democracy and freedom and an all-too-real present of authoritarianism and repression on the one hand, and the so-called demonstration effect (or contagion factor) of other Eastern European countries on the other. As a result, the Czechoslovak people, especially the urban intelligentsia of Prague who led the Velvet Revolution, were increasingly feeling relatively deprived and were rebelling in increasingly public ways, while inspiring and mobilizing many others along with them.[16]

---

[15] Hirschman, "Exit, Voice, and the Fate of the GDR", pp. 175-76

[16] *Cf.* Richard J. Barnet, *Intervention & Revolution*, Revised and Updated (New York and Scarborough, Ontario: Mentor Book, 1968, 1972), p. 66: "The communists themselves learned in the midst of their success in Russia that revolution, contrary to what Trotsky believed, cannot be spread by example. Revolutionary ideas travel; revolutions do not.... a successful revolution in one country may incite rebels in other countries to attempt to make their own, but the outcome will depend entirely on local conditions".

Chapter IX.

Acquiescence of the Military

"There is a tendency ... to under-estimate the importance of control over the instruments of violence—the army and the police—and the significance of decisions taken by political leaders"
— Barrington Moore[1]

Momentum was building in the opposition to the Communist Party regime in Czechoslovakia with growing and more frequent public protests and threats of strikes; however, the Communist Party was still in full control of the means of coercion and violence. Although there were substantial grievances against the government, "popular suffering by itself never explains the occurrence of state breakdown and revolution.... [Indeed,] diffuse popular discontent can express itself in a variety of ways; it is unlikely to have any political impact against a strong state supported

---

[1] Moore, *Injustice*, pp. 82-83

by a unified elite".[2]

Speaking of the French Revolution of 1789, for example, Goldstone asserts that "The police (and the army) were reluctant to act against French [citizens] voicing demands that they themselves considered valid".[3] The regime in France had substantially lost legitimacy and therefore it also lost much of its powers to coerce. One could say much the same of Czechoslovakia (and the rest of Eastern Europe, with the notable exception of Romania) in late 1989. By this time, Przeworski maintains, the "party bureaucrats did not believe in their speech. And to shoot one must believe in something: when those who hold the trigger have absolutely nothing to say, they have no force to pull it".[4] This was not so of China, however, where (poor) peasant soldiers—who were isolated from the media—were "imported" into Beijing to violently repress (middle class) urban students.[5]

Katharine Chorley was perhaps the first student of revolution to emphasize the role of the military—doing so during World War II—and is still virtually alone in the field. She argues that "little serious attention has been given to an effort to make an historical analysis of [revolution] in its relation to the character and strengths of the defending force of the *status quo* government which the [revolution] is designed to overthrow".[6] Doing this herself, Chorley concludes that "governments of the *status quo* who are in full control of their armed forces and are in a position to use them to full effect have a decisive superiority which no rebel force can

---

[2] Goldstone, *Revolution and Rebellion in the Early Modern World*, p. 86. *Cf.* Robert Michels, *Political Parties* [1915], trans. by Eden and Cedar Paul (New York: Collier Books, 1962), p. 168: "When there is a struggle between the leaders and the masses, the former are always victorious if only they remain united".

[3] Goldstone, *Revolution and Rebellion in the Early Modern World*, p. 270

[4] Przeworski, "The 'East' Becomes the 'South'?", p. 22

[5] See, *e.g.*, Bradshaw and Wallace, *Global Inequalities*, p. 128

[6] Katharine C. Chorley, *Armies and the Art of Revolution* (London: Faber & Faber, 1943), p. 11. This is still largely true.

hope to overcome".[7] Huntington concurs, arguing that the military is the "necessary support" of authoritarian regimes: "In the last analysis, whether the regime collapses or not depends on whether [the military] support[s] the regime, join[s the] opposition to it, or stand[s] by on the sidelines".[8] More than half a century later, Chorley's analyses and conclusions still appear to be empirically accurate.

East German officials' decision to cancel Erich Honecker's direct order to open fire on the hundreds of thousands of peaceful protestors in Leipzig was a significant turning point in the revolutionary situations in Eastern Europe. After those demonstrations, many people, especially in East Germany, sensed that it was now safer to demonstrate against the government and, all over Eastern Europe, they accordingly translated their "private political preferences" into public action, establishing a "latent bandwagon" effect.[9] This belief was strongly reinforced in many people's minds, both in the regimes and in the oppositions, by Gorbachev's repeated remarks that the USSR had no right to interfere in its neighbors' affairs and that the threatened or actual use of military force should not be employed as a weapon of foreign policy.

The Communist Party leaders throughout Eastern Europe were losing legitimacy amongst the masses, were losing support from their long-time superpower ally, and were losing faith in their own authority to rule amongst themselves. Feelings of being in crisis were pervasive throughout the region. These factors, combined, led to the Communist Party regimes losing their power and authority, along with their legitimacy, to force their will onto the citizens, as they had so brutally done in the past.

The tide was clearly turning within Czechoslovakia as well. Prime Minister Adamec emphasized that he would not declare martial law. More directly, when General Milán Vaclavík, the Minister of Defense, *publicly* announced on television on the evening of 23 November 1989 that the military would not be used to repress the people, the regime's days were clearly numbered. The Czechoslovak government was "divided between those too frightened to budge and those scared enough to risk reform", while facing an opposition that was largely united under the

---

[7] *Ibid.*

[8] Huntington, *The Third Wave*, p. 150. *Cf.* Gurr and Goldstone, "Comparisons and Policy Implications" in Keddie, ed., *Debating Revolutions*, pp. 333-34

[9] Kuran, "The East European Revolution of 1989", pp. 122-23

umbrella organization of Civic Forum and the charismatic leadership of Václav Havel.[10]

Three weeks later, further, the Communist Party announced that all party activity within the military was suspended. "As against the party's perception of its future role", according to Barbara Misztal, "the military elites knew that the army had to stay, whatever the characteristics of the new system". Therefore, "its lack of a 'force solution' can be attributed to the military elite's understanding that such action would have damaged its future relations with the majority in society".[11] The ruling elites, as well as the middle echelons, in the party and the military decided to give up on repressing the people, thereby opting out of the totalitarian paradigm of the past and implicitly looking forward to the democratic and capitalist paradigms of the future.[12]

In her discussion of the collapse of Communist Party regimes in Eastern Europe, Rubie Watson exposes a paradox caused by simple answers having been given to complex problems. She reminds us that Communist Party regimes were "never as omnipotent as the cold war warriors of the 1950s claimed [them] to be, nor w[ere they] the paper tiger that some present-day celebrants of [their] demise proclaim. It is also important not to lose sight of the fact that [Communist Party] regimes had the capacity to be both brutally coercive and vulnerable at the same time".[13] The militaries, especially, proved this to be true in 1989.

In Czechoslovakia, the military was the last obstacle toward a legitimate opposition movement overthrowing a government with almost no legitimacy. As Guillermo O'Donnell and Philippe Schmitter maintain, "no transition can be forced purely by opponents against a regime which

---

[10] Frankland, *The Patriots' Revolution*, p. 271

[11] Barbara A. Misztal, "Understanding Political Change in Eastern Europe: A Sociological Perspective", *Sociology*, August 1993, p. 464

[12] S.N. Eisenstadt, "The Breakdown of Communist Regimes and the Vicissitudes of Modernity", *Daedalus*, Spring 1992, pp. 24, 33

[13] Rubie S. Watson, "Memory, History, and Opposition Under State Socialism: An Introduction" in Rubie S. Watson, *Memory, History, and Opposition Under State Socialism* (Santa Fe, NM: School of American Research Press, 1994), p. 2

maintains the cohesion, capacity, and disposition to apply repression".[14] With the fear of an external or internal military intervention and suppression removed in Czechoslovakia, the path was clear for a revolutionary transformation. Indeed, this sort of governmental crisis is what the resource mobilization model, or especially its more sophisticated variant, the political process model,[15] might predict prior to a social or political movement's victory. This is the social and political opportunity *par excellence*.

As with the elimination of the threat of Soviet military intervention, the acquiescence of the Czechoslovak military was clearly necessary for a peaceful transfer of power and is also necessary for the success of the Revolution, yet it is clearly not sufficient. Military acquiescence does not make revolutions, and it certainly did not do so in Czechoslovakia, but it does make it more possible, and more likely, for social movements and the rebellions they sometimes help spawn to become successful revolutionary movements. Furthermore, the military's role in staying out of the political process also bodes well for the future of democracy. Czechoslovakia is fortunate, like Hungary, in that it does "not

---

[14] Guillermo O'Donnell and Philippe C. Schmitter, *Transitions from Authoritarian Rule: Tentative Conclusions About Uncertain Democracies* (Baltimore and London: Johns Hopkins University Press, 1986), p. 21. On the one hand, the experiences of China, especially in light of the events of the Beijing Spring of 1989, not to mention the violent and repressive histories of Indonesia, El Salvador, Guatemala, and Haiti, as well as the mostly-peaceful democratic transitions in Zimbabwe in 1980, the Philippines in 1986, South Africa in 1994, East Timor in 2002, and Georgia in 2003, on the other hand, appear to support this contention.

[15] The political process model is more sophisticated than the resource mobilization model due to its analyses of the state and the dialectics of power relationships, in addition to its conception of resources broadly conceived. *Cf.* Anne N. Costain, *Inviting Women's Rebellion* (Baltimore and London: Johns Hopkins University Press, 1992), pp. 11-12: "The political process approach grew out of resource mobilization, but instead of concentrating exclusively on resources, it places more emphasis on the political system, indigenous accumulation of resources, and psychological aspects of movement identification". For a good exposition of these models, see Doug McAdam, *Political Process and the Development of Black Insurgency, 1930-1970* (Chicago and London: University of Chicago Press, 1982), esp. ch. 2 ["Resource Mobilization"] and ch. 3 ["The Political Process Model"]. The best book-length explication of the political process model, however, is Tarrow, *Power in Movement*.

have a historical background of interventionism by the military in political affairs".[16] The subordination, and non-interference, of the military to the political process is a requisite condition for stable, legitimate and, indeed, meaningful democracy.

[16] Grilli di Cortona, "From Communism to Democracy", p. 326. The limits to this historical fortune, though, was clearly shown by the August 1991 attempted *coup d'état* against Gorbachev in the Soviet Union, another country with a history of military non-intervention in political affairs.

Chapter X.

Revolutionary Rehearsal and the Case(s) of China[1]

"When China wakes, it will shake the world"
— Napoleon Bonaparte[2]

---

[1] A much different and earlier version of this chapter was presented as "The Beijing Spring and Beyond: Modern Revolution in China" at the *Second International Conference on Alternative Futures and Popular Protest*, Manchester, England, 26-28 March 1996 and published in Colin Barker and Mike Tyldesley, eds., *Alternative Futures and Popular Protest II* (Manchester: Manchester Metropolitan University, 1996). Portions of this chapter were also published as "Comparisons of Coercion, Consent, and Change in China", *Chinese Community Forum*, 22 January 1997, and as "Democratic Daydreams and Communist Party Nightmares", *Chinese Community Forum*, 5 February 1997.

[2] Cited in Nicholas D. Kristof and Sheryl WuDunn, *China Wakes: The Struggle for the Soul of a Rising Power* (New York: Vintage Books, 1994), frontisquote. *Cf.* W.A.P. Martin, *The Awakening of China*, 1907 cited in *Ibid.*:

"...even China is now on the way to a revolution"
— Friedrich Engels[3]

In 1989, the world witnessed revolutionary situations in Eastern Europe and China. The rebellions and revolutions of that year shook beliefs as well as political parties and toppled theories as well as governments. While the revolutions were successful in Czechoslovakia and Hungary, the revolution in China failed. Therefore, China in 1989 represents a negative case of revolution (*geming*, literally heavenly change), despite it depicting a positive case of rebellion. Not only did China not experience revolution in 1989 (as Czechoslovakia and Hungary did), but it also failed to have a regime change (as Romania and Bulgaria did). Interestingly, however, China shares most of the causal characteristics of modern revolution with Czechoslovakia and its Velvet Revolution of 1989. The focus of this analysis, a decade after the Tiananmen Square rebellion and massacre, therefore, lies in the apparent differences between Czechoslovakia and China—a history of democracy and, especially, the role of the domestic military—as well as between China then and now. The historical component of this social scientific method is another form of comparison as, in many ways, "the past is another country", with its "memories" and "mis-memories" which are consequently "shaping and misshaping" both the "myths" and "realities" of the past, present, and future.[4]

The similarities are, nevertheless, worth recounting. Even though China does not have a history of democracy as does Czechoslovakia, it

---

"China is the theatre of the greatest movement now taking place on the face of the globe. In comparison with it, the agitation in Russia shrinks into insignificance.... It promises nothing short of the complete renovation of the oldest, most populous and most conservative of empires". Also see Andre Gunder Frank, *ReORIENT: Global Economy in the Asian Age* (Berkeley: University of California Press, 1998) and Paul Bracken, "Will China Be Number 1?", *Time*, 22 May 2000.

[3] Friedrich Engels, *Principles of Communism* [1847], #11, <http://csf.colorado.edu/psn/ marx/archive/1847-prin/main.htm>

[4] Tony Judt, "The Past is Another Country: Myth and Memory in Postwar Europe", *Daedalus*, Fall 1992

does have a history of democratic movements in opposition to its authoritarian regimes both before and after the Revolution of 1949. The 1989 Democracy Movement drew heavily on this tradition, engaging in what Elizabeth Perry calls the "recycling of tradition" and what James Chace calls "a usable past".[5] Democracy Movement protesters consciously made reference to, and skillfully employed the symbols of, the French Revolution and the signing of the U.S. Constitution (1789), the founding of the Second International (1889), the May 4th Movement (1919), a revolutionary student movement (1926), the Chinese Revolution (1949), the April 5th Movement (1976), the Democracy Wall Movement (1978-79), the Student Movement (1986), and the recent strike wave (1987-88). On 29 May 1989, the protesters theatrically constructed and centrally displayed a thirty-foot statue in Tiananmen Square—located spatially between a huge portrait of Mao and the imposing Monument of the People's Heroes depicting the May 4th student struggle from 1919—which became known as the Goddess of Democracy.

Mao Zedong, representing the past, and the Goddess of Democracy, representing the future, both larger than life, were facing off and staring at each other as the present unfolded before them and as the media transmitted this iconographic scene around the world. Like many of the secret societies of China's past, the Democracy Movement, and especially its student leadership, both opposed and mirrored the regime it was fighting against, just as it mirrored many past political movements in China.[6] In this way, the political economic history and trajectory of China

---

[5] Elizabeth J. Perry, "Casting a Chinese 'Democracy' Movement: The Roles of Students, Workers, and Entrepreneurs" in Jeffrey N. Wasserstrom and Elizabeth J. Perry, eds., *Popular Protest and Political Culture in Modern China: Learning from 1989* (Boulder, CO: Westview Press, 1992), p. 149; James Chace, "'Managing' China's Ascent", *World Policy Journal*, Summer 1996, p. 87. Claude Lévi-Strauss used the term "mythemes" to describe similar phenomena. Also see Gennie Bull and Feng Ouyang, "On Culture, Democracy, et al.", *Chinese Community Forum*, 30 September 1998.

[6] Even the use of Tiananmen Square itself, the site where Mao declared the establishment of the "People's Republic", is in this cultural vein, as the documentary *The Gate of Heavenly Peace* suggests. *Cf.* Alexander Groth, *Revolution and Elite Access: Some Hypotheses on Aspects of Political Change* (Davis, CA: Institute of Government Affairs, 1966), p. 1; Lee Feigon, "Gender and the Chinese Student Movement" in Jeffrey N. Wasserstrom and Elizabeth J. Perry, eds., *Popular Protest and Political Culture in Modern China*, Second Ed.

exhibit both social change and cultural continuity.[7]

The Chinese, like the Czechs, also had a unifying issue which was, broadly speaking, democracy (*minzhu*); democracy was and remains the "master frame" through which dissident individuals and groups in China organize their claims. For most dissidents, these claims did not (originally) necessitate multiparty democracy; rather, the Communist Party could, with modifications, retain its (historical, Leninist, and self-proclaimed) vanguard role. Though democracy was sometimes confused with capitalism (*e.g.*, when Wuer Kaixi, a student leader, spoke of the *right* to wear Nike sneakers), issues of freedom and liberty were pervasive in the Democracy Movement. It is sometimes unclear, however, whether Chinese student protestors want the "struggle fruits" of their social movement to be primarily political or economic. That is probably why it has been said that "China is a country caught between a hard rock and the Hard Rock Café".[8]

The students, and other protestors, initially rallied in mourning for Hu Yaobang, the reformist and purged former Communist Party General Secretary who died on 15 April 1989. In a authoritarian system where open calls for political change are viewed as threatening and therefore can be dangerous, public mourning for Hu, the purged reformer, was a metaphorical vehicle for demands for reform. The metaphor soon became more literal and calls for change began to be publicly vocalized. The core of the popular demands for change during the Beijing Spring of 1989 comprised calls for freedom of speech and press, the right of peaceable assembly, an end to the 'campaign against bourgeois

---

(Boulder, San Francisco, and Oxford: Westview Press, 1992, 1994); Jeffrey N. Wasserstrom, "Mass Media and Mass Actions in Urban China, 1919-1989" in Jeremy D. Popkin, ed., *Media and Revolution: Comparative Perspectives* (Lexington: University of Kentucky Press, 1995).

[7] Craig Calhoun, *Neither Gods Nor Emperors: Students and the Struggle for Democracy in China* (Berkeley: University of California Press, 1994)

[8] Anonymous, told to Geraldo Rivera, in Beijing during President Bill Clinton's visit to China, June 1998. Adding more *commercial* legitimacy in China, there is now a portrait of Colonel Sanders that spans several stories on the side of a building that houses the largest KFC in the world. The portrait of Colonel Sanders, near Mao's mausoleum, dwarfs the bus-size one of Chairman Mao on the opposite side of Tiananmen Square (Paul Martin, "Face-Off in Tiananmen Square", *National Geographic Traveler*, January/February 2001, p. 102).

liberalism', an increase in the education budget, and an end to governmental and Party corruption. These demands were shortly followed by certain other more narrow demands, such as the resignations of Prime Minister Li Peng and of Deng Xiaoping. Shortly thereafter, some students began to call for the suicide of Li, suggesting that hanging himself would be an appropriate method. The verbal attacks against Deng were generally less common and much less severe.[9] Deng's fear, exemplified by his so-called "Polish nightmare", was "that political concessions made in response to popular demands would be perceived as a sign of weakness, leading to further escalation of demands and ending in chaos, as in Poland in 1980-81".[10] In spite of Deng's strategy, more radical and militant demands were later voiced by student protestors, including "down with military government" and "down with fascists". The students also chanted "Long live freedom, long live democracy". Echoing the big character statement (*dazibao*) that Wei Jingsheng posted on Democracy Wall in Beijing on 5 December 1978, the protestors demanded China's "Fifth Modernization: Democracy".[11]

---

[9] Deng officially resigned from all posts five months later on 9 November (the same day, ironically, that the Berlin Wall fell), however as he was (and is) still venerated in the Communist Party, he continued to wield much power and was widely believed to be in control until his death in February 1997. Indeed, "[i]n a televised discussion with Mikhail Gorbachev, Zhao [Ziyang, then Communist Party General Secretary and potential president] revealed a secret 1987 party agreement by which leaders had agreed to consult Deng on all major policy decisions" (Melanie Manion, "Introduction: Reluctant Duelists: The Logic of the 1989 Protests and Massacre" in Michel Oksenberg, Lawrence R. Sullivan, and Marc Lambert, eds., *Beijing Spring, 1989: Confrontation and Conflict: The Basic Documents* (Armonk, NY and London: M.E. Sharpe, 1990), p. xxxv).

[10] Richard Baum, "China After Deng: Ten Scenarios in Search of Reality", *China Quarterly*, March 1996, p. 162

[11] Deng Xiaoping stated, in 1978, at the first session of the Fifth National People's Congress of China, that the "Four Modernizations" should be "for the all-round modernization of agriculture, industry, national defense, and science and technology" so that, by the end of the century, "China will have a new look and will stand *unshakably* in the East as a modern, powerful socialist country" (Deng Xiaoping, "The Four Modernizations" in Molly Joel Coye and Jon Livingston, eds., *China Yesterday and Today*, Second Ed. (New York: Bantam Books, 1975, 1979), pp. 510-12, emphasis added). Wei Jingsheng was arrested a few months later and then sentenced in the Fall of 1979 to fifteen years in prison for his simple

Unfortunately for China, the various demands and movements for democracy may not be coherent and concrete enough of a tradition to act as a functional substitute for an *actual* history of democracy. A history of democracy, such as that which exists in Czechoslovakia, may not cause revolution *per se*; however, it can serve to inspire and unite the opposition(s) to (re)imagine the past and (re)create an honorable and legitimate aspect of national political culture. Whereas the Czechs used their histories of democracy and the power of human rights to rally the masses around a popular national tradition and against the authoritarian regime, the Chinese dissidents were denied this particular social opportunity by their own history, or lack thereof.[12]

Throughout the 1980s, many associations and organizations, like the secret societies in China's past, were formed that would later play an important role in the dissemination of ideas and information. These organizations were also instrumental as social networks which facilitated mobilization amongst its similarly situated members. These groups are called conversation associations, Democracy Salons, democracy associations, and action committees. With the loosening of ideological control over work committees beginning in 1979, these networks were also employed as modes of popular communication and action in Simmelian fashion.[13]

---

action. Interestingly, "the sort of things Wei said with great daring... years ago are now on the lips of any taxi driver" (Jasper Becker, "The Fading Voices of Dissent", *World Press Review*, March 1996 [*South China Morning Post*, 3 December 1995], p. 21).

[12] *Cf.* Raphael Samuel, *Theatres of Memory*, Vol. I (London: Verso, 1995) and Raphael Samuel, *Island Stories: Unravelling Britain: Theatres of Memory*, Vol. II (London: Verso, 1998)

[13] *Cf.* E. Pierre Deess, "Social Change in the German Democratic Republic: The Role of Institutional Pre-Mobilization Practices (IPPs)", Paper presented at the 91st Annual Meetings of the American Sociological Association on *Social Change: Opportunities and Constraints*, New York, New York, 16-20 August 1996, pp. 1-2: "Where a sophisticated secret police oversees all political activity and effectively smashes opposition groups, movements cannot rely on the usual means to prepare popular mobilization.... [The IPP approach] looks for the development of social change through institutions controlled by the state. This approach holds, fundamentally, that the process of change can be furthered by the unintended consequences of official institutions". Also see Dingxin Zhao,

The protesters also made use of street theatre, photocopiers, big character posters, newspapers, radio broadcasting, audio and video cassette recorders, telephones and fax machines (subsidized by AT&T), and both domestic and foreign television. Students and others in the U.S. and Hong Kong also faxed news reports and photographs back to the protesters in Beijing, thereby (re)cycling information of the ongoing revolutionary situation across national borders at the speed of light and electrically exemplifying Marshall McLuhan's concept of a "global village".[14] The mass media, through their global dissemination of information and images, were clearly important in mobilizing the masses, just as they were in Eastern Europe in 1989. The mass media taught many Chinese people that their individual private problems were also mass political issues. It showed citizens of China that they were feeling similarly to each other and to people in other countries, as well. The mass media, in this way, was (unwittingly?) helping to "manufacture consent" and to instill a "sociological imagination" in the people, which they sensationally encouraged to run wild.[15]

"Ecologies of Social Movements: Student Mobilization during the 1989 Prodemocracy Movement in Beijing", *American Journal of Sociology*, May 1998. On the concept of "everyday forms of resistance", see James C. Scott, *Weapons of the Weak* (New Haven: Yale University Press, 1990) and James C. Scott, *Domination and the Arts of Resistance: Hidden Transcripts* (New Haven: Yale University Press, 1995), as well as John Markoff, *Waves of Democracy: Social Movements and Political Change* (Thousand Oaks, CA: Pine Forge Press, 1996), p. 23.

[14] Marshall McLuhan and Quentin Fiore, *The Medium is the Massage: An Inventory of Effects*, Produced by Jerome Agel (San Francisco: Hardwired, 1996 [1967])

[15] *Cf.* Edward S. Herman and Noam Chomsky, *Manufacturing Consent: The Political Economy of the Mass Media* (New York: Pantheon, 1988). For an earlier study employing the same concept with regard to corporations and the labor process, see Michael Burawoy, *Manufacturing Consent: Changes in the Labor Process Under Monopoly Capitalism* (Chicago, IL: University of Chicago Press, 1979). Further, E.E. Schattschneider in *The Semi-Sovereign People* (New York: Holt, Rinehart and Winston, 1960) discusses a "mobilization of bias", while Ralph Miliband refers to an "engineering of consent". Also see Ethan Huang, "Disinformation in Democratic Society", *Chinese Community Forum*, 23 October 1996. On the sociological imagination which connects societal histories to personal biographies, see C. Wright Mills, *The Sociological Imagination* (London:

Following President George Bush's visit to China in February 1989, Mikhail Gorbachev arrived in Beijing on 15 May, for the first Sino-Soviet summit in thirty years, and was greeted with much more excitement from the citizenry and the media. Many of the Chinese protestors regarded changes in the Soviet Union not so much as a model to be replicated, but rather as a socially legitimate and relatively safe political metaphor to agitate for social change within their own country. When Gorbachev came to China, so too did the international mass media and, by proxy, the world. Gorbachev's itinerary was repeatedly modified in attempts to avoid the hundreds of thousands of protestors in and around Tiananmen Square, some of whom were even holding banners in Russian and English—as well as in Chinese—hailing Gorbachev as a great reformer. Other banners, often large and colorful, announced the protesting delegations of teachers and professors, students and scholars, factory workers and entrepreneurs, writers and artists, young children and Buddhist monks, low-level government officials and *People's Daily* journalists, among others, in support of the Democracy Movement.

Along with Gorbachev, the media saw hunger strikers in Tiananmen Square, as well as hundreds of thousands of protestors calling for democratic reform and changes in leadership. The mass media sent the reports and photographs of these events throughout China and around the world. Just outside of where a banquet was being held for Gorbachev, some protestors sang the Internationale (a revolutionary workers' anthem, the Chinese version of which includes "There has never been a savior, nor should we rely on gods and emperors" and "To create happiness for humankind, we must rely on ourselves"), some chanted various anti-government slogans (*e.g.*, "Long live democracy" and "Down with corruption"), while others shouted more practical demands, such as "sell the Mercedes-Benzes to pay the national debt".[16]

Realizing that the rebellion was being internationalized through the use of instantaneous global communications technologies, both the government and the students began "staging" actions and events for particular foreign audiences and "cultivating" international sympathies. Indeed, with regard to the 1989 Democracy Movement, as well as earlier

---

Oxford University Press, 1959).

[16] Sheryl WuDunn, "150,000 Lift Their Voices for Change" in Bernard Gwertzman and Michael T. Kaufman, eds., *The Collapse of Communism* [an anthology of *New York Times* articles] (New York: Times Books, 1990), p. 52

social movements in modern Chinese history, "there have always been two audiences: eyewitnesses and those exposed to representations".[17] Protest banners written in English and Russian are a clear example of this; the Goddess of Democracy statue, although a little less clear, is another. The Goddess of Democracy statue and the way in which it was transported into and displayed in Tiananmen Square was a complex cultural amalgam of democratic symbolism, socialist realism, Chinese nationalism, and folk deificationism. Interestingly, though not coincidentally, in the 1940s and then again in the 1960s, statues of Chiang Kai-shek and Mao Zedong, respectively, were paraded through the streets and the one of Mao was placed on the very same spot where the Goddess of Democracy came to rest in 1989.[18]

Beginning on Karl Marx's birthday (5 May), coincidentally, official Chinese media coverage went from ignoring the pro-democracy protests in Tiananmen Square to covering them prominently and even quite favorably. Sympathetic articles were accompanied by large, color photographs of the demonstrations. In a veiled criticism of their government, the *China Youth News* published a lengthy narrative of a Soviet citizen who said, in part, that prior to Gorbachev the Soviet Union was "run by old and sickly people who need help to walk, who lack the breath to speak, whose minds are stiff and muddled", unlike the "young and strong" Gorbachev.[19] This account was, no doubt, clearly understood as a metaphor by its many youthful readers.

In a particularly stunning incident of revolutionary political theatre which was broadcast on national television, Prime Minister Li Peng and other government officials had a "meeting" in the Great Hall of the People alongside Tiananmen Square with Wuer Kaixi, Wang Dan, and other representatives of the Student Leadership Federation, on 18 May, a month into the movement. Wuer Kaixi was dressed in a hospital gown, having come directly from the hospital after having been recently hospitalized due to his participation in the hunger strike. During the televised discussion with the Prime Minister, Wuer Kaixi even

---

[17] Wasserstrom, "Mass Media and Mass Actions in Urban China, 1919-1989" in Popkin, ed., *Media and Revolution*, pp. 211, 214

[18] *Ibid.*, pp. 211-213

[19] Nicholas D. Kristof, "China's Hero of Democracy: Gorbachev" in Gwertzman and Kaufman, eds., *The Collapse of Communism*, p. 50

conspicuously pulled at his nose tube while making a trenchant political point, and "for a fittingly tragic/heroic ending to the dialogue, Wuer Kaixi fainted".[20] Another "meeting, not a dialogue" between top government officials and the students was held and televised the following day in Tiananmen Square.

Popular modes of communication, especially the mass media, further fueled the mass mobilization of a student-led coalition of workers and others. With the support of the Chinese (and foreign) media, huge rallies grew into enormous crowds. Major support by students was also garnered by more traditional and more low-tech methods, intimately based on Chinese culture and university campus ecology, such as posting large character messages on campus walls in Beijing University's "Triangle" in the Haidian University District.[21] At various times, gigantic throngs of people marched through the streets of Beijing, often along a zig-zag path which began in the University District, joined by various types of vehicles, while hoards of other people packed the sidewalks.

A million or more people may have been in and around the more than one hundred acres of Tiananmen Square on many days during May through early June. Certain special days (notably the seventieth anniversary of the May 4th Movement,[22] the beginning of the hunger strike on 13 May, and the 17th and 18th of May when government leaders were meeting with both Gorbachev and the student leaders in separate venues) mobilized even larger numbers of people, perhaps as many as three million.

If, as Lenin claims, revolutions are the "festivals of the oppressed and the exploited", then Beijing in the spring of 1989 was rather

---

[20] Douglas J. Guthrie, "Political Theater and Student Organizations in the 1989 Chinese Movement: A Multivariate Analysis of Tiananmen", *Sociological Forum*, September 1995, p. 440

[21] Zhao, "Ecologies of Social Movements"

[22] The May 4th Movement of 1919 was a student-led movement in Beijing (the first major one to occur in China) that demanded political and cultural modernization, scientific rationalization, and western democracy. The May 4th Movement foreshadowed the birth of the Chinese Communist Party in 1921. Since shortly after the founding of the People's Republic in 1949, the fourth of May has also been National Youth Day. *Cf.* Lucien Bianco, *Origins of the Chinese Revolution, 1915-1949*, trans. Muriel Bell (Stanford, CA: Stanford University Press, 1971 [1967]), esp. pp. 31-52

revolutionary.[23] Many Beijing citizens donated clothes, blankets, food, and refreshments, in addition to voicing moral support, to the students occupying Tiananmen Square, the largest public space in the world. The crisis was clearly escalating. Although crisis, in the words of Georg Lukács, is simply the "intensification of everyday life", it is further infused with symbolic meaning in Chinese. As the Chinese ideogram for the word suggests, crisis (*weiji*) encompasses the seemingly oppositional concepts of danger and opportunity, both of which are chock-full of choice, chance, contingency, and cultural interplay.[24]

At the same time as the students were protesting in Tiananmen Square, millions of other people gathered and rallied in at least eighty other cities, and even some villages, across the country, representing all of China's provinces (excluding occupied Tibet). In addition, solidarity hunger strikes were staged in Shanghai, Xian, Chengdu Shenyang, and Harbin.[25] Sympathy rallies in the U.S., Taipei, and especially Hong Kong also helped to raise both international consciousness and vast amounts of money and matériel for the dissident student organizations in Beijing. Ironically for orthodox Marxists (of which Marx himself claimed not to be one), China's communist revolution of 1949 is attributable primarily to peasant activity in the countryside (Mao's estimate was 70 percent), while China's modern revolution (*i.e.*, its democratic revolution) is shaping up to be a largely urban affair led by the middle class. Once again, the "rules of revolution" derived from theory are being broken in practice.[26]

The 1989 Democracy Movement easily dwarfed many others in recent Chinese history and is probably only surpassed by the Revolution itself. Part of this is surely due to the fact that the Democracy Movement

---

[23] Stephan T. Possony, ed., *The Lenin Reader* (Chicago: Henry Regnery, 1966), p. 349. *Cf.* Liu Xiaobo, "That Holy Word, 'Revolution'" in Wasserstrom and Perry, eds., *Popular Protest and Political Culture in Modern China*, Second Ed.

[24] *Cf.* Calhoun, *Neither Gods Nor Emperors*. Along with chaos, crisis is also something that many Chinese, especially Chinese leaders, fear the most.

[25] *Cf.* Jonathan Unger, ed., *The Pro-Democracy Protests in China: Reports from the Provinces* (Armonk, NY: M.E. Sharpe, 1991)

[26] Clifton B. Kroeber, "Theory and History of Revolution", *Journal of World History*, Spring 1996, pp. 26, 36. Also see Charles Tilly, *European Revolutions, 1492-1992* (Oxford and Cambridge, MA: Blackwell Publishers, 1993), p. 237.

was the first anti-government collective action in China to receive encouragement and support from reformers in the government itself, most notably Communist Party General Secretary Zhao Ziyang. Zhao, in fact, in his "tearful farewell to the students" in Tiananmen Square (correctly expecting that he would soon be purged from power, as his predecessor Hu Yaobang was two years earlier), courageously "commented to the students that as a young man he had been involved in student demonstrations against [Chiang Kai-shek's Nationalist] Guomindang, going so far as to lie on railroad tracks to disrupt rail traffic—an act later emulated by students and workers in several cities after the June 4 crackdown".

Zhao's inspiring and self-sacrificing statement that 'it doesn't matter what happens to me' was also "later mimicked by Beijing residents in daily confrontations with authorities".[27] Zhao's words and past deeds, along with the hunger strike itself, became what Sidney Tarrow terms "modular actions" for the Chinese dissidents, *i.e.*, actions, like petitions and strikes for example, which are easily convertible and reusable from one political-historic context to another, regardless of actor(s), issue(s), or target(s). "It was when flexible, adaptable and indirect forms of collective action", Tarrow says, describing what he refers to as the "*modular* repertoire", "were diffused through print, association and state building that national social movements developed. They brought together broad coalitions of supporters around general claims", he continues, "using the political opportunities created by the expansion of the national state to do so".[28] This, too, is a "recycling of tradition" and the student protestors were ardent recyclers.

Although there was no threat of foreign intervention in China, there was strong domestic military opposition—at least amongst its leadership—to the Democracy Movement. This characteristic represents the major relevant difference between China and Czechoslovakia in 1989. The Czechoslovak and other Eastern European militaries, as well as the Soviet Red Army, were unwilling or incapable of violently suppressing

---

[27] Michel Oksenberg with Lawrence R. Sullivan, "Preface" in Oksenberg *et al.*, eds., *Beijing Spring, 1989*, p. x

[28] Sidney Tarrow, *Power in Movement: Social Movements, Collective Action and Politics* (Cambridge: Cambridge University Press, 1994), p. 6, original emphasis; also see pp. 19, 33, 39-45, 73, 114-15

their own citizens.[29] This proved to be pivotal.

In China, there was an initial possibility of a split in the military, and perhaps even a civil war as some army units were reported to have fired upon other units outside of Beijing. Among various other incidents, open letters were sent by military officers, journalists, trade unionists, and others in support of dialogue and peaceful reform.[30] On 25 May, Prime Minister Li had to call on the soldiers to "overcome difficulties and carry out martial law" in the face of clear and open non-compliance by officers and soldiers alike.[31] There were incidents not only of soldiers being pushed back by protestors, which was problematic enough for the political leaders, but also incidents in which thousands of soldiers and protestors sat down *together* to talk about issues and sing patriotic songs. At other times, citizens gave food and refreshments to the soldiers while reminding them that the People's Army should never repress the people.

On 21 May, further, "marshals Nie Rongzhen and Xu Xiangqian had apparently telephoned Deng Xiaoping to urge against the use of force to end the movement, and seven veteran generals had apparently sent a letter to the Military Affairs Commission and the Martial Law Command demanding that the army remain outside [Beijing]".[32] The veracity of these rumors were less important than the fact that they were widely circulated and widely believed. In fact, though, "[c]opies of the letter by the seven generals were dropped on [Tiananmen] Square by helicopters",

---

[29] It is true, however, that whereas the Eastern European countries were to some extent colonized by the Soviet Union, China is much more independent and sovereign in this regard. Some scholars have used this type of logic, along with the concept of homegrown revolutions, as opposed to imposed ones, to explain the absence of modern revolution in Cuba and Vietnam, in addition to China. The cases of modern revolutionary situations in the Soviet Union and Yugoslavia, where revolutions were not originally imposed, are explained away by powerful extenuating conditions. The Soviet Union and Yugoslavia, for example, despite their other serious problems, were eventually torn apart by vicious ethnic rivalries and populist nationalist movements for secession.

[30] Oksenberg *et al.*, eds., *Beijing Spring, 1989*

[31] The Editors of *Time* Magazine, *Massacre in Beijing: China's Struggle for Democracy* (New York: Time Inc. Books, 1989), p. 260

[32] Manion, "Introduction" in Oksenberg *et al.*, eds., *Beijing Spring, 1989*, pp. xxvi-xxvii

graphically indicating the divisions within the military and government while spreading the news.[33]

Other top military leaders openly opposed the use of violence against the people, as well. Of the seven designated military regions of China, the leaders of three of them, including Beijing, refused to support the martial law declarations. Additionally, over one hundred high-ranking officers signed a petition declaring that "The People's Army belongs to the people.... It should under no circumstances fire at the people and create any bloody incidents".[34]

The People's Liberation Army, however, finally fell into line under the control of the Party and was used to violently suppress the movement. "In [late May and early June] 1989 the Chinese government... finding that the units committed to the occupation of Beijing were fraternizing [with the protesters]... withdrew them and sent in fresh troops drawn from many parts of the country (and hence speaking strange dialects and held together only by institutional loyalties) who had been isolated from the news media for a period of two weeks in advance of the operation".[35] An ultimatum was issued by the government on 3 June (following the martial law curfew announced on 20 May) warning the people of Beijing to leave Tiananmen Square and to stay off the streets that night. The language was ominous, as government actions would later prove.

Commencing the night of the ultimatum and continuing throughout the next day (and week, in some areas of the capital), the army arrested, silenced, beat, disabled, disappeared, crushed, and killed up to

---

[33] *Ibid.*

[34] Christopher Tuck, "Is the Party Over?", *World Press Review*, March 1996 [*Contemporary Review*, May 1995], pp. 17-18. In May, there were incidents of police officers proclaiming "Victory to the Students" and soldiers declaring "the PLA [People's Liberation Army] supports you". Citizens also pledged *with soldiers* not to harm the students. On 23 May, and on other days through 3 June, the PLA even retreated after being blocked by a large crowd in Beijing (Support Democracy in China and Christus Rex et Redemptor Mundi, "Tiananmen, April-June 1989", Revised and Updated on 28 February 1998, <http://www.christusrex.org/www1/sdc/tiananmen.html>).

[35] Peter Calvert, *Revolution and Counter-Revolution* (Minneapolis: University of Minnesota Press, 1990), p. 43. It was, in a sense, a "reversed reality" (to use Laila Kabeer's pithy phrase out of context) of the Long March.

several thousand people who continued to protest, whether individually or collectively. Tanks, driven by (peasant) soldiers from the countryside, some even from distant Inner Mongolia and Sichuan provinces, rolled through the capital city of Beijing on the Avenue of Eternal Peace and into Tiananmen Square, brutally retaking control of the city.

As Mao famously says, "political power grows out of the barrel of a gun". The latest wave of the Democracy Movement abruptly ended in a blood bath. Along with the Goddess of Democracy statue, which was *physically* destroyed but otherwise remains in existence and intact, another powerful iconographic image was created when a 19-year-old student named Wang Weilin courageously stood in front of a line of tanks, after the massacre, and effectively blocked them singlehandedly for about six minutes while the world watched in suspense on television.[36] These commanding images will live on in the underground cultures of resistance in China (and elsewhere) and will serve to further inspire the next wave(s) of democratic dissidence.

Although the Chinese students had the broad-based moral, physical, and financial support of millions of people both in and out of China, representing all classes and various ethnicities, this vast mobilization of people and resources was still not enough to overcome the government and its ultimate control of the military forces. As was noted earlier, the "rules of revolution" do not always seem to hold in the expected ways.[37]

The window of political opportunity was again closed to opponents of the regime—for the time being. The struggle for democracy

---

[36] John Kamm, the executive director of the San Francisco human rights Dui Hua Foundation, says "For me, he represents the unknown soldier of the Chinese democratic revolution" (John M. Glionna, "An Icon, And Then He's Gone", *Los Angeles Times*, 4 June 2004). When asked by Barbara Walters in 1992 about the whereabouts of Wang Weilin, Jiang Zemin simply and coldly responded, "I think never killed". His fate or whereabouts have not yet been determined.

[37] For excellent and concise critiques of the resource mobilization approach, see Doug McAdam, *Political Process and the Development of Black Insurgency, 1930-1970* (Chicago, IL and London: University of Chicago Press, 1982), ch. 2; John Walton, *Western Times and Water Wars: State, Culture, and Rebellion in California* (Berkeley and Los Angeles: University of California Press, 1992), pp. 320-26; and also Aldon D. Morris & Carol McClurg Mueller, eds., *Frontiers in Social Movement Theory* (New Haven, CT and London: Yale University Press, 1992).

is part of a long political process, punctuated by events, which confers both opportunities and constraints on *all* of its participants. Those with the biggest "war chests" of mobilized resources, though clearly advantaged, do not necessarily or automatically prevail in revolutionary situations.

In the years since, many of the causal characteristics that led to social upheaval in 1989 either have remained the same or have been exacerbated. There is reason to believe that "the storm is gathering in the disillusioned sectors of China's society".[38] It is, however, not yet a thunderstorm. Indeed, a young woman who lives in Beijing commented that "Chinese people often don't like to say things directly but we do think about them".[39] The desire for democracy is still strong and is more coherent, and there is now another movement to draw from (*i.e.*, the events of 1989), both domestically and in Eastern Europe.[40] Additionally, "the sophistication and political experience of the pro-democracy people (both in and out of the governance system) has increased dramatically".[41]

Although there has been substantial and rapid economic growth in China in the last several years, the gains have not nearly been equally distributed and there are growing class and regional polarizations. "From 1985 to 1994 the average urban-rural income differential rose by almost 40%—from 1.9:1 to 2.65:1" and "[i]n 1993, two Chinese social scientists noted that regional income disparities—estimated to be as high as 8:1—were equal to or greater than those existing in Yugoslavia on the eve

---

[38] Drew Liu, "The Unfolding of Post-Deng Era: Reports from China", *China Backgrounder No. 2*, <http://www.ned.org/page_3/China/publ/backg/back2.html>, p. 1. *Cf.* David Shambaugh, "China's Fragile Future", *World Policy Journal*, Fall 1994

[39] Julia Wilkinson, "Heart of the Celestial Empire", *National Geographic Traveler*, September/October 1998, p. 91

[40] *Cf.* Wang Dan, "The Star of Hope Rises in Eastern Europe" [4 March 1989] in Mok Chiu Yu and J. Frank Harrison, eds., *Voices from Tiananmen Square: Beijing Spring and the Democracy Movement* (Montreal and New York: Black Rose Books, 1990), p. 38: "Only when China follows in the footsteps of these Eastern European countries, and only then, will full democracy and full development be successfully accomplished".

[41] Cited in Liu, "The Unfolding of Post-Deng Era", p. 2. And as Carlos Fuentes has stated, "Democracy generates confidence".

of its disintegration".[42]

Inflation, furthermore, which has been a significant problem since the mid-1980s, signifies that nominal economic growth has been greater than real economic growth and also greater than what people would reasonably expect and feel that they deserve, thereby likely increasing feelings of frustration and relative deprivation. "Rising inflation is pinching urban incomes, and rural incomes have actually declined over the last [few] years".[43] Yet, the (private) business community has grown and has greater resources, and more independence, both of which can, and probably will, be employed against the government during the (inevitable) next social movement for expanded rights. Many have heard Deng's slogan that "to get rich is glorious", and they no longer want the political constraints on their attempts to do so.

The state sector is not faring nearly as well, however, with about two-thirds of the 13,000 medium to large state industries operating at a loss and about 70 percent of all state factories unable to pay their employees on a regular basis.[44] It is still unclear how China's entry into the

---

[42] Baum, "China After Deng", p. 158, fn. 10. Also see Azizur Rahman Khan and Carl Riskin, "Income and Inequality in China: Composition, Distribution and Growth of Household Income, 1988 to 1995", *China Quarterly*, June 1998. *Cf.* Henry Rosemont, Jr., "Why the Chinese Economic Miracle Isn't One", *Z Magazine*, October 1995; and Jack A. Goldstone, "Gender, Work, and Culture: Why the Industrial Revolution Came Early to England But Late to China", *Sociological Perspectives*, Spring 1996, pp. 5, 8-9, 17

[43] Shambaugh, "China's Fragile Future", p. 44. Despite the feelings of relative deprivation in some quarters, paradoxically it is also the feelings of aspiration and optimism regarding the Chinese economy that may limit and blunt political attacks against the government in other quarters. The Chinese equivalent of the American Dream is a powerfully conservative force in Chinese society and it may forestall political rebellion. Additionally, economic pursuits, like the market itself, individualize people's thoughts and actions, thereby redirecting their efforts from the social and political to the personal.

[44] According to *The Economist* (13 September 1997), there are a total of about 305,000 state-owned firms employing over 100 million people and accounting for up to 90 percent of loans granted by China's state-owned banks, many of which are considered "policy loans", *i.e.*, loans made for political rather than strictly economic reasons and are not expected to be repaid. For a look at China's largest state-owned enterprise, the 2.4 million employee Xinjiang Construction and Production Corporation, see James Harding, "China's Sleeping Giant Starts to

World Trade Organization will affect the economic situation there, but it likely will be beneficial for the economic élite but will not be positive for the majority of people, further exacerbating economic polarization.

The agricultural industry where the majority of Chinese are employed, in particular, will undoubtedly face severe pressures. In any case, "With unemployment in double digits and rising, with a banking crisis that observers say has China's financial institutions bankrupt three times over, with state-owned enterprise productivity plummeting and privatization moving slower than planned, with their currency softening and the threat of devaluation looming, China's leaders have plenty on their minds".[45] As always, they are also thinking about how to keep order.

Moreover, the Chinese population is expanding dramatically despite the contraction in the growth rate, while the food and water supplies are stagnating or diminishing. So severe are the food shortages in China that it has, in the 1990s, gone from being a net exporter of grain to becoming the world's second largest importer. Moreover, China's agricultural sector has been in a recession for at least the past decade and a half, largely due to the fact that since 1979, well over ten million acres of farm land have either been washed away, been used for commercial cash cropping, been built on with factories and new housing, or have been otherwise transformed into non-food producing ventures.[46]

Stir", *Financial Times*, 3 August 1999, p. 10.

[45] Rebecca Weiner, "Grassroots Conservatism Comes of (New) Age: The Falun Gong Phenomenon", *Tikkun*, January/February 2000, p. 13

[46] Floris-Jan Van Luyn, "Will China Eat Up the World?", *World Press Review*, March 1996 [*NRC Handelsblad*, 26 October 1995], p. 39; B.M. Bhatia, "Famine Math", *Ibid.* [*Hindustan Times*, 16 June 1995]; Lester R. Brown, "Who Will Feed China?", *World Watch*, 1994; Lester R. Brown, "China's Food Problem: The Massive Imports Begin", *World Watch*, 1995; Lester R. Brown, *Who Will Feed China?* (Island Press, 1995). *Cf.* Martin Walker, "China and the New Era of Resource Scarcity", *World Policy Journal*, Spring 1996; Lester R. Brown and Brian Halweil, "China's Water Shortage Could Shake World Food Security", *World Watch*, July/August 1998. (Alarmed by *World Watch*'s investigation, the CIA launched its MEDEA project which, two years later, confirmed China's serious food problems.) Some of Brown's other books, including *Eco-Economy* and *Plan B*, also address these issues. But see "Self-Sufficiency in Grain Ensured", *Beijing Review*, 28 October-3 November 1996, p. 5 for an official and optimistic scenario. China has also been importing massive quantities of oil,

Most ominous of all demographic trends, perhaps, is the gigantic "floating population", officially estimated to be as high as 105 million people. Millions of families and individuals are no longer rooted to a particular geographical place, while there is no other particular place to go. Therefore, many "floaters" are becoming unofficial residents of the already overcrowded megacities of China. The depth of the government's fear of the floaters is illustrated by a book published by Shanxi People's Press in 1994 by a confidant of government insider Chen Yuan, entitled *Viewing China Through a Third Eye*. The book warns of an imminent social apocalypse brought on by a combination of massive rural emigration and epidemic lawlessness, and describes the floaters as a "seething volcano".[47]

Combined with the restrictions on family size,[48] continuing official (*i.e.*, party, government, military, and police) and now corporate corruption,[49] the appearance of "conspicuous consumption" among the

---

copper, aluminum, concrete, and other basic resource commodities to satisfy its seemingly insatiable economic growth.

[47] Jiang Zemin reportedly praised the book, giving special attention to the section on agriculture. *Cf.* Baum, "China After Deng", pp. 155, 158

[48] For an analysis of how Communist policies relied on family politics among the peasantry during the Chinese Revolution, see Judith Stacey, *Patriarchy and Socialist Revolution in China* (Berkeley and Los Angeles: University of California Press, 1983). For an assessment of how the student protestors mirrored the sexism of the government, see Feigon, "Gender and the Chinese Student Movement" in Wasserstrom and Perry, eds., *Popular Protest and Political Culture in Modern China*, Second Ed.

[49] A survey conducted in October 1994 found that 71 percent of the 2,500 people questioned were angry at the level of governmental corruption. When last asked in late 1988, furthermore, 55 percent of respondents claimed they would be willing to protest in the streets "if necessary" (Bruce Gilley, "Vox Populi", *World Press Review*, March 1996 [*Far Eastern Economic Review*, 7 December 1995], p. 16). Ironically, the anger towards corruption, in particular, helped the Communist Party gain many adherents in the 1940s and greatly aided the cause of the 1949 Chinese Revolution. *Cf.* Abbe Huc, *L'Empire Chinois*, 1854 cited in Kristof and WuDunn, *China Wakes*, p. 184: "We've seen the most hideous corruption spread everywhere. Magistrates sell justice to the highest bidder, and Mandarins at every level—instead of protecting the people—use every imaginable means to oppress them and pillage them"; Liu Binyan, *People or Monsters?*, 1997

political and economic élite (*e.g.*, luxury cars), encroaching marketization, rising crime rates (including prostitution, drugs, guns, gambling, and even the disappearance of over 21,000 66-pound sewer hole covers in Beijing during 2004), declining healthcare and worker safety,[50] deteriorating environmental conditions (including heavily polluted air and waterways, flooding, acid rain, deforestation, and desertification), worsening educational conditions, rampant inflation, growing unemployment, shrinking budgets, growing tax avoidance, and the knowledge of Eastern Europe and other viable political economic alternatives to the authoritarian present, frustration and anger have increased and are increasing.[51]

There have also been numerous, albeit (so far) isolated, protests all over the country. In 1993 there were more than 12,000 "large-scale" labor disputes and 1994 saw more than 10,000 sit-ins, strikes, and rallies before the Chinese government stopped publishing this type of data. Recent data suggests that throughout the early 2000s, there may have been about 40,000 protest events in each year, with their size, and possibly intensity, growing. In fact, with economic reforms and the closing of bankrupt state industries pushing millions of people out of work, the Associated Press reports that "[p]rotests by the unemployed have become an almost daily occurrence in China".[52] Furthermore, provincial governments have scarce funds to buoy the unemployed, while a national

---

cited in Michael S. Duke, *The Iron House* (Layton, UT: Gibbs Smith Publ., 1990), p. 22: "The Communist Party regulates everything, but it does not regulate the Communist Party".

[50] In the most prosperous province of Guangdong, where foreign firms are increasing their presence, "accidents abound. In some factories, workers are chastised, beaten, strip-searched, and even forbidden to use the bathroom during work hours". In total, the province officially reported 45,000 industrial accidents in 1993 alone, which claimed the lives of over 8,700 workers (cited in David C. Korten, *When Corporations Rule the World* (West Hartford, CT and San Francisco, CA: Kumarian Press and Berrett-Koehler Publishers, 1995), p. 231).

[51] *Cf.* Rosemont, "Why the Chinese Economic Miracle Isn't One". Also see Henry Rosemont, Jr., "China & U.S. Morality", *Z Magazine*, December 1995.

[52] "Report: Chinese Police Scuffle with Protesting Factory Workers", *Associated Press*, 5 November 1999. *Cf.* Joe McDonald, "Miners Riot to Protest Layoffs as China Tries to Close Unprofitable State Companies", *Associated Press*, 5 April 2000

social welfare system does not yet exist to meet their needs.

According to Louie Kin Sheun, "the 1990s ha[d] been a period of rising expectations", as many people seem to want "something more".[53] That "something more" appears to include positive political and economic rights, *i.e.*, a focus on the "freedom to" of (narrowly defined) democracy and capitalism as opposed to the "freedom from" of the Communist Party's paternal authoritarianism. And indeed, the divergence between the Chinese people's daily reality and the Communist Party's relentless ideology is probably wider now than at any other time, except perhaps for June 1989.[54]

Gorbachev's visit to China may have had more immediate and noticeable effects on the protestors, however President Bill Clinton's visit in the Summer of 1998 may ultimately have a more profound and long-term influence on the movement for democracy. In one of the events of his visit, President Clinton appeared on live television with President Jiang, deftly answering questions and discussing issues related to democracy and human rights, along with independence for Tibet and other matters rarely discussed so candidly in China. People are increasingly resentful of their government's monopolization of public discourse on so many of the issues that matter dearly to them. Economic growth and the lure of wealth cannot permanently put aside all other conceptions of the public good. The "ties that bind" in Chinese society are fraying and loosening.

One particularly striking example of fiscal crisis and market mania is worth noting here:

> Universities, and their individual departments, have also been obliged to enter the market in a variety of ways, most of which have little or nothing to do with education. One department at a distinguished institution, for example, formed a company in 1993, and took money from its operating budget to hire a consultant on investment opportunities. The advice given was

[53] Cited in Gilley, "Vox Populi", p. 16

[54] Baum, "China After Deng"

> to purchase a large quantity of a chemical used in food processing which was for sale immediately at a low price. Much more money was taken from the operating budget to purchase the chemical, which, unfortunately, is seldom used anymore by food processing firms. Consequently, a couple of classrooms had to be emptied in order to store the chemical—a ton of it—where the containers of it continue to sit, gathering dust.[55]

An article in *China Daily* in March 1994 even boasted that Shanghai "is trying to promote the development of its college-run businesses to boost educational and economic development".[56] Going too far, perhaps, the International Politics Department at Beijing University was warned by the Chinese Education Ministry to focus more on political thought and less on its economic ventures, such as its lucrative business of selling women's underwear. Likewise, the University's History Department was ordered to close its gift and souvenir shop.[57]

Popular communications networks also appear to be even more dense and more autonomous than in 1989. Just as Benedict Anderson "imagined communities" of "reading publics" which encouraged the development of nationalist social movements, one could also begin to imagine electronic communities of both domestic and diasporic Chinese in urban China.[58] An increase in the use of cellular telephones (many provided by corporate employers) and long-distance phone calls (doubling from 1989 to 1991), short-wave radios, televisions, fax machines, and computers (especially with regard to the internet generally and e-mail specifically; *e.g.*, Beijing and Shanghai now boast hundreds of internet

---

[55] Rosemont, "Why the Chinese Miracle Isn't One", p. 44

[56] *Ibid.*, p. 45

[57] R.J. Lambrose, "Department Stores", *Lingua Franca*, January/February 1994, p. 6

[58] Benedict Anderson, *Imagined Communities* (London: Verso, 1991)

cafes which are only nominally censored) all aid in this process. So do the presence of the Voice of America on the radio, CNN and MTV on television, and *Newsweek* on the streets, not to mention news and entertainment sources from Australia, France, and Taiwan, as well. People can even view the BBC in Chinese or watch the many Star Television programs from Hong Kong on one of the at least 1,800 cable television systems and the hundreds of thousands of satellite dishes in this era of "borderless television".

Interestingly, even government ministries, including the Army General Staff Department, are selling satellite equipment, despite the ban on doing so. Furthermore, since 1994, ten newly released western movies have been (officially) imported annually, with many more showing up unofficially. President Jiang Zemin even recommended that the people go to see the movie *Titanic*. This flow of information, and how it is received and ultimately consumed, cannot be censored or coopted by the Communist Party. For example, "American cops-and-robbers shows sometimes play on Chinese television, and viewers often find the plot twists full of surprises—like the moments when the bad guys are read their rights and allowed to call a lawyer. To some Chinese, that kind of novelty is more memorable than the plot itself".[59]

As evidence of China's new appetite for global communications, "China has become a major producer and consumer of TVs, VCRs, satellite dishes, and, in a recent emerging trend, PCs with Internet connections". And, as George Koo continues, "[i]nformation and knowledge change attitudes".[60] In May 1995, ChinaNet was established for "public" access to the internet. Mostly used by students and faculty of the universities, there are hundreds of thousands of users and they are increasing rapidly. This is not to be confused with another important network with a similar name, China-Net, which was established in May 1989, and is a electronic network that serves the overseas community of

---

[59] Nicholas D. Kristof, "Satellites Bring Information Revolution to China", *New York Times*, 11 April 1993, p. A12. *Cf.* John Lippman, "Tuning In the Global Village: How TV is Transforming World Culture and Politics", *Los Angeles Times*, 20 October 1992, esp. p. 2: "Marshall McLuhan coined the phrase 'global village' to describe how the electronics revolution [is] shrinking the world and shortening the time between thought and action".

[60] George Koo, "An Asian American Perspective on China", *Asian Week*, 17 January 1997, reprinted in *Chinese Community Forum*, 29 January 1997

students and scholars interested in China. Both of these computer networks help spread and cycle information and ideas amongst the Chinese communities in and out of China. There are three other public servers approved by the state, along with over 100 internet service providers (ISPs) and at least several hundred internet cafes.[61] A Beijing University lecturer boasts that "I am now talking to my friends on almost everything, even politically sensitive issues, without the worry of being bugged.... A friend of mine communicates frequently with an old friend who fled to the United States because of his involvement in the prodemocracy movement".[62]

Presently, there are millions of personal computer owners in China, while tens of millions of middle class Chinese now have a computer at the top of their latest consumer wish list.[63] There are between one and two million Chinese online and, with about four thousand new computers being sold each day, the numbers are sure to continue to increase rapidly.[64]

The lesson from the events during the spring of 1998 in Indonesia

---

[61] Wei Liming, "Are You On Line?", *Beijing Review*, 30 November-6 December 1998, pp. 8-10. The first internet café was started in Shekou, Shenzhen in 1993 and the idea caught on. Beijing now has over 200 internet cafes, while Shanghai has over 400. Fully one-quarter of internet users in China are in Beijing, and 80 percent of users are between the ages of 21 and 35.

[62] "Invasion from Cyberspace", *World Press Review*, March 1996 [*Asiaweek*, 8 September 1995], p. 40

[63] While the "old three big things" include a wristwatch, a bicycle, and a sewing machine, and the "new three big things" include a color television, a refrigerator, and a washing machine, all of which are now commonplace in Beijing, the "super three big things" now sought by the urban middle class are a computer, a car, and a private house. Of the super three, obtaining a computer is presently the most realistic (Teresa Poole, "The Long March to Affluence", *World Press Review*, March 1996 [*Independent on Sunday*, 31 December 1995], p. 32).

[64] There are also about 1,000 mobile phones being sold each day. Though not nearly so in the rest of the country, "out of every 100 Beijing households: 99 have a television... 56 have a stationary phone... 19 have a personal computer... [and] 12 have a mobile phone" (William Lindesay, "The New Consumers", *National Geographic Traveler*, September/October 1998, p. 102). These numbers are undoubtedly increasing with time.

are not lost on either the Chinese government or the dissidents. Indonesian students, in their successful struggle to oust authoritarian President Suharto, used the internet to communicate with each other and to send messages to journalists, U.S. government officials, human rights groups, and others. The international community was successfully mobilized along with the Indonesian people. Further, the use of cellular telephones, including the use of text messaging, is growing exponentially, especially amongst the young.

More than two centuries ago, Emperor Qianlong demanded: "Be sure to prevent any contact between the barbarians and the population", thereby ordering his authorities to block communication between foreigners and Chinese.[65] As usual, however, politics could not keep up with technology. If ever it were possible to honor Qianlong's fearful demand, his contemporary Communist Party counterparts know this to be a futile exercise. Even under an authoritarian regime, the possibilities of contact in the global village between "barbarian" ideas and Chinese minds are ceaseless.

Lastly, and perhaps most importantly, the Chinese military leaders seem to be much less enthralled with their political leaders *and* their official ideology, and also are distancing themselves from the 1989 violent crackdown. Military leaders giving public lectures often comment that their units were neither involved in the suppression nor even in Beijing in June 1989, insisting that they would not do such things. This is not just talk. Hundreds of officers, including several high-ranking officials, and thousands of soldiers refused to carry out direct orders to violently repress civilians in June 1989. Other soldiers who did participate are now bitter and disillusioned. Whereas "[s]tudents are the universal opposition", "[t]he military are the ultimate support of regimes. If they withdraw their support, if they carry out a coup against the regime, or if they refuse to use force against those who threaten to overthrow the regime, the regime falls".[66]

---

[65] Emperor Qianlong (of the Qing Dynasty [1644-1911]), 11 October 1793, cited in Kristof and WuDunn, *China Wakes*, p. 2

[66] Samuel P. Huntington, *The Third Wave: Democratization in the Late Twentieth Century* (Norman and London: University of Oklahoma Press, 1991), pp. 144-45. Huntington, no friend of democracy beyond occasional lip service (sounding similar to Mao, he elsewhere speaks of an "excess of democracy"), thankfully claims to keep his values detached from his otherwise insightful

Katharine Chorley was perhaps the first student of revolution to emphasize the role of the military and is still virtually alone in the field. She argues that "little serious attention has been given to an effort to make an historical analysis of [revolution] in its relation to the character and strengths of the defending force of the *status quo* government which the [revolution] is designed to overthrow".[67] Doing this herself, Chorley concludes that "governments of the *status quo* who are in full control of their armed forces and are in a position to use them to full effect have a decisive superiority which no rebel force can hope to overcome".[68] Huntington concurs, arguing that the military is the "necessary support" of authoritarian regimes: "In the last analysis, whether the regime collapses or not depends on whether [the military] support[s] the regime, join[s the] opposition to it, or stand[s] by on the sidelines".[69] More than half a century later, Chorley's analyses and conclusions still appear to be empirically accurate.

East German officials' decision in 1989 to cancel Erich Honecker's direct order to open fire on the hundreds of thousands of peaceful protestors in Leipzig was a significant turning point in the revolutionary situations throughout Eastern Europe.[70] After those demonstrations, many people, especially in East Germany, sensed that it was now safer to demonstrate against the government and, all over Eastern Europe, they accordingly translated their "private political preferences"

---

analyses "95 percent" of the time.

[67] Katharine C. Chorley, *Armies and the Art of Revolution* (London: Faber & Faber, 1943), p. 11. This is still largely true.

[68] *Ibid.*

[69] Huntington, *The Third Wave*, p. 150. *Cf.* Ted Robert Gurr and Jack A. Goldstone, "Comparisons and Policy Implications" in Nikki R. Keddie, ed., *Debating Revolutions* (New York and London: New York University Press, 1995), pp. 333-34

[70] In the last of the Eastern European rebellions against the Communist Party regimes, the Romanian military captured, quickly tried, and summarily executed Nicolae Ceausescu and his wife Elena on 25 December 1989.

into public action, establishing a "latent bandwagon" effect.[71] This belief was strongly reinforced in many people's minds, both in the regimes and in the oppositions, by Gorbachev's repeated remarks that the USSR had no right to interfere in its neighbors' affairs and that the threatened or actual use of military force should not be employed as a weapon of foreign policy. The Communist Party leaders throughout Eastern Europe were losing legitimacy amongst the masses, were losing support from their long-time superpower ally, and were losing faith in their authority to rule amongst themselves. Feelings of being in crisis were pervasive throughout the region. These factors, combined, led to the Communist Party regimes losing their power and authority to force their will onto the citizens, as they had so brutally done in the past. China appears to be on a similar, albeit unique, trajectory.

All tolled, the "iron rice bowl" appears to be rusting from the inside out. It is in this sense that like East Germany in 1953, Hungary in 1956, Czechoslovakia in 1968, and Poland in 1980-81, China's Democracy Movement in 1989 may be viewed as a "revolutionary rehearsal" for the inevitable next round of collective action.[72] "As Marx remarked about the 1848 [rebellions]", Colin Barker reminds us, "a movement sometimes needs the 'whip of reaction' to stimulate it forward".[73] For as the students say, "you can't kill an idea!". Indeed, during a "Free Speech Hour" at Beida just one week before the massacre, a young woman read her riveting poem aloud:

> There is one sentence,
> Spoken aloud it brings calamity.
> There is one sentence,
> That can cause conflagration.
> Don't divulge it!
> Youth did not disclose it.
> You can understand
> Our silence deep as a volcano.
> Perhaps we'll suddenly be possessed,

---

[71] Timur Kuran, "The East European Revolution of 1989: Is It Surprising That We Were Surprised?", *American Economic Review*, May 1991, pp. 122-23

[72] Colin Barker, ed., *Revolutionary Rehearsals* (London: Bookmarks, 1987)

[73] Colin Barker, "Perspectives" in *Ibid.*, p. 236

> Lightning suddenly strikes from the sky,
> *Our* China [will] be born from the thunder!
> How's that, how can I express it today?
> It's all right if you don't believe an iron tree can still blossom.
> But
> There is one sentence, just listen:
> Like a volcano that cannot bear the silence,
> Shakes its head, sticks out its tongue, stamps its feet,
> When lightning strikes from the sky,
> *Our* China will be born from the thunder!

The sentence that cannot be "spoken aloud", but is often thought, is "Down with the Communist Party!". The students will be the buds on the iron tree of China that will make it blossom again.[74]

Jack Goldstone also makes a convincing case that the next mass mobilization against the Chinese government will likely have different results than those from 1989. "Should nationwide disturbances recur, particularly after [a national leader's] death" or some other major crisis or event, Goldstone suggests, "it seems highly unlikely that any party leader would be able to persuade the army to take actions similar to those of spring 1989".[75] This appears all the more likely given the possibility that

---

[74] Duke, *The Iron House*, pp. 65-66

[75] Jack A. Goldstone, "The Coming Chinese Collapse", *Foreign Policy*, Summer 1995. Goldstone also predicts that the crisis will occur within fifteen years. "Deng's death" or a similarly significant event, Goldstone suggests, could "touch off popular protests, power struggles within the party, and the formation of provincial coalitions of business[people] and local officials, perhaps supported by workers, proclaiming greater autonomy". *Cf.* Jack A. Goldstone, *Revolution and Rebellion in the Early Modern World* (Berkeley and Los Angeles: University of California Press, 1992), p. 482, fn. 2. Also see Martin King Whyte, "The Social Sources of the Student Demonstrations in China, 1989" in Jack A. Goldstone, ed., *Revolutions: Theoretical, Comparative, and Historical Studies*, Second Ed. (Fort Worth, TX: Harcourt Brace College Publishers, 1994), p. 192: "The shift of mood in China is symbolized by the sad fact that many who in the early 1980s used to pray for Deng's longevity [began to] hope for his early demise [by the early 1990s]". Their hopes and fears materialized on 19 February 1997 when Deng finally died at the age of 92. The successor was, of course, President Jiang Zemin, Deng's political heir. Though he lacks charisma, Jiang maintained the top

the post-Deng leaders will "reevaluate" and "rehabilitate" the 1989 Democracy Movement (what many students called "The Great Revolution For Democracy and Against Dictatorship", but what is officially labeled the "counter-revolutionary rebellion"), and its sympathizers, just as was done with other past popular movements. Already, official accounts have referred to it as a "political disturbance", or more neutrally as the "June 4th Movement".

The April 5th Movement of 1976, for example, officially went from being maligned as a "counter-revolutionary political incident" to being positively termed a "revolutionary action".[76] A would-be successor might choose to seize this terminology early, so as to beat, rather than to catch or follow, the political wave of the future. Zhao Ziyang, the purged leader of the Communist Party under house arrest from 1989 to his death, purportedly wrote a letter which was read at the 1997 five-yearly Party conference advocating such a re-evaluation, while warning that "The problem of reassessing June 4 will have to be resolved sooner or later".[77]

As the students did with Zhao's predecessor Hu Yaobang, they

---

positions in the Communist Party, the Chinese government, and the People's Liberation Army, and had shored up his position in each of these spheres. On 15 March 2003, Hu Jintao was selected as president as well as becoming chair of the communist Party and chair of the military. Other possibilities for future top leadership include former State Chairman Yang Shangkun, who supported the approach of Zhao Ziyang up until the massacre, former chair of the National People's Congress Wan Li, and its current chair and Politburo member Qiao Shi. Prime Minister Li Peng, the adopted son of Zhou Enlai, can also make a bid for leadership, while one cannot rule out some former leader's political resurrection, just as Deng himself had done. Some also have speculated about the eventual possibility of a collective leadership. For these and other possibilities, see Baum, "China After Deng".

[76] Bruce Gilley, "The Sound of Silence", *Far Eastern Economic Review*, 18 April 1996. While the government since Spring 1989 employed the terms "chaos" and "turmoil" (*dongluan*), which is the chronic fear of Chinese leaders, the students preferred the phrase "free-form dancing" (*luandong*), derived from a syllabic reversal of the same word, which came to symbolize a new hope of many Chinese citizens. The students may have been performing political jazz, but they were not creating chaos. They were, they said, "dancing in spontaneous order" (Calhoun, *Neither Gods Nor Emperors*, p. 1).

[77] "New Rumbles of Democracy", *World Press Review*, November 1997 [Marcus Gee, *Globe and Mail*, 17 September 1997], p. 8

might have again "spontaneously" risen up in mourning and protest after the death of Zhao in January 2005, but it was not to be: there might be more economic hope, especially given China's high growth rates; security was *much* tighter; and the weather was quite cold; to name a few possible reasons. Of course, "revolutions do not occur haphazardly or purely spontaneously. A syndrome of variables coalesce before... revolutions take place. These variables consist of an array of observable economic, political, social, and psychological changes or occurrences".[78] These changes have been quietly taking place for some time now, especially since the 1980s.

However, since 1990, the military, under the at least nominal control of President Jiang and then his successor Hu Jintao, since March 2003, has received steady and huge increases in its official budget (more than 200 percent in the decade following 1989), in addition to the military's non-budget revenue derived from its vast network of profit-making ventures (a $5 billion industry of around 20,000 companies).[79] Ironically, it was Deng Xiaoping who once remarked to German Chancellor Helmut Schmidt that "one of the reasons why the Soviet economy suffers from paralysis is that the Russians spend too much money on the military".[80] The increased expenditure on the military, especially in the current context of an increasingly fiscally constrained state, is being pursued, according to Li-Cheng Wang, "for three reasons: to solidify

---

[78] Mostafa Rejai, "Survey Essay on the Study of Revolution", *Journal of Political and Military Sociology*, Fall 1973, p. 302

[79] "China's New Model Army", *The Economist*, 11 June 1994, p. 29. In the summer of 1998, however, Jiang ordered the Army to fully divest itself of all business operations. It still remains to be seen if this order will be fully carried out. The 1990s have also seen the replacement of the top few military commanders and the shifting of all seven regional leaders. The military now accounts for a quarter of the 190 members of the Central Committee. Additionally, the Party has substituted the People's Armed Police, of which 40,000 now occupy Beijing, for the People's Liberation Army as the first wave of defense against unarmed citizens. *Cf. China Quarterly*, June 1996 [special issue on "China's Military in Transition"]

[80] Thomas Bernstein, "Domestic Politics" in Steven Goldstein, ed., *China Briefing, 1984* (Boulder, CO: Westview Press, 1985), p. 9 cited in Nancy Bernkopf Tucker, "China as a Factor in the Collapse of the Soviet Empire", *Political Science Quarterly*, Winter 1994-95, p. 505

military-civilian relations, to curtail military corruption, and to distract social frustration with aggressive military policies. These three policies [a]re all aimed at increasing Party authority, support, and credibility, in order to counter internal threats".[81]

Max Weber long ago noted, for example, how domestic legitimacy and support often can be purchased through international power plays. Military posturing, especially towards Taiwan, and perhaps to a lesser extend Hong Kong and Tibet, may be seen as just this sort of attempt. More generally, Chalmers Johnson notes that the "ideological shift from an all-embracing communism to an all-embracing nationalism [has] helped to hold Chinese society together, giving it a certain intellectual and emotional energy and stability under the intense pressures of economic transformation".[82]

Yet the Chinese government, and its chaos-averse leaders, still appears to be worried. Even more so, it seems, since the overthrow of the Communist Party regimes of Eastern Europe in 1989 and the disintegration of the Soviet Union in 1991. Poignantly, the Czech writer Ludvik Vaculik, noting that his "[g]overnment always seemed to be frightened", asked "[w]hy does it not conduct itself so that it does not have to be afraid?".[83]

Qiao Shi, chair of the National People's Congress and member of the Politburo, delivered a speech in October 1994 on "sudden incidents" that could shake the Chinese government.[84] Qiao did not ask or answer Vaculik's trenchant question, but he did outline twelve of these possible "sudden incidents" that apparently keep the Communist Party in a chronic fear of chaos. They are: (1) social and political movements

---

[81] Li-Cheng Wang, "Chinese Military Expenditures in the 1990s", *Stanford Journal of International Affairs*, Spring/Summer 1995, p. 153

[82] Chalmers Johnson, *Blowback: The Costs and Consequences of American Empire* (New York: Metropolitan Books, 2000), p. 50. Also see Chalmers Johnson, *Sorrows of Empire: Militarism, Secrecy, and the End of the Republic* (New York: Metropolitan Books, 2004)

[83] Cited in Mark Frankland, *The Patriots' Revolution: How East Europe Won Its Freedom* (London: Sinclair-Stevenson, 1990), p. 259

[84] Li Zijing, "Twelve Nightmares for Beijing", *World Press Review*, March 1996 [*Cheng Ming*, December 1995], p. 19

similar to the Democracy Movement of 1989; (2) a disruption during a major conference or event in China, such as the Olympics in 2008 or the World Expo in 2010, thereby "causing chaos and attracting international attention"; (3) the potential that enemies of the state might attempt to subvert or overthrow the government when the older revolutionaries die; (4) opportunists could start power struggles by exploiting internal party disagreements; (5) the U.S. could remove MFN status or otherwise impose economic sanctions on China which could cause an economic downturn and social instability; (6) a Taiwanese declaration of independence could force military intervention on the island; (7) U.S. support of Taiwan could jeopardize Sino-U.S. relations and instigate military action; (8) Hong Kong (or Macau) could declare itself an "independent entity" which might force the central government to put it under martial law in order to quell the rebellion; (9) overseas Chinese dissidents could secretly return to China by the sea, land, or air in order to create upheavals, as some U.S.-based Cuban-Americans have tried to do with Cuba; (10) anger at corruption from both inside and outside the Communist Party could cause massive dissatisfaction if the party's corruption problem is not resolved; (11) peasant discontent could evolve into large-scale rebellion, as it has many times in Chinese history; and (12) Xinjiang Uygur, Inner Mongolia, Tibet, and other remote and/or autonomous areas could develop stronger separatist movements and foment rebellion.

The reversion of Hong Kong on 1 July 1997 and the re-incorporation of Macau on 21 December 1999, where these different political economic entities now have to coexist as "one country, two systems", may also increase the pressures on the Chinese government and the demands for democracy. So too would an independence (or secessionist) bid by either of these two territories, by Taiwan, by any of China's five "autonomous regions", especially Tibet and Xinjiang Uygur (both of which have had sporadic incidents and uprisings), or by one of the newly prosperous provinces such as Guangdong, Fujian, or Hainan. Guangdong, for example, which is "the fastest growing provincial economy in China", "is now largely self-financing, receiving little cash from [the] central government and, in return, paying little in taxes".[85] This,

---

[85] Tuck, "Is the Party Over?", p. 17. Ye Xuanping, the outspoken governor of Guangdong, was removed from office in 1991. The breakup of the Soviet Union and the Eastern Bloc increased the calls for autonomy and independence, especially in the north and west of China. In 1994, Deng warned that if a Soviet-style disintegration was to be avoided in China the political leaders needed to

of course, only exacerbates China's ballooning budget deficits, compounded by its general revenue collection problem. It is in this sense that the Communist Party of China "reigns but it does not rule. It is a hollow shell of an organization to which officials and citizens alike feign compliance at best and ignore in normal circumstances".[86] Therefore, in sum, China in 1989 represents a negative case of revolution; however, the case of China in the medium term (within a generation) will almost certainly experience a modern revolution.

One wonders about the relevance of the *I Ching* (*Book of Changes*), an ancient Chinese text of prophesy and wisdom that "does not describe the past; rather, it establishes a mythological treatment of the actor's present and potential futures, charted among a myriad set of interlinked possibilities".[87] The "judgment" for the 49th hexagram, "*Ko*", is: "Revolution. On your own day/ You are believed./ Supreme success,/

"handle well the relations between the party centre and the localities" (cited in Baum, "China After Deng", p. 164). It is highly questionable, though, whether Chinese leaders will be more successful at this than was Gorbachev with the USSR, Václav Havel with Czechoslovakia, or the leaders of the former Yugoslavia and former Yemen.

[86] Shambaugh, "China's Fragile Future", p. 43. "It survives through its monopoly of political power; the suppression of dissent and lack of any organized political rival; by pushing economic growth; and by playing the nationalism card." But also see Koo, "An Asian American Perspective on China". Koo cites Michael Dowdle as stating that "[t]he 1982 constitution is becoming increasingly relevant to China's decision making process... [and that the National People's Congress] is beginning to take independent action and [is] getting away with it [as happened in some Eastern European countries in the late 1980s]... [including] rewriting the criminal law to state that defendants shall not be presumed guilty, that they shall have lawyers, and that the police shall no longer be able to hold them without charge". Koo also claims that "the Chinese Minister of Justice, Xiao Yang, has publicly stated that China needs to govern all affairs by the rule of law [and] admitted that China is not there yet". Furthermore, the Chinese legislature on 6 March 1997 approved a new civil code which, importantly, no longer contains a category for "counterrevolutionary" crimes, and on 5 October 1998 China signed the International Covenant on Civil and Political Rights.

[87] John R. Hall, *Cultures of Inquiry* (Cambridge: Cambridge University Press, 1999), ch. 3. The *I Ching*, reputed to be the oldest book in the world, is premised on the belief that everything changes except change itself. The text contains a total of 64 hexagrams.

Furthering through perseverance...". One specific line for that hexagram reads: "When one's own day comes, one may create revolution./ Starting brings good fortune. No blame".[88] This day may indeed soon be upon us. And with more than one-fifth of the world's population (1.3 billion out of a total 6 billion people) and an economy predicted to be the largest in the world early next century, China's awakening certainly will, as Napoleon prophesied, "shake the world".

---

[88] Cited in *Ibid.*

Chapter XI.

Conclusion:

Looking Back and Looking Forward

"The origins of the Revolution are one story; the story of the Revolution from that point onward is quite another"
— D. Mornet[1]

In one sense, the revolution in Czechoslovakia took a few days, but in another more fundamental sense, it took a few generations and is

---

[1] Cited in Goldstone, *Revolution and Rebellion in the Early Modern World*, p. 416

still continuing. Theoretically, the causes of the revolution may have been infinite, producing a completely unique social phenomenon. Indeed, according to Hirschman, "Large-scale social change typically occurs as the result of a unique constellation of highly disparate events and is therefore amenable to paradigmatic thinking only in a very special sense".[2] However, more practically in a heuristic sense, there appears to be several major factors that contributed to a revolutionary transformation resulting in the "Prague Autumn" of 1989, or what Przeworski refers to in Eastern Europe as the "Autumn of the People" and what Tarrow terms a "cycle of protest",[3] and a rebellion in China which resulted in a massacre and repression. This study has presented these factors in rough chronological order. Unfortunately, yet inherently, whether they all were necessary is unclear; whether there are others that are necessary is uncertain.

"Of necessity", according to Ragin (and many others), "the social sciences must make room for imprecision and incompleteness in the study of human affairs".[4] Yet, at least for Czechoslovakia, certain factors, some more basic and others more superficial, seem to have collectively and synergistically played a sufficiently important causal role in the (so far) successful democratic transition. In their convergence, these causes comprise, to paraphrase Roy Hofheinz, the ecology of revolutionary success.[5]

First, the histories of democracy in Czechoslovakia, with its relatively civic culture, provided a national collective memory/myth of how society should be. Indeed, for many, the memory of the Prague Spring was from personal experience, while the democratic interwar years are

---

[2] Albert O. Hirschman, "The Search for Paradigms as a Hindrance to Understanding", *World Politics*, April 1970, p. 329 cited in Guiseppe di Palma, "Legitimation from the Top to Civil Society: Politico-Cultural Change in Eastern Europe", *World Politics*, October 1991, p. 79

[3] Przeworski, *Democracy and the Market*, p. 1 and Przeworski, "The 'East' Becomes the 'South'?: The 'Autumn of the People' and the Future of Eastern Europe"; Tarrow, *Power in Movement*, p. 7, ch. 9

[4] Charles C. Ragin with Mary Driscoll, "Afterword: The Promise of Social Research" in Ragin, *Constructing Social Research*, p. 162

[5] Roy Hofheinz, Jr., "The Ecology of Chinese Communist Success: Rural Influence Patterns 1932-45" in A.D. Barnett, ed., *Chinese Communist Politics in Action* (Seattle, WA, 1969)

cherished amongst the Czechs like a national treasure. Although this factor may not have been necessary for the Revolution *per se*, it may have been a facilitating factor and is invaluable for the long-term success of the Revolution. In China this factor is largely absent and may make China less likely than Czechoslovakia to have a revolution and more vulnerable to counter-revolution if it does have one. In Iran, by contrast to Czechoslovakia, a democratic past makes the government potentially less stable because it goes against the logic of the current politico-cultural system in Iran. Czechoslovakia has a democratic past and political entrepreneurs who are perennially willing to resurrect it. Havel clearly follows in the liberal democratic tradition of Czech history and many Czech intellectuals, including Jan Hus, Tomas Masaryk, Eduard Benes, and Karel Capek, who were "naive dreamer[s] who always tr[ied] to combine the incompatible: politics and morality".[6] Histories of democracy can be understood as forms of path dependency, though never as path determinacy.

The issue of human rights, secondly, became a strong external pressure which in turn produced indigenous human rights organizations which created pressure internally. The non-violent and non-partisan demands for human rights also broadened and unified the diverse and disaggregated elements of the opposition.

Third, the economy played a quidditous role; initially by growing in the 1960s, then stagnating in the 1970s, and finally declining in the 1980s, thereby encouraging rising expectations to be frustrated. Economic conditions were not a factor directly, or by themselves, yet these conditions contributed by the ways in which they deeply affected other societal phenomena.

Fourth, rather than being a cause *per se,* the important role of Gorbachev was in the removal of an historical obstacle toward change in Eastern Europe, *i.e.* the Soviet Red Army. Gorbachev did not foment revolution in Czechoslovakia and the rest of Eastern Europe, but through word and deed he provided the social and political *opportunities* for others to do so.

The role of the mass media, fifthly, was to nationalize and unify the opposition movement. The mass media also alerted people as to what was happening both within their own country and in the neighboring countries, further contributing, sixthly, to relative deprivation. People

---

[6] Václav Havel, *Summer Meditations*, trans. Paul Wilson (New York: Alfred A. Knopf, 1992), p. 4

learned about what was happening in both Eastern and Western Europe and acted accordingly based on their perceptions and interpretations.

Seventh and finally, like the (in)actions of Gorbachev, the domestic military played a significant role by removing the obstacle of physical repression. When the military was no longer willing or able to repress the popular movement, time was running short for the government with little legitimacy.

All in all, the combination of these several major factors seem to have worked interactively to contribute to the making of the Velvet Revolution. In short, the seemingly sudden "willingness of the party bureaucrats to surrender their power position can be seen as the result of ideological bankruptcy and their growing interest in converting political into economic power. The previous experience of military solutions and the calculation of their costs and benefits contributed to adoption of a non-violent approach in the majority of Soviet bloc countries".[7]

The role of a nation's location within international centers of power and its position within the global economy is also not insignificant. Regarding international relations and the global economy, the Czechoslovak state (along with the other Eastern European states) was opposed by Western European and North American states. Its main supporter, the Soviet Union, however, became neutral and its regional supporters, especially Poland and Hungary, were weak and retreating. The Czechoslovak state was therefore seriously weakened in 1989. The Chinese state is similarly opposed by various other powerful states and has no main supporter. Yet, China's massive size (*i.e.*, geographic, demographic, and economic) may temper the latter concern to some extent. Further, China is opposed primarily on political grounds, as opposed to economic ones, mostly due to its large and opening economy and its great potential for increased business ties with the West. When domestic crises turn revolutionary in these politically isolated countries, therefore, revolution is more likely to obtain, as rebellions against these weakened states may be less defensible.[8]

---

[7] Misztal, "Understanding Political Change in Eastern Europe", p. 465

[8] In contrast, the Mexican state has a powerful neighbor and supporter, the U.S., without any opponents, diplomatically or militarily. In 1968 and 1994, therefore, when rebellions emerged, or in 1982 and 1988, when they could have, the oppositional movements were coopted, crushed, or contained. Mexico also (continued...)

It should be clear that I have not been simply offering either a structuralist or an idealist analysis; to do so would be too simplistic and self-limiting. Neither individuals nor institutions nor ideas alone make history; history is made through the ensemble of all of these. Like micro-level phenomena, macro-level phenomena rarely operate in a vacuum. Indeed, this analysis follows the Weberian methodology of "causal pluralism",[9] or what I have termed causal convergence. All analyses of social change must, in some way or another, address both structures and agents, in addition to relevant historical events and cultural phenomena, in the making of social change.[10] However, one must be cautious, as Jenson suggests, against theorizing "agentless structures" and

---

[8](...continued)
maintains a facade of democracy which makes it more resistant to revolution. Domestic crises in Mexico, for now, are not likely to lead to revolution. Cuba, Vietnam, and North Korea are somewhere between China and Mexico on this conceptual map. *Cf.* Immanuel Wallerstein, *The Modern World System*, Vols. 1-3 (New York: Academic Press, 1974, 1980, 1989). Also see Noam Chomsky, *World Orders Old and New* (New York: Columbia University Press, 1994).

[9] Gerth and Mills, eds., *From Max Weber*, esp. pp. 34, 58-59, 65. *Cf.* John R. Hall, "The Patrimonial Dynamic in Colonial Brazil" in Richard Graham, ed., *Brazil and the World System* (Austin: University of Texas Press, 1991), p. 61: "The neo-Weberian approach counters theories based in holism and necessitism, which force events into the matrix of a universal history founded on some prime mover---materialist, idealist, or otherwise". Weber refers to the revolutionary moment as a "carnival we decorate with the proud name of 'revolution'" (Max Weber, "Politics as a Vocation" in *op. cit.*, p. 115).

[10] See William H. Sewell, Jr., "Collective Violence and Collective Loyalties in France: Why the French Revolution Made a Difference", *Politics & Society*, December 1990 and William H. Sewell, Jr., "A Theory of Structure: Duality, Agency, and Transformation", *American Journal of Sociology*, July 1992. (When asked why the title of his article wasn't "A Theory of Transformation: Structure, Agency, and Duality", Sewell responded that "it could have been" that or any combination of those words.) *Cf.* Griswold, *Cultures and Societies in a Changing World*, p. 105, fn. 2: "we need to understand the impact of both culture and structure on social processes; neither is sufficient by itself".

"structureless agents".[11] To this end, Nitin Nohria and Ranjay Gulati argue that "people are *in* structures the way cells are in bodies: they do not just fill a framework; in an important sense, they *are* this framework".[12] As McDaniel so eloquently states,

> Ideas become effective only when they interpret social realities in a persuasive way and so provide guides for action; in this sense, they are not 'autonomous'. Similarly... structural possibilities for change require actors driven on by ideas. To insist on the primacy of ideology against structural preconditions, or the reverse, is to separate what in actual revolutions are always found together; each is a necessary complement to the other.[13]

---

[11] Cited in Peet, "Cultural Production of Economic Forms in the New England Discursive Formation". In this sense, the analysis offered here approaches so-called post-structuralism (and post-agentism). I choose to employ the term post-structuralism differently than the "conventional" post-structuralism of post-modernism. For the purposes of this book, post-stiucturalism refers to a transcendence of uni-deterministic models, whether based on structures or on agents. For the clearest and most "objective" exposition of post-modernism, see Pauline Marie Rosenau, *Postmodernism and the Social Sciences: Insights, Inroads, and Intrusions* (Princeton, NJ: Princeton University Press, 1992).

[12] Nitin Nohria and Ranjay Gulati, "Firms and Their Environments" in Smelser and Swedberg, eds., *The Handbook of Economic Sociology*, p. 549, original emphasis. In an address to Parliament during World War II, Winston Churchill commented that "We shape our buildings, and afterwards our buildings shape us". Marshall McLuhan later elaborated on this theme of human creations in turn re-creating humans.

[13] McDaniel, *Autocracy, Modernization, and Revolution in Russia and Iran*, p. 188. *Cf.* Alexis de Tocqueville, *Democracy in America* [1835, 1840], edited by Richard D. Heffner (New York: Mentor Books, 1956), pp. 266, 317; Frances Fox Piven and Richard A. Cloward, *Poor People's Movements: Why They Succeed, How They Fail* (New York: Vintage Books, 1977), p. 20; Louis Althusser, *For*
(continued...)

This is certainly true of Czechoslovakia in 1989, in addition to the rest of Eastern Europe and China. Moreover, it also echoes Lenin's "fundamental law of revolution", which states (at length) that

> It is not sufficient for revolution that the exploited and oppressed masses understand the impossibility of living in the old way and demand changes; for revolution, it is necessary that the exploiters should not be able to live and rule in the old way. Only when the 'lower classes' do not want the old way, and when the 'upper classes' cannot carry on in the old way—only then can revolution triumph. This truth may be expressed in other words: revolution is impossible without a nationwide crisis (affecting both the exploited and the exploiters). It follows that for revolution it is essential, first, that a majority of the workers (or at least a majority of the class-conscious, thinking, politically active workers) should fully understand that revolution is necessary and be ready to sacrifice their lives for it; secondly, that the ruling classes be in a state of governmental crisis which draws even the most backward masses into politics... a crisis which weakens the government and makes it possible for the revolutionaries to

---

[13](...continued)
Marx (London: Verso, 1977), pp. 100-01; Fox, *Lions of the Punjab, passim.* For the related view within the field of existential psychology, see the "existential-integrative position" also known as the "freedom-limitation dialectic" in Kirk J. Schneider and Rollo May, eds., *The Psychology of Existence* (New York: McGraw-Hill, 1995), p. 321.

overthrow it rapidly.[14]

Whether one can formulate a general theory from these Czechoslovak phenomena is still an open question. Geoff Eley states, speaking of the rise of fascism specifically but large-scale social change generally, that "In the end both perspectives are necessary—the one stressing deep historical or long-term structures *and* the one stressing the immediate crisis".[15] It is relevant that "Czechoslovakia in 1989 had

---

[14] Cited in Christopher Hill, *Lenin and the Russian Revolution* (New York: Penguin Books, 1984 [1947]), p. 30 and in Dunn, *Modern Revolutions*, p. 14. I have combined both citations to form a composite quote.

[15] Geoff Eley, "What Produces Fascism: Preindustrial Traditions or a Crisis of a Capitalist State", *Politics & Society*, 1983, p. 82. With respect to the deep historical perspective, I do not include Skocpol's "nonvoluntarist, structural" approach as it treats human actors as mere automatons playing determined roles. Furthermore, although Barrington Moore can explain the absence of revolution in India, for example, his student Skocpol cannot. The structural approach is likewise silent with respect to the absence of revolution in modern Mexico in 1982, 1988, and 1994-95, in addition to Cuba, Libya, and Zaire through the mid-1990s, for example, because the explanations for revolutions are surely social and cultural as well as structural. It also fails to explain why revolution, though not a modern one, occurred in Zaire (now the so-called Democratic Republic of The Congo) in 1996-97.

With respect to the more immediate perspective, I discard the "rational choice" approach because it contains major flaws which render it unacceptable. It assumes universal individual selfishness and it is tautological. The rational choice approach also contains what Ferree describes as "dehumanizing [deculturizing?] assumptions" based on "a neglect of value differences". Further, it assumes people's goals and constraints to be static when we should know them to be dynamic. Unfortunately, all of the theories herein presuppose "pseudo-universal human actor[s]" irrespective of class, race/ethnicity, and sex/gender which effectively silences the roles of the powerless *within* the powerless (Myra Marx Ferree, "The Political Context of Rationality: Rational Choice Theory and Resource Mobilization" in Morris & Mueller, eds., *Frontiers in Social Movement Theory*, esp. p. 31). Rational choice theory has also been criticized for being overly schematic, ethnocentric, phallocentric, and temporocentric.

It is interesting to note that on 18 November 1989, two women students *qua* citizens went to Prime Minister Adamec's house and privately secured his agreement to officially investigate the violent crackdown on the peaceful protestors from the previous day. This action was neither "rational" nor backed by

(continued...)

undergone no gradual political liberalization, no partial economic reform. The regime put in place by Soviet tanks after 1968 was still there, its leaders and policies substantially unaltered".[16] In one sense, then, the revolutionary upheavals that swept through Eastern Europe and China in 1989 can be considered "inevitable revolutions",[17] however "[t]he assumption that socialism ha[s] to fail... takes too much for granted and does not hold up under critical scrutiny".[18] Neither capitalism nor socialism, authoritarianism nor democracy, success nor failure, is

---

[15](...continued)
"resources" of *any* kind, yet it was quite successful. As with the rational choice approach, the resource mobilization approach, aside from its theoretical deficiencies, does not appear to make a very good empirical fit in Czechoslovakia, despite some superficial coincidence. For a cogent discussion of the theoretical deficiencies of resource mobilization theory, see Walton, *Western Times and Water Wars*, pp. 321-26. But for a defense of rational choice, see Little's (misleadingly titled) *Varieties of Social Explanation*. A classic statement of rational choice is Mancur Olson, Jr., *The Logic of Collective Action* (New York: Schocken Books (Harvard University Press), 1965). For more directly relevant statements, see the essays in Michael Taylor, ed., *Rationality and Revolution* (Cambridge: Cambridge University Press, 1988).

[16] Tony R. Judt, "Metamorphosis: The Democratic Revolution in Czechoslovakia" in Banac, ed., *Eastern Europe in Revolution*, p. 96. Tocqueville's speculation that governments are more susceptible to revolution "when [they] seek to mend [their] ways" rather than "when things are going from bad to worse" does not seem to apply to Czechoslovakia (Alexis de Tocqueville, *The Old Regime and the French Revolution* (New York: Anchor Books/Doubleday, 1955 [1856]), pp. 176-77. Also see Tocqueville, *Democracy in America*, p. 57; and Eric Hoffer, *The Ordeal of Change* (New York: Harper & Row, 1963), p. 6). *Cf.* Goldstone, *Revolution and Rebellion in the Early Modern World*, pp. 316-18. Neither Marxian nor Burkean in his view of revolution, Tocqueville believes revolutions to be beneficial only when they lead to and encourage the formation and strengthening of democratic governance.

[17] Walter LaFeber, "Inevitable Revolutions", *Atlantic Monthly*, June 1982; and LaFeber, *Inevitable Revolutions*. LaFeber, however, refers to the countries of Central America, specifically, and the role of the U.S. Hannah Arendt refers to this concept as an "irresistible process" (Hannah Arendt, *On Revolution* (New York: Penguin Books, 1990 [1963]), p. 49).

[18] Szelenyi, Beckett, and King, "The Socialist Economic System" in Smelser and Swedberg, eds., *The Handbook of Economic Sociology*, p. 248

teleologically determined.

The situation of Eastern Europe and China does indeed have similarities with anti-colonial revolutions. Indeed, *all* pre-revolutionary governments have been authoritarian—which we can triadically typologize as personalistic dictatorships (*viz.* England, France, Mexico, Russia, China, Cuba, Iran, and Nicaragua), colonial dictatorships (*viz.* the U.S., Haiti, Algeria, Indochina, Mozambique, and Angola), and (post)totalitarian dictatorships (*viz.* Eastern Europe, China)—though not all authoritarian governments, as we certainly know too well, end in revolution. Authoritarianism appears to be a necessary, though insufficient, structural precondition for revolution.

Whereas authoritarian regimes are susceptible to revolution, democracies, in contradistinction, appear to be resistant to revolution, as was first suggested by Lenin, just prior to the Russian Revolution:

> A democratic republic is the best possible political shell for capitalism, and, therefore, once capital has gained control of this very best shell... it establishes its power so securely, so firmly, that *no* change, either of persons, of institutions, or of parties in the bourgeois-democratic republic, can shake it.[19]

---

[19] V. I. Lenin, *The State and Revolution* (Peking [Beijing]: Foreign Languages Press, 1970 [1917]), pp. 15-16, original emphasis. *Cf.* Tocqueville, *Democracy in America*, pp. 99-100, 107-08, 164-65, 264-68; Che Guevara, *Guerilla Warfare* (New York: Vintage Books, 1961), p. 2: "Where a government has come into power through some form of popular vote, fraudulent or not, and maintains at least an appearance of constitutional legality, the guerrilla outbreak cannot be promoted" (advice Che himself did not take in Bolivia, with well-known disastrous ends); Huntington, *Political Order in Changing Societies*, p. 275: "Perhaps the most important and obvious but also most neglected fact about successful great revolutions is that they do not occur in democratic political systems"; Michael Parenti, *Power and the Powerless*, 2nd Ed. (NY: St. Martin's Press, 1978), p. 201: "[E]lections serve as a great asset in consolidating the existing social order by propagating the appearances of popular rule. History demonstrates that the people might be moved to overthrow a tyrant who shows himself provocatively indifferent to their woes, but they are far less inclined to

(continued...)

Judging by the experiences of Czechoslovakia, we might hypothesize that the collectively sufficient factors for a *long-term successful* modern revolution include a cultural memory/myth, especially a democratic or "civic" history, a force or theme to broaden and unify the opposition, economic decline or distress, the spread of relevant information, the desire for better conditions, and, *at minimum*, the neutrality of superior military forces, both foreign and domestic. On the one side, the Czech Republic appears to have fully met these conditions. The Czech Republic evidences a history and culture of moral resistance and velvet social change. It is similarly true of Hungary, which experienced the same basic causal convergence. On the other side, Slovakia may not have met the necessary conditions. Neither has Romania or Bulgaria. Based on their configuration of causes, Slovakia, Romania, and Bulgaria each experienced regime change, but not a revolution as it is defined here. Indeed, it is fair to say that Romania and Bulgaria in 1989 experienced *coups d'état*, or perhaps more specifically, a putsch in

---

[19](...continued)
make war upon a state... if it preserves what [James] Madison called 'the spirit and form of popular government'"; Wickham-Crowley, *Guerrillas & Revolution in Latin America*, p. 299: "elected democratic regimes appear to be the strongest of all in the face of insurgency"; Dietrich Rueschemeyer, Evelyne Stephens, and John Stephens, *Capitalist Development & Democracy* (Chicago: University of Chicago Press, 1992), p. 57: "It is a telling fact that revolutions from below, Marxist-Leninist or otherwise, are always carried out against authoritarian systems, not democracies"; Skocpol, "Reflections on Recent Scholarship about Social Revolutions and How to Study Them" in Skocpol, ed., *Social Revolutions in the Modern World*, p. 311. It appears that democracies do politically what Barrington Moore claims India does socio-culturally (and politically), namely absorb and coopt new ideas and movements through the channeling of political energies as well as continuous and gradual reform (although violent repression, both actual and potential, is also employed by all states). Individuals, of course, are generally much more precarious than are institutions. Additionally, so-called electoral revolutions are possible within democracies (*e.g.* the democratic socialist Indian state of Kerala, the Italian city of Bologna, *et al.*), despite Marx's contention that "revolutions are not made with laws" (Marx, *Capital*, p. 915. In 1872, however, Marx, as well as Engels, seems to have considerably softened on this position, arguing that it might be possible in developed countries.). It should be noted that the above typological categories are Weberian ideal-types constructed for heuristic purposes. In actuality, social phenomena are less cooperative and rarely can be situated on precise endpoints, but instead fall within an inexact range on a vast continuum of infinite possibilities.

Romania and a palace *coup* in Bulgaria.[20] It is also fair to say that these three countries will probably revert to their traditional role in the world economy, as will Albania and most or all of the former Yugoslavia and the former Soviet Union.

China, too, did not experience a complete causal convergence and, instead, had a different configuration of causes (than Czechoslovakia), which led to a revolutionary situation resulting neither in regime change nor in revolution. However, due to the fact that China did not have a change in regime as did Romania, it remains more likely than Romania to experience a revolution in the short to medium term. Half-way reform, as in Romania, is in some ways worse than no reform at all, as in China, because it forestalls the more necessary radical reform (or revolution), sometimes for as long as a generation or more. Some of the possible results of collective action in countries that have configurations of causes that are less than complete include riots, resistance, revolts and rebellions, reaction and repression, reorganization and reconstruction, radical reform, and even regime changes. However, the countries that have an incomplete causal convergence will *not* undergo revolution.

If and when China—*or any other country with an authoritarian government*—realizes the same *type* of causal convergence that the Czech Republic did in the Autumn of 1989, that country will also realize revolution. Although the causes are likely to be similar, all of the causes do not need to be identical; they need only to have identical *effects*.[21]

Employing Boolean algebra, the causes of modern revolution can be simplified. Factors such as a unifying issue (*e.g.* human rights), economic decline after growth, and popular communication (*e.g.* mass media) are only necessary to the extent that they give rise to relatively unified and directed mass mobilization. When mass mobilization against

---

[20] See, *e.g.*, Krishan Kumar, "The Revolutions of 1989: Socialism, Capitalism, and Democracy" [1992] in Stephen K. Sanderson, ed., *Sociological Worlds: Comparative and Historical Readings on Society* (Los Angeles: Roxbury Publishing Co., 1995), p. 126, fn. 29

[21] *Cf.* Goldstone, "Methodological Issues in Comparative Macrosociology, p. 9: "In real life, different factors can be functional substitutes". Also see Jack A. Goldstone, "Introduction" in Goldstone, Gurr, and Moshiri, eds., *Revolutions of the Late Twentieth Century*, p. 3, original emphasis: "Not all revolutions stem from the same causes. Thus, to foresee the coming of a revolution, it is necessary to be able to perceive critical *combinations* of elements that may, in isolation or in different combinations, otherwise be innocuous."

an authoritarian regime (especially in the capital city and other major urban areas)[22] is coupled with an absence of (especially full scale) military intervention and suppression, revolution may occur. Yet these factors do not obtain without the other supporting factors already mentioned. A history of democracy, therefore, does not cause democratic revolution, but rather makes this outcome more stable and less susceptible to reversal.

It is likely that the Czech Republic (and Hungary) will be able to achieve First World (or core) status, or perhaps belong to a newly conceptualized Second World (or semi-periphery). It is equally likely that Slovakia (along with Albania, Bulgaria, Romania, most of the former Soviet Union, and most of the former Yugoslavia) will fall back into its traditional and peripheral Third World role, as yet another source of cheap raw materials, cheap (albeit educated and disciplined) labor, consumer markets of goods and services for the more advanced capitalist countries, and dumping grounds for outdated, unwanted, and/or polluting products and production facilities.[23]

Whereas Plato thought that all polities inevitably proceed from aristocracy to democracy to tyranny, the countries of Eastern Europe appear to be reversing this ancient claim. We must await further research to test these hypotheses and to develop, if possible, a general theory of modern revolution.[24] To date, "less is known about revolution than is

---

[22] *Cf.* Mark Traugott, "Capital Cities and Revolution", *Social Science History*, Spring 1995. Traugott discusses what he calls the "capital cities phenomenon", specifically as it applies to the history of Paris vis-a-vis social change in France.

[23] *Cf.* Chomsky, *What Uncle Sam Really Wants* ["The Prospects for Eastern Europe"]; Przeworski, "The 'East' Becomes the 'South'?: The 'Autumn of the People' and the Future of Eastern Europe"; and Arpad Abonyi, "Eastern Europe's Reintegration" in Christopher K. Chase-Dunn, ed., *Socialist States in the World-System* (Beverly Hills, CA, London, and New Delhi: Sage Publications, 1982). Also see George Konrad, "From Communism to Democracy" in Mary Caldor, ed., *Europe From Below: An East-West Dialogue* (London and New York: Verso, 1991), p. 58: "We used to be the Western fringe of the East, more developed than the centre. Now we shall be the Eastern fringe of Western Europe, more primitive than the centre".

[24] *Cf.* Edgar Kiser and Michael Hechter, "The Role of General Theory in Comparative-Historical Sociology", *American Journal of Sociology*, July 1991, p. 4: "those who seek causal explanations of historical events cannot hope to

(continued...)

unknown, and much of what is known remains subject to debate and doubt".[25] Yet as Durkheim cautions, speaking of sociology generally, "There is nothing necessarily discouraging in the incompleteness of the results thus far obtained. They should arouse new efforts, not surrender".[26] Indeed, that is the very nature and enduring strength of science, including social science.

---

[24](...continued)
dispense with general theories".

[25] William E. Lipsky, "Comparative Approaches to the Study of Revolution: A Historiographic Essay", *Review of Politics*, October 1976, p. 509

[26] Emile Durkheim, *Suicide: A Study in Sociology* (New York: The Free Press, 1951 [1897]), p. 36. *Cf.* Moore, *Social Origins of Dictatorship and Democracy*, p. 135: "That such a search is endless, that the discovered relations are themselves only partial truths, does not mean that the search ought to be abandoned".

Appendix 1:

Selected Chronology of Event-Processes

600
Czechs and Slovaks settle in Bohemia and Moravia.

1372-1415
Jan Hus, a critic of the Church, is excommunicated and then burned at the stake with his ashes spread by the wind. He was Rector of Prague University and his dictum that "the truth prevails" became incorporated into the official seal of the Czechoslovak Republic five hundred years later. "I, Master Jan Hus, in chains and in prison, now standing on the shore of this present life and expecting on the morrow a dreadful death, which I hope will purge away my sins, find no heresy in myself."

1620
The Czech nobility is defeated by the Hapsburg Emperor Ferdinand II at the Battle of White Mountain.

1848
The *Communist Manifesto* is published. Rebellions break out across Europe.

15 March 1848
Free Press Day

18 March-27 May 1871
The Paris Commune is established for two months.

1891
The Bulgarian Communist Party is founded, one of the first in the world.

1906
Universal suffrage is granted in Czechoslovakia, but no power is given to it.

1911-12
The Manchu Dynasty, ruling China since 1644, falls and is replaced by a republic headed by President Sun Yat-sen.

1914-18
Tomás G. Masaryk and Eduard Benes form a provisional government. Masaryk demands "Let Truth Prevail", a concept which runs through Czech thought from Hus to Havel, becoming a slogan that is voiced during the 1989 Velvet Revolution.

1915
The New Culture Movement emerges in China, a precursor to the Democracy Wall Movement of 1978-79.

1917
The Bolsheviks assume power with the Russian Revolution.

1918-19
U.S. and western European troops invade Russia, trying to suppress the Bolsheviks and overturn the Russian Revolution.

28 October 1918
In the wake of World War I, Czechoslovakia is granted a velvet

independence with Professor Masaryk as founder and President.

4 May 1919
A student-led movement in Beijing, the first major one to occur in China, demands political and cultural modernization, scientific rationalization, and western democracy.

August 1919
Romania defeats the Hungarian Red Army and loots Budapest.

1920
A liberal democratic constitution is promulgated in Czechoslovakia.

July 1921
The Communist Party of China is formed.

October 1921
The Communist Party of Czechoslovakia is formed, uniting the leftists of various ethnicities into one party.

Mid-1930s
Czechoslovakia ranks 10th in the league of economically developed nations.

29-30 September 1938
The Munich Agreement cedes Sudetenland to Germany without armed resistance.

14 March 1939
Compelled by Hitler, Slovakia declares independence. Czechs and Slovaks are disunited and the country is occupied by the Nazis. The Czech section is a victim and the Slovak section is an ally of Nazi Germany.

November 1939
The Nazis close the Czech universities.

17 November 1939
At a protest demonstration against the occupation of Czechoslovakia and the closing of the universities, Jan Opletal, a university student, is killed by the Nazis.

1943
Czechoslovakia's government-in-exile in London signs a friendship treaty with the Soviet Union.

August 1944
Democratic and communist groups in Slovakia launch an armed uprising against the Nazis and assert their control for four months before being suppressed.

1945
Parliamentary democracy is restored in Czechoslovakia. Communist Party governments are established in Albania and Yugoslavia.

1946
The Czechoslovak Communist Party wins a plurality of nearly 38 percent of the vote in a free and fair election. Communist Party governments replace coalition ones in Bulgaria, Hungary, Poland, and Romania.

1947
Participation in the U.S. Marshall Plan is rejected by President Benes of Czechoslovakia.

21 February 1948
After the voluntary resignations of the non-Communist Party ministers following a police crisis, the Communist Party launches a successful velvet coup d'état.

10 March 1948
Jan Masaryk, the foreign minister and former president Tomas Masaryk's son, is found dead in the foreign ministry's courtyard. He apparently died from impact having either committed suicide or having been pushed out of a window (defenestration).

7 June 1948
President Benes resigns. He dies three months later.

1948
Yugoslavia breaks with the Soviet Union.

10 December 1948

The United Nations Universal Declaration of Human Rights is adopted.

1949
The Council for Mutual Economic Assistance (COMECON) is established.

21 September 1949
The Communist Party of China assumes national power following the Revolution and proclaims the birth of the People's Republic of China on 1 October in Tiananmen Square. The Nationalist forces are all on Formosa/Taiwan by 8 December.

1950
Britain recognizes Communist China. China and the Soviet Union sign a 30 year pact. Chiang Kai-shek resumes his presidency of "Nationalist China" on Taiwan.

21 October 1950
The Chinese military invades Tibet following Tibet's rejection of China's offer to join the Communist system with regional authority.

5 March 1953
Stalin dies.

June 1953
A worker revolt breaks out in Plzen (Pilsen), Czechoslovakia in response to higher prices and stricter work rules. Demonstrations spread to other areas. This first collective protest against a Communist Party regime in Eastern Europe causes the Party to back down on most of its recent policies.

17 June 1953
The East Berlin Revolt of construction workers erupts. Other workers join the protest which spreads to other cities, escalating into anti-government riots. The uprising is crushed with the help of thousands of Soviet troops and tanks. More than 125 people are killed.

1955
The Warsaw Pact, a military alliance between the Soviet Union and the countries of Eastern Europe, is formed. Yugoslavia refuses to join.

1956

Khrushchev denounces Stalin at the Twentieth Congress of the Communist Party of the Soviet Union. Following Khrushchev's 1955 visit with Tito in Yugoslavia, the Soviet Party Congress publicly recognizes the right of each Party to choose its own path toward socialism.

June 1956

Over 50,000 workers in Poznan, Poland riot against higher prices and work quotas, demanding "bread and freedom". Many students join the protests which spread and become anti-government. The uprising is crushed by the army. The formerly purged Wladyslaw Gomulka is named the new party chief in October.

23 October 1956

The Hungarian Revolt begins with a major anti-government demonstration calling for the return to power of the purged Imre Nagy, free elections, and the removal of Soviet troops from Hungary. After several people are shot to death by security forces, a large group storms the police headquarters and kills police officers. Another group pulls down a huge statue of Stalin. The revolt expands across the country, where collective farms disaggregate, workers take over their factories, and citizens take over their local governments. On 30 October, Nagy takes power and forms a multi-party coalition, promising a benign non-Soviet socialism, a middle way between capitalism and communism. Nagy withdraws from the Warsaw Pact, declares neutrality, and asks for western help.

4 November 1956

After pretending to withdraw on 1 November, Soviet troops and tanks invade Budapest and crush the rebellion after several days of street fighting. The western powers offer no assistance. About 32,000 people are killed and more than 250,000 Hungarians escape to the West. Instead of the promised safe passage out of the country, Nagy and his associates are arrested, convicted, and executed in 1958 and buried in unmarked graves in Budapest.

1957

Mao declares the policy of "let one hundred flowers bloom, let one hundred schools contend" in an act of openness. Yet half a year later, the window of opportunity was closed and Mao's new plans became "dredging up the rightists" and "luring the snake out of its hole", metaphorically killing the flowers and closing the schools.

January 1959
Fidel Castro assumes power following the Cuban Revolution.

1959
Chinese troops crush a rebellion in Tibet, following a Tibetan rebellion within China in 1956. Approximately 100,000 people are killed and many temples destroyed. The Dalai Lama and 100,000 other Tibetans flee to India.

1960
China breaks with the Soviet Union.

17-18 August 1961
The Berlin Wall is built overnight to stem the continuing and growing "exit" of East Germans to the West.

1962
Khrushchev renews his denunciation of Stalin at the Twenty Second Party Congress. Albania leaves COMECON.

1963
Václav Havel's first play, *A Garden Party*, is performed.

1967
A mass women's organization is (re)created in Czechoslovakia.

Late-1967
Student unrest in Czechoslovakia is harshly suppressed.

1968
Havel visits the U.S., mostly Manhattan, for six weeks and participates in demonstrations, rallies, be-ins, and student protests. He also visits Yale and MIT and gives a talk while the university is on strike.

April 1968
Following meetings in October and December of 1967, Antonin Novotny resigns as First Secretary and is replaced by Alexander Dubcek in January, who then initiates the "action program" of the Prague Spring. Censorship

effectively ceases. Many mass organizations form.

21 August 1968
The Warsaw Pact, led by the Soviet Red Army, invades Czechoslovakia with 500,000 troops and crushes the Prague Spring. Romania refuses to take part. Albania leaves the Warsaw Pact in protest. China also condemns the invasion. The Moscow Protocols are signed. A "consolidation" (later called "normalization") regime is begun in Czechoslovakia. Passive resistance is punctuated by more dramatic acts of resistance to defend the reforms.

23 August 1968
A symbolic one-hour general work stoppage occurs in Czechoslovakia.

25 September 1968
Pravda publishes an article entitled "Sovereignty and International Duties of Socialist Countries", which outlines what is later referred to as the Brezhnev Doctrine.

16 January 1969
Jan Palach, a university student, publicly immolates himself to protest the replacement of reformers in Czechoslovakia.

March 1969
Anti-Soviet demonstrations break out following the Czechoslovak victory over the Soviet Union in the World Ice Hockey Championships.

17 April 1969
Dubcek is finally forced to resign and is replaced by Gustáv Husák.

September 1969
Censorship is re-established in Czechoslovakia.

January 1970
Echoing Janos Kádár of Hungary from December 1961, Husák states that "He who is not against us is our potential ally".

Fall 1970
Ex-communist intelligentsia organize the Socialist Movement of Czechoslovak Citizens in support of the goals of 1968. Many of the

movement's leaders are arrested.

December 1970
Demonstrations and violence erupt in Gdansk, Poland in reaction to price hikes and wage cuts. Workers strike and occupy the Lenin Shipyards, refusing to leave. As the protests begin to spread, troops move into the shipyard and massacre striking workers. Gomulka suffers a heart attack or stroke and resigns.

1972
The first trials of opponents to the "normalization" regime take place, while the word "reform" is officially outlawed from the public vocabulary in Czechoslovakia.

1975
The U.S. Council on Foreign Relations (CFR), until 1980, engaged in its "1980s Project" which included an appeal for an international campaign for "human rights". Vietnam is unified under the command of the Communist Party. The Communist-led Pathet Lao assumes power in Laos.

8 April 1975
Václav Havel sends an "Open Letter to Gustáv Husák" protesting "normalization".

29 May 1975
Husák becomes President of Czechoslovakia.

1 August 1975
Czechoslovakia signs the Helsinki Final Act of the Conference on Security and Cooperation in Europe. The Act becomes Czechoslovak law.

1976
The underground Czech rock group *Plastic People of the Universe* is arrested for "disturbing the peace". Mao and Zhao Enlai die.

1976
New strikes break out in Poland, this time openly supported by intellectuals. One group of intellectual dissidents, including the sociologist Jacek Kuron and the historian Adam Michnik, form the Workers' Defense Committee (KOR). University students also form a group called

Committee for Student Solidarity, and these two groups combine to form a "flying university", offering underground education.

1 January 1977
Charter 77 is established by Jan Patocka, Jirí Hájek, and Václav Havel. The Charter is first published in West German newspapers on 6 January and is immediately reprinted throughout the world. Havel is sent to prison for the first time.

20 January 1977
Jimmy Carter assumes the U.S. presidency and adopts the CFR program and many of its members into his administration.

March 1977
Patocka dies after police interrogation.

27 April 1978
The Committee for the Defense of the Unjustly Prosecuted (VONS) is co-founded by Havel.

August-Sept. 1978
Charter 77 meets with its Polish counterpart.

November 1978-April 1979
Thousand of people place stories, essays, poems, and posters on a wall—quickly dubbed Democracy Wall—in Beijing describing their grievances and calling for various freedoms.

December 1978
The Chinese Communist Party adopts the program of "reform and opening up to the outside world".

5 December 1978
Wei Jingsheng posts a big character wall poster on "Democracy Wall" in Beijing calling for "The Fifth Modernization: Democracy". Wei is arrested a few months later and eventually sentenced to prison for 15 years.

15 December 1978
The U.S. formally recognizes the People's Republic of China.

1979
Havel is sentenced to prison for four years. Charter 77 begins to issue "position papers", variously called "situation reports".

February 1979
Ayatollah Khomeini assumes power following the theocratic Iranian Revolution.

July 1979
The Sandinistas assume power following the Nicaraguan Revolution.

December 1979
The Soviet Union invades Afghanistan.

1980
The Czechoslovak Government announces a decline in GNP for the first time. It also announces that only 2 percent of Czechoslovak products are equivalent to those in the developed countries.

August 1980
Solidarity is founded in Gdansk, Poland by Lech Walesa as the first free trade union in Eastern Europe.

1980-81
Months of labor turmoil in Poland lead to the recognition of independent trade unions and the right to strike. But after Solidarity leaders call for a national referendum on Communist Party rule and with the fear of a Soviet invasion, the army declares martial law on 13 December 1981. General Wojciech Jaruzelski names himself first secretary and prime minister in what amounts to a military coup, and he then rescinds many rights. After a failed general strike, many solidarity leaders are arrested. Solidarity (now with 7 million members) goes underground.

March 1982
Brezhnev accepts the legitimacy of Chinese socialism.

10 November 1982
Brezhnev dies.

11 March 1985

Mikhail Gorbachev becomes the leader of the Soviet Union.

March 1985
The Jazz Section of the Union of Musicians in Czechoslovakia is dissolved for "counterrevolutionary activities", but continues to operate.

1986
Gorbachev begins his plans of *Perestroika* (Restructuring) and *Glasnost* (Openness), defining them as "qualitatively different". Vietnam begins its program of *doi moi*, or economic reform.

26 April 1986
A reactor at the Chernobyl nuclear power plant in the Ukraine explodes and emits tremendous amounts of radioactivity. Soviet leaders try to cover it up completely for 3 days and then downplay this massive disaster for many more days.

18 November 1986
Fang Lizhi, a physicist, gives a speech at Tongji University in Shanghai entitled "Democracy, Reform and Modernization", which calls for "complete openness, the removal of restrictions in every sphere".

December 1986
Chinese student protestors in Shanghai and Beijing demand greater freedom and democracy.

January 1987
The Chinese government condemns the students and initiates the "campaign against bourgeois liberalism".

1987
Democratic Initiative is formed in Czechoslovakia.

Early-1987
Leaders of the Czechoslovak Union of Musicians' Jazz Section are arrested and put in jail for publishing censored materials.

March 1987
Charter 77 activists are allowed to meet at Jan Patocka's grave without harassment.

April-May 1987
Gorbachev visits Czechoslovakia.

July 1987
Friends of Czechoslovak-Polish Solidarity is formed.

October 1987
Zhao Ziyang, who recently succeeded the purged reformer Hu Yaobang, presents his report on "the first stage of socialism" which eventually seeks to "establish a socialist regime that is highly democratic, fully equipped with legal systems, efficient, and full of vitality". Zhao also proposes separating the party from the state.

November 1987
It is reported that Dubcek sent a telegram to Gorbachev wishing him luck with his reform program.

December 1987
Husák is replaced by Milos Jakes as General Secretary, but remains as president. Jakes was one of the leaders of the purges following the Prague Spring.

1988
Gorbachev pledges to cut the Soviet military budget.

January 1988
Dubcek gives an interview in which he praises Gorbachev, draws a parallel between Perestroika and the Prague Spring, and criticizes the Czechoslovak government for talking about reform without instituting it.

March 1988
Over 600,000 people in Czechoslovakia sign a petition in support of religious freedom. Large demonstrations follow. The Association of Friends of the USA is formed. Gorbachev visits Yugoslavia and promises no "interference in the internal affairs of other states under any pretext whatsoever". He also says that all countries must take "their own roads of social development".

April 1988
Independent Peace Association is formed in Czechoslovakia.

May 1988
Czech Children, a playful political group, is formed.

21 August 1988
A spontaneous demonstration erupts in Prague marking the 20th anniversary of the Warsaw Pact invasion. The crowd is forcefully dispersed.

15 October 1988
The Movement for Civil Liberties (HOS) is founded in Czechoslovakia.

28 October 1988
The anniversary of the founding of the Czechoslovak Republic is declared a holiday and independent demonstrations take place.

January 1989
Gorbachev recalls nearly all of the Soviet troops from Afghanistan, despite the fact that the Communist Party government there is under heavy siege.

15-21 January 1989
Massive spontaneous demonstrations erupt in Czechoslovakia, especially Prague, to commemorate the self-immolation of Jan Palach twenty years earlier.

Late-January 1989
Havel is arrested for "incitement", among hundreds of others. Workers send letters of support to Havel.

Early-1989
The Czechoslovak Government announces the bail-out of over 100 bankrupt firms.

February 1989
Three generals walk out of a Central Committee meeting in Poland. Hungary legalizes non-communist political parties. President Bush visits China.

6 February 1989
`Round Table' talks begin in Poland between the government and Solidarity. A photo of the round table is printed around the world,

including Eastern Europe.

15 February 1989
The last Soviet troops withdraw from Afghanistan.

March 1989
75,000 people march in Budapest demanding free elections and the withdrawal of Soviet troops.

26 March 1989
The freest elections in Soviet history oust some high-ranking Party members in what is viewed as a humiliating defeat.

April 1989
The Czechoslovak Socialist Party requests autonomy. The Tbilisi riots are repressed.

4 April 1989
The Czechoslovak Government condemns an interview with Dubcek on Hungarian TV.

5 April 1989
The Round Table talks in Poland conclude with the signing of a long and complex document of which the preamble declares it to be `the beginning of the road to parliamentary democracy'. Solidarity is re-legalized.

15 April 1989
Student-led pro-democracy demonstrations erupt in Beijing following the death of Hu Yaobang.

May 1989
Havel is released from prison on parole.

2 May 1989
Hungary opens its border with Austria by having its troops cut the barbed-wire fence separating the two countries.

13 May 1989
Students begin their hunger strike in Tiananmen Square.

15-18 May 1989
Gorbachev visits China for the first Sino-Soviet summit since 1959.

20 May 1989
Martial law is imposed in Beijing, but is mostly ignored.

29 May 1989
The Goddess of Democracy statue is erected in Tiananmen Square.

June 1989
The Czechoslovak Popular Party requests autonomy. Imre Nagy and four of his associates are reburied with full honors in the presence of a quarter of a million Hungarians, including government ministers.

4 June 1989
The Chinese government violently attacks the peaceful student demonstrators in Tiananmen Square, killing, wounding, and arresting thousands. A general strike is called for, but does not materialize. Sporadic protesting and fighting occurs throughout the week with more deaths, injuries, and arrests.

5 June 1989
Solidarity sweeps the Polish elections, installing the first non-communist prime minister in Eastern Europe in forty years.

14 June 1989
The Czechoslovak Government praises the Chinese massacre.

16 June 1989
The Czechoslovak Government condemns the rehabilitation of Imre Nagy and the Hungarian Uprising of 1956.

Summer 1989
30,000 people sign the 'Several Sentences' Manifesto that calls for political freedom and an end to censorship. Thousands sign a petition entitled `Just a Few Sentences' calling for democratic reforms and dialogue between the government and the people.

6 July 1989
Gorbachev effectively declares an end to the Brezhnev Doctrine in a

speech to the European Parliament in Strasbourg. He states that people have the right to choose and change their social system without any interference, or attempts to limit their sovereignty, by the USSR. Gorbachev thereby announces the end of the era in which the USSR intervenes in the internal affairs of "friends, allies or anyone else".

21 July 1989
Solidarity leaders, including Jacek Kuron, Adam Michnik, and Zbigniew Bujak, visit Czechoslovakia and meet with Havel, Dubcek, and others.

8 August 1989
The first of many thousands of East Germans cram into the West German embassy in Prague.

11 August 1989
The Polish Senate unanimously condemns the Warsaw Pact invasion of Czechoslovakia in 1968 and apologizes for its participation.

21 August 1989
A commemorative demonstration in Prague against the Warsaw Pact invasion of 1968 is broken up by police. Some Hungarians are also arrested for their participation in the protest demonstration.

30 August 1989
30 percent of Czechoslovak industrial enterprises are declared "uneconomical".

September 1989
Havel urges people to continue the struggle despite little hope of victory. Hungary completely opens its border with Austria.

28 September 1989
The Hungarian Parliament condemns the 1968 invasion of Czechoslovakia.

October 1989
After sporadic detainments, Havel is released for the last time.

8 October 1989
Spurred on by Gorbachev's visit, East Germans hold anti-government

protests in various cities on the 40th anniversary of the government. Gorbachev encourages reform and tells Erich Honecher that "Life punishes those who delay".

18 October 1989
Honecker resigns amidst growing demonstrations in East Germany.

25 October 1989
The Czech Philharmonic and official journalists announce a boycott of Czechoslovak TV.

28 October 1989
A huge group of demonstrators chant for civil rights and democratic reform in Prague.

4 November 1989
Over 1,000,000 demonstrators call for democracy in Berlin. The East German Politburo and many others resign. East Germans are allowed to emigrate through Czechoslovakia.

6 November 1989
The Czechoslovak Government condemns an interview with Havel on Hungarian TV.

9 November 1989
The Berlin Wall falls and with it the East German Government soon after. Deng Xiaoping "officially" resigns from all positions.

11 November 1989
Over the weekend, four million East Germans emigrate to West Germany.

13 November 1989
Democratic Initiative becomes the first independent political party in Czechoslovakia since 1948. Demonstrations against environmental degradation take place in Western Bohemia.

15 November 1989
An environmental demonstration in Prague approaches Hradcany Castle.

17 November 1989

Students commemorate the closing of Czech universities and the death of Jan Opletal by the Nazis. This officially sanctioned demonstration attracts 100,000 people demanding freedom and democracy. Protestors sing "We Shall Overcome". Police and special forces beat and wound hundreds of people. One student is (falsely) reported killed. Two thousand videocassettes of the crackdown are distributed in Prague and throughout the country. This day marks the beginning of the end to Communist Party rule in Czechoslovakia. There are now demonstrations and public anti-regime activities everyday.

18 November 1989
Students occupy university buildings and call for a general strike on 27 November. Actors decide to boycott all performances. Theatres become political centers. Posters and photographs appear everywhere. Computers print out flyers. Two women students go to Prime Minister Ladislav Adamec's home to discuss the crackdown of the previous day. Adamec agrees to an official investigation.

19 November 1989
Civic Forum is established in Prague at 11 P.M.

20 November 1989
Public Against Violence, the Slovak counterpart to Civic Forum, is formed in Bratislava. Demonstrations spread to other cities. Even the Communist Party press publishes articles condemning police violence.

21 November 1989
With over 200,000 people in attendance, Havel speaks to the demonstrators for the first time and reiterates the threat of general strike for 27 November. The rally concludes with Marta Kubisova, banned since 1968, singing the (world's only federal) national anthem. Student strikes spread to many other cities. Civic Forum sends letters to Presidents Bush and Gorbachev informing them of the crisis.

22 November 1989
Students begin to camp out in Wenceslas Square in downtown Prague. Dubcek addresses a crowd, 100,000 strong, in Bratislava, for the first time since 1969.

23 November 1989

10,000 workers from a huge engineering enterprise join at least 300,000 other demonstrators and declare the support of "the workers", as the first snow of winter falls during an extremely cold night. Civic Forum calls for free elections and the removal of the Communist Party's "leading role" Constitutional status. Prague demonstrations are aired on Czechoslovak TV. A Czech newspaper advises its readers to talk with their fellow citizens and not be misled by the mass media! General Milán Vaclavík, the Minister of Defense, declares on evening TV that the army will not fight the people. He is later rushed to the hospital.

24 November 1989
Dubcek speaks in Prague, to 350,000, for the first time since 1969. The Swedish foreign minister gives Havel the Olaf Palme Prize. Jakes and the entire Politburo resign.

25 November 1989
Havel urges the nearly 750,000 protestors to put public pressure on the government. General Secretary Karel Urbánek opens the way for talks. Many hard-liners resign. The mass media are opened up to the opposition.

26 November 1989
Civic Forum, led by Havel, meets with Prime Minister Adamec in Prague City Hall. 500,000 people gather nearby and a long human chain is formed. In an afternoon rally, Adamec is first applauded, then booed. Lieutenant Ludvik Pinc, a young soldier involved the violent repression of 17 November, apologizes for his participation. There are now 6,000 strike committees. People are able to see dissident leaders like Havel and thousands of protestors on Czechoslovak television. Soviet TV broadcasts a program about the Prague Spring, including a *samizdat* interview with Dubcek.

27 November 1989
A two-hour general strike in Czechoslovakia is 80 percent successful. People ring bells, sound horns and sirens, and rattle keys in a massive show of popular support. (The two hours of missed work is made up at the end of the day.) Many Czech fairy tales conclude with the line, "And the bell rang and that's the end of the story"; therefore, the potent and almost primeval symbolism of ringing bells and rattling keys was well understood in Czechoslovakia. A TV anchorman declares support for the general strike and shows pictures of crowds in the streets of Prague. The Ministry

of Culture releases previously censored books and films.

28 November 1989
Civic Forum again meets with Prime Minister Adamec. Article 4, the constitutional article guaranteeing the Communist Party's leading role, is rescinded. Marxism-Leninism will no longer be compulsory in the universities. The remaining political prisoners will be released.

2 December 1989
Havel is interviewed by *Rudo Pravo* and recommends that the Communist Party become a regular political party. People start wearing "Havel for President" badges.

3 December 1989
Adamec proposes power-sharing with "only three-quarters" of the government consisting of the Communist Party. It is rejected and demonstrations are called for. Another general strike is threatened for 11 December. All leaders of the East German Communist Party quit.

4 December 1989
Hundreds of thousands of people demonstrate against Adamec's proposal. Students continue to occupy university buildings. The Warsaw Pact condemns its invasion of Czechoslovakia in 1968. All visa requirements for travel abroad are canceled.

7 December 1989
Adamec and his government resign. Lithuania legalizes a multiparty system.

8 December 1989
Husák declares a general amnesty for political prisoners.

10 December 1989
On International Human Rights Day, Husák swears in a "government of national understanding" formed by Marián Calfa with the Communist Party in the minority. Husák then resigns. An enormous demonstration celebrates the announcement. In Bulgaria, Todor Zhivkov is ousted in a coup led by a reform Communist. The Democratic League, the first non-communist political party in Mongolia, is formed and is inaugurated as the Mongol Democratic Party on 18 February 1990.

11 December 1989
Students in Prague decide to continue their strike.

15 December 1989
Defense Minister Miroslav Vacek announces that all Communist Party activity in the military has been suspended.

19 December 1989
The Adamec government resigns and a new coalition government is formed by Calfa.

20 December 1989
The Communist Party of Czechoslovakia changes its structure, declares support for multi-party democracy, disbands the militia, and apologizes for the events of 1968 and after.

21 December 1989
The Czechoslovak State Security is put under collective government control.

23 December 1989
The government of Romania collapses amidst a revolt involving the military. Fresh mass graves of tortured protestors are discovered 500 miles west of Bucharest. The Army and the Security Forces fight each other. The Interior Minister and the Deputy Prime Minister are arrested. All political prisoners are freed. The mass media are free until shut down after midnight. Nicolae Ceausescu and his wife Elena, also his chief deputy, are captured after fleeing Bucharest and are summarily executed two days later by the Army for "genocide".

28 December 1989
Dubcek is elected Chairman of the Federal Assembly.

29 December 1989
Havel is *unanimously* elected President of the Czechoslovak Republic by the Federal Assembly.

January 1990
Martial law is lifted in Beijing.

25 January 1990
Foreign Minister Jirí Dienstbier announces that Czechoslovakia is planning to stop the export of arms.

26 January 1990
Czechoslovak radio announces the rebirth of over forty political parties.

February 1990
President Havel visits the United States and addresses a joint session of the U.S. Congress.

7 February 1990
After a huge demonstration in Moscow a few days earlier, the Soviet Communist Party agrees to give up its monopoly on power.

March 1990
The Sandinistas, despite winning a plurality of about 41 percent of the popular vote, lose power in the Nicaraguan elections to a 14-party coalition supported by the U.S.

9 March 1990
The Mongol Communist Party agrees to revise the constitution and introduce a multiparty system.

11 March 1990
Lithuania declares independence.

29 March 1990
The Federal Assembly votes to change the name of the country to the Czecho-slovak Republic.

30 March 1990
Estonia makes moves toward independence.

April 1990
Less than three weeks after changing the country's name, which produced protest, the name is again changed to The Czech and Slovak Federal Republic. Chai Ling, after ten months of hiding in China, escapes the country.

19 April 1990
Laws ending monopolies and establishing the right to free enterprise are passed in Czechoslovakia.

2 May 1990
Czechoslovakia abolishes the death penalty.

4 May 1990
Latvia declares a transition period leading to independence.

21 May 1990
The pre-election Federal Assembly of Czechoslovakia votes to expropriate, as of 1 June, all of the property that the Communist Party had been given by the old regime.

22 May 1990
Yemen reunifies.

8-9 June 1990
A total of at least 334 associations and 58 political parties have obtained registration, of which 23 participate in the election. 96 percent of the electorate participates. Dubcek is re-elected as chair. Only 6 of the parties win seats in the 300 seat Federal Assembly:

Party	Seats
Civic Forum / Public Against Violence	170
Communist Party of Czechoslovakia	47
Christian and Democratic Union	40
Association for Moravia and Silesia	16
Slovak National Party	15
Coexistence (Hungarian Christian Democratic Party)	12

Havel names Calfa, who has only left the Communist Party less than six months earlier, to form another new government.

5 July 1990
Havel is re-elected as president of Czechoslovakia.

29 July 1990

The Mongol Communist Party wins a majority of seats in free elections. In early September, the Communist Party forms a coalition government. Marketization plans are announced in November.

September 1990
Czechoslovakia is readmitted to the International Monetary Fund and World Bank.

4 October 1990
Germany reunifies.

November 1990
The U.S. grants most-favored nation [MFN] status to Czechoslovakia.

11 December 1990
In Albania, Ramiz Alia accepts student demands for the creation of independent political parties. Three and a half months later, multi-party elections are held.

1991
Yugoslavia disintegrates and war breaks out in Bosnia-Hercegovina and Croatia.

21 June 1991
The last Soviet troops leave Czechoslovakia.

28 June 1991
COMECON is dissolved in Budapest.

July 1991
The Warsaw Pact dissolves itself in Prague.

6 September 1991
Estonia, Latvia, and Lithuania, having regained their independence, are recognized by the Soviet Union.

19 August 1991
A military coup against Gorbachev fails after a few tense days of popular pressure and splits in the military.

December 1991
The Soviet Union disintegrates. Czechoslovakia (along with Hungary and Poland) is granted associate membership in the European Community. 45 percent of respondents to a survey report a lower standard of living in Czechoslovakia; only 6 percent report a higher one.

27 February 1992
A treaty signed in Prague de facto nullifies the Munich Agreement.

November 1992
Charter 77 is disbanded.

7 November 1992
Dubcek dies of wounds sustained from an automobile accident on 1 September 1992.

25 November 1992
The Federal Assembly approves the dissolution of the Czechoslovak federation.

1 January 1993
The Czechs and Slovaks separate into two independent republics, the Czech Republic and Slovakia, in a velvet divorce.

26 January 1993
Havel is elected President of the new Czech Republic.

May 1994
President Clinton delinks human rights from Most Favored Nation [MFN] trade status for China.

December 1994
The son-in-law of Brezhnev is tried for bribery.

Spring 1995
A wave of legislative petitions and open letters are addressed to China's top leaders and are circulated in Beijing prior to the annual meeting of the National People's Congress.

November 1995

The Czech Republic becomes the first post-communist state admitted to the Organization for Economic Cooperation and Development [OECD]. Nine Chinese dissidents make public pro-democracy announcements and are detained.

19 February 1997
Deng Xiaoping dies.

6 March 1997
The Chinese legislature enacts a new civil code which no longer contains a category for "counterrevolutionary" crimes.

1 July 1997
Hong Kong reverts to Chinese control.

November 1997
Wei Jingsheng is released and exiled to the U.S. on the 16th. President Jiang visits the U.S.

April 1998
Wang Dan is released and exiled to the U.S.

June-July 1998
President Clinton visits China. He appears on live television with President Jiang at Beijing University, answering questions and discussing issues related to democracy and human rights.

5 October 1998
China signs the International Covenant on Civil and Political Rights.

1999
Czech Republic is admitted into NATO.

21 December 1999
Macau reverts to Chinese control.

13 June 2003
The Czech Republic votes to join the European Union. Poland, Hungary, Lithuania, Malta, Slovenia and Slovakia have already voted to join.

1 May 2004
In its largest expansion ever, Czech Republic and Slovakia, as well as eight other nations (Cyprus, Estonia, Hungary, Latvia, Lithuania, Malta, Poland, and Slovenia), join the now 25-member European Union.

17 January 2005
Zhao Ziyang dies at the age of 85. No large scale movement emerges in response, as it did following the death of his predecessor and fellow reformer, Hu Yaobang.

2008?
Turkey to join the EU.

Appendix 2:

Charter 77 Declaration

In the Czechoslovak Register of Laws No. 120 of 13 October 1976, texts were published of the International Covenant on Civil and Political Rights, and of the International Covenant on Economic, Social and Cultural Rights, which were signed on behalf of our republic in 1968, reiterated at Helsinki in 1975 and came into force in our country on 23 March 1976. From that date our citizens have enjoyed the rights, and our state the duties, ensuing from them.

The human rights and freedoms underwritten by these Covenants constitute features of civilized life for which many progressive movements have striven throughout history, and whose codification could greatly assist humane developments in our society.

We accordingly welcome the Czechoslovak Socialist Republic's accession to those agreements.

Their publication, however, serves as a powerful reminder of the extent to which basic human rights in our country exist, regrettably, on paper alone.

The right to freedom of expression, for example, guaranteed by article 19 of the first-mentioned Covenant, is in our case purely illusory. Tens of thousands of our citizens are prevented from working in their own fields for the sole reason that they hold views differing from official ones, and are discriminated against and harassed in all kinds of ways by the authorities and public organizations. Deprived as they are of any means to defend themselves, they become victims of a virtual apartheid.

Hundreds of thousands of other citizens are denied that `freedom from fear' mentioned in the preamble to the first Covenant, being condemned to the constant risk of unemployment or other penalties if they voice their own opinions.

In violation of article 13 of the second-mentioned Covenant, guaranteeing everyone the right to education, countless young people are prevented from studying because of their own views or even their parents'. Innumerable citizens live in fear of their own, or their children's right to education being withdrawn if they should ever speak up in accordance with their convictions.

Any exercise of the right to `seek, receive and impart information and ideas of all kinds, regardless of frontiers, either orally, in writing or in print' or `in the form of art' specified in article 19, clause 2 of the first covenant is followed by extra-judicial and even judicial sanctions, often in the form of criminal charges as in the recent trial of young musicians.

Freedom of public expression is inhibited by the centralized control of all the communication media and of publishing and cultural institutions. No philosophical, political or scientific view or artistic activity that departs ever so slightly from the narrow bounds of official ideology or aesthetics is allowed to be published; no open criticism can be made of abnormal social phenomena; no public defense is possible against false and insulting charges made in official propaganda; the legal protection against 'attacks on honour and reputation' clearly guaranteed by article 17 of the first Covenant is in practice non-existent; false accusations cannot be rebutted and any attempt to secure compensation or correction through the courts is futile; no open debate is allowed in the domain of thought and art. Many scholars, writers, artists and others are penalized for having legally published or expressed, years ago, opinions which are condemned by those who hold political power today.

Freedom of religious confession, emphatically guaranteed by article 18 of the first covenant, is continually curtailed by arbitrary official action; by interference with the activity of churchmen, who are constantly threatened by the refusal of the state to permit them the exercise of their functions, or by the withdrawal of such permission; by financial or other transactions against those who express their religious faith in word or action; by constraints on religious training, and so forth.

One instrument for the curtailment or, in many cases, complete elimination of many civic rights is the system by which all national institutions and organizations are in effect subject to political directives from the machinery of the ruling party and to decisions made by powerful individuals.

The Constitution of the Republic, its laws and legal norms do not regulate the form or content, the issuing or application of such decisions; they are often only given out verbally, unknown to the public at large and beyond its powers to check; their originators are responsible to no one but themselves and their own hierarchy; yet they have a decisive impact on the decision-making and executive organs of government, justice, trade unions, interest groups and all other organizations, of the other political parties, enterprises, factories, institutions, offices and so on, for whom these instructions have precedence even before the law.

Where organizations or individuals, in the interpretation of their rights and duties, come into conflict with such directives, they cannot have recourse to any non-party authority, since none such exists. This constitutes, of course, a serious limitation of the right ensuing from articles 21 and 22 of the first-mentioned Covenant, which provides for freedom of association and forbids any restriction on its exercise; from article 25 on the right to take part in the conduct of public affairs, and from article 26 stipulating equal protection by the law without discrimination.

This state of affairs likewise prevents workers and others from exercising the unrestricted right to establish trade unions and other organizations to protect their economic and social interests, and from freely enjoying the right to strike provided for in clause 1 of article 8 in the second-mentioned Covenant.

Further civil rights, including the explicit prohibition of `arbitrary interference with privacy, family, home or correspondence' (article 17 of the first Covenant), are seriously vitiated by the various forms of interference in the private life of citizens exercised by the Ministry of the Interior, for example, by bugging telephones and houses, opening mail, following personal movements, searching homes, setting up networks of neighbourhood informers (often recruited by illicit threats or promises), and in other ways.

The Ministry frequently interferes in employers' decisions, instigates acts of discrimination by authorities and organizations, brings weight to bear on the organs of justice and even orchestrates propaganda campaigns in the media. This activity is governed by no law and, being clandestine, affords citizens no chance of defending themselves.

In cases of prosecution on political grounds the investigative and judicial organs violate the rights of those charged and of those defending them, as guaranteed by article 14 of the first Covenant and, indeed, by Czechoslovak law. The prison treatment of those sentenced in such cases is an affront to their human dignity and a menace to their health, being aimed at breaking their morale.

Clause 2, article 12 of the first Covenant, guaranteeing every citizen the right to leave the country, is consistently violated, or under the pretense of `defense of national security' is subjected to various unjustifiable conditions (clause 3). The granting of entry visas to foreigners is also treated arbitrarily, and many are unable to visit Czechoslovakia merely because of professional or personal contacts with those of our citizens who are subject to discrimination.

Some of our people—either in private, at their places of work or by the only feasible public channel, the foreign media—have drawn attention to the systematic violation of human rights and democratic freedoms and demanded amends in specific cases. But their pleas have remained largely ignored or been made grounds for police investigation.

Responsibility for the maintenance of civil rights in our country naturally devolves in the first place on the political and state authorities. Yet not only on them: everyone bears his or her share of responsibility for the conditions that prevail and accordingly also for the observance of legally enshrined agreements, binding upon all individuals as well as upon governments.

In this sense of co-responsibility, our belief in the importance of its conscious public acceptance and the general need to give it new and more effective expression, that led us to the idea of creating Charter 77, whose inception we today publicly announce.

Charter 77 is a loose, informal and open association of people of various shades of opinion, faiths and professions united by the will to strive individually and collectively for the respecting of civil and human rights in our own country and throughout the world—rights accorded to all people by the two mentioned international Covenants, by the Final Act of the Helsinki conference and by numerous other international documents opposing war, violence and social or spiritual oppression, and which are comprehensively laid down in the United Nations Universal Declaration of Human Rights.

Charter 77 springs from a background of friendship and solidarity among people who share our concern for those ideals that have inspired, and continue to inspire, their lives and their work.

Charter 77 is not an organization; it has no rules, permanent bodies or formal membership. It embraces everyone who agrees with its ideas and participates in its work. It does not form the basis for any oppositional political activity. Like many similar citizen initiatives in various countries, West and East, it seeks to promote the general public interest.

It does not aim, then, to set out its own platform of political or social reform or change, but within its own field of impact to conduct a constructive dialogue with the political and state authorities, particularly by drawing attention to individual cases where human and civil rights are violated, to document such grievances and suggest remedies, to make proposals of a more general character calculated to reinforce such rights and machinery for protecting them, to act as intermediary in situations of conflict which may lead to violation of rights, and so forth.

By its symbolic name, Charter 77 denotes that it has come into being at the start of a year proclaimed as Political Prisoners' Year—a year in which a conference in Belgrade is due to review the implementation of the obligations assumed at Helsinki.

As signatories, we hereby authorize Professor Dr. Jan Patocka, Václav Havel and Professor Jirí Hájek to act as the spokespersons for the Charter. These spokespersons are endowed with full authority to represent it vis-à-vis state and other bodies, and the public at home and abroad, and their signatures attest the authenticity of documents issued by the Charter. They will have us and others who join us as their colleagues, taking part in any necessary negotiations, shouldering particular tasks and sharing every responsibility.

We believe that Charter 77 will help to enable all the citizens of Czechoslovakia to work and live as free human beings.

Appendix 3:

Hunger Strike Announcement [from the Chinese Students][1]

In this bright sunny month of May, we are on a hunger strike. In this the best moment of our youth, we have no choice but to leave behind us everything beautiful about life. But how reluctant, how unwilling we are!

However, the country has come to this juncture: rampant inflation; widespread illegal business dealings by corrupt officials; the dominance of abusive power; the corruption of bureaucrats; the fleeing of a large number of good people to other countries; and the deterioration of law and order. Compatriots and all fellow citizens with a conscience, at this critical moment of life and death of our people, please listen to our voice:

This is our country.
The people are our people.

---

[1] Originally printed at Tiananmen Square in a pamphlet called *Xinwen daobao* (*News express*) on 12 May 1989

The government is our government.
Who will shout if we don't?
Who will act if we don't?

Although our shoulders are still tender, although death for us is still seemingly too harsh to bear, we have to part with life. When history demands us to do so, we have no choice but to die.

Our national sentiment at its purest and our loyalty at its best are labeled as "chaotic disturbance"; as "with an ulterior motive"; and as "manipulated by a small gang".

We request all honorable Chinese, every worker, peasant, soldier, ordinary citizen, intellectual, and renowned individuals, government officials, police and those who fabricated our crimes to put their hands over their hearts and examine their conscience: what crime have we committed? Are we creating chaotic disturbances? We walk out of classrooms, we march, we hunger strike, we hide. Yet our feelings are betrayed time after time. We bear the suffering of hunger to pursue the truth, and all we get is the beatings of the police. When we kneel down to beg for democracy, we are being ignored. Our request for dialogue on equal terms is met with delay after delay. Our student leaders encounter personal dangers.

What do we do?

Democracy is the most noble meaning of life; freedom is a basic human right. But the price of democracy and freedom is our life. Can the Chinese people be proud of this?

We have no other alternative but to hunger strike. We have to strike.

It is with the spirit of death that we fight for life.

But we are still children, we are still children! Mother China, please take a hard look at your children. Hunger is ruthlessly destroying their youth. Are you really not touched when death is approaching them?

We do not want to die. In fact, we wish to continue to live comfortably because we are in the prime years of our lives. We do not wish to die; we want to be able to study properly. Our homeland is so poor. It seems irresponsible of us to desert our homeland to die. Death is definitely not our pursuit. But if the death of a single person or a number of persons would enable a larger number of people to live better, or if the death can make our homeland stronger and more prosperous, then we have no right to drag on an ignoble existence.

When we are suffering from hunger, moms and dads, please don't be sad. When we bid farewell to life, uncles and aunts, please don't be heart-broken. Our only hope is that the Chinese people will live better. We have only one request: please don't forget that we are definitely not after death. Democracy is not the private matter of a few individuals, and the enterprise of building democracy is definitely not to be accomplished in a single generation.

It is through death that we await a far-reaching and perpetual echo by others.

When a person is about to die, he speaks from his heart. When a horse is about to die, its cries are sad.

Farewell comrades, take care, the same loyalty and faith bind the living and the dead.

Farewell loved ones, take care. I don't want to leave you, but I have to part with life.

Farewell moms and dads, please forgive us. Your children cannot have loyalty to our country and filial piety to you at the same time.

Farewell fellow citizens, please permit us to repay our country in the only way left to us. The pledge that is delivered by death will one day clear the sky of our republic.

The reasons of our hunger strike are: first, to protest the cold and apathetic attitude of our government towards the students' strike; second, to protest the delay of our higher learning; and third, to protest the government's continuous distortions in its reporting of this patriotic and democratic movement of students, and their labeling it as "chaotic disturbance".

The demands from the hunger strikers are: first, on equal basis, the government should immediately conduct concrete and substantial dialogues with the delegation of Beijing institutes of higher learning. Second, the government should give this movement a correct name, a fair and unbiased assessment, and should affirm that this is a patriotic and democratic students' movement.

The date for the hunger strike is 2:00 P.M., 13 May [1989]; location, Tiananmen Square.

This is not a chaotic disturbance. Its name should be immediately rectified. Immediate dialogue! No more delays! Hunger strike for the people! We have no choice. We appeal to world opinion to support us. We appeal to all democratic forces to support us.

Beijing, China

Bibliography

Abonyi, Arpad. "Eastern Europe's Reintegration" in Christopher K. Chase-Dunn, ed., *Socialist States in the World System* (Beverly Hills, CA, London, and New Delhi: Sage Publications, 1982)

Abrams, Philip. *Historical Sociology* (Ithaca, NY: Cornell University Press, 1982)

Almond, Gabriel A. and Sidney Verba. *The Civic Culture* (Newbury Park, CA: Sage Publications, 1989 [1963])

Althusser, Louis. *For Marx* (London: Verso, 1977)

Angelou, Maya. "On the Pulse of the Morning", Poem read at the U.S. Presidential Inauguration, 20 January 1993

Arato, Andrew. "Interpreting 1989", *Social Research*, Fall 1993

Arendt, Hannah. *The Origins of Totalitarianism*, Second Enlarged Ed. (Cleveland, OH and New York: Meridian Books, 1951, 1958)

Arendt, Hannah. *On Revolution* (New York: Penguin Books, 1990 [1963])

Ash, Timothy Garton. *The Magic Lantern: The Revolution of '89 Witnessed in Warsaw, Budapest, Berlin, and Prague* (New York: Random House, 1990)

Ash, Timothy Garton. *The Uses of Adversity* (New York: Random House, 1983-89)

Ash, Timothy Garton. "Czechoslovakia Under Ice" [February 1984] in Timothy Garton Ash, *The Uses of Adversity* (New York: Random House, 1983-89)

Ash, Timothy Garton. "The Revolution of the Magic Lantern", *New York Review of Books*, 18 January 1990

Banac, Ivo, ed. *Eastern Europe in Revolution* (Ithaca, NY and London: Cornell University Press, 1992)

Barker, Colin. "Perspectives" in Colin Barker, ed., *Revolutionary Rehearsals* (London: Bookmarks, 1987)

Barker, Colin, ed. *Revolutionary Rehearsals* (London: Bookmarks, 1987)

Barker, Colin. "'The Mass Strike' and 'The Cycle of Protest'", unpublished manuscript

Barker, Colin and Michael Tyldesley, eds. *Alternative Futures and Popular Protest II* (Manchester: Manchester Metropolitan University, 1996)

Barker-Plummer, Bernadette. "The Dialogic of Media and Social Movements", *Peace Review*, March 1996

Barnet, Richard J. *Intervention & Revolution*, Revised and Updated (New York and Scarborough, Ontario: Mentor Book, 1972 [1968])

Barnett, A.D., ed. *Chinese Communist Politics in Action* (Seattle, WA: 1969)

Batt, Judy. "East-Central Europe: From Reform to Transformation" in Gilbert Rozman *et al.*, eds.,*Dismantling Communism: Common*

Causes and Regional Variations (Washington, D.C.: Woodrow Wilson Center Press & Baltimore, MD and London: Johns Hopkins University Press, 1992)

Baum, Richard. "China After Deng: Ten Scenarios in Search of Reality", *China Quarterly*, March 1996

Becker, Jasper. "The Fading Voices of Dissent", *World Press Review*, March 1996 [*South China Morning Post*, 3 December 1995]

Becker, Howard S. *Writing for Social Scientists* (Chicago and London: University of Chicago Press, 1986)

Benda, Václav. "The Parallel 'Polis'" [originally distributed in *samizdat* form, May 1978] in H. Gordon Skilling and Paul Wilson, eds., *Civic Freedom in Central Europe: Voices from Czechoslovakia* (New York: St. Martin's Press, 1991)

Berger, Peter L. and Thomas Luckmann. *The Social Construction of Reality* (New York: Anchor Books, 1966)

Bernstein, Thomas. "Domestic Politics" in Steven Goldstein, ed., *China Briefing, 1984* (Boulder, CO: Westview Press, 1985)

Bhatia, B.M. "Famine Math", *World Press Review*, March 1996 [*Hindustan Times*, 16 June 1995]

Block, Fred. *Postindustrial Possibilities: A Critique of Economic Discourse* (Berkeley and Los Angeles: University of California Press, 1990)

Block, Fred. "The Roles of the State in the Economy" in Neil J. Smelser and Richard Swedberg, eds., *The Handbook of Economic Sociology* (Princeton, NJ and New York: Princeton University Press and Russell Sage Foundation, 1994)

Blumberg, Rae Lesser, ed. *Gender, Family, and the Economy: The Triple Overlap* (Newbury Park, CA: Sage Publications, 1991)

Booth, John A. *The End and the Beginning: The Nicaraguan Revolution*

(Boulder, CO and London: Westview Press, 1985)

Bottomore, Tom. *The Frankfurt School* (London and New York: Tavistock Publications, 1984)

Bourdieu, Pierre. *Outline of a Theory of Practice*, trans. Richard Nice (Cambridge: Cambridge University Press, 1977 [1972])

Bourdieu, Pierre. "Viva la Crise!: For Heterodoxy in Social Science", *Theory and Society*, 1988

Bourdieu, Pierre. *The Logic of Practice* (Stanford, CA: Stanford University Press, 1990)

Bracken, Paul. "Will China Be Number 1?", *Time*, 22 May 2000

Bradley, John F.N. *Czechoslovakia's Velvet Revolution: A Political Analysis* (New York: Columbia University Press, 1992)

Bradshaw, York W. and Michael Wallace. *Global Inequalities* (Thousand Oaks, CA, London, and New Delhi: Pine Forge Press, 1996)

Brightman, Robert. "Forget Culture: Replacement, Transcendence, Relexification", *Cultural Anthropology*, November 1995

Brinton, William M. "The Role of Media in a Telerevolution" in William M. Brinton and Alan Rinzler, eds., *Without Force or Lies: Voices from the Revolution of Central Europe in 1989-90* (San Francisco, CA: Mercury House, 1990)

Brinton, Crane. *The Anatomy of Revolution*, Revised and Expanded Ed. (New York: Vintage Books, 1965 [1938])

Brinton, William M. and Alan Rinzler, eds. *Without Force or Lies: Voices from the Revolution of Central Europe in 1989-90* (San Francisco, CA: Mercury House, 1990)

Brook, Daniel. "Review" of *EcoPopulism* by Andrew Szasz, *Journal of Political Ecology*, 1994

Brook, Daniel. "The Great Transformation—Its Relevance Continues", *American Journal of Economics and Sociology*, October 1994

Brook, Daniel. "The Beijing Spring and Beyond: Modern Revolution in China", Paper presented at the Second International Conference on *Alternative Futures and Popular Protest*, Manchester, England, 26-28 March 1996 and published in Colin Barker and Michael Tyldesley, eds., *Alternative Futures and Popular Protest II* (Manchester: Manchester Metropolitan University, 1996)

Brook, Daniel. "The (Re)Production of Velvet: On the Dynamics of Czechoslovakia's Modern Revolution", Paper presented at the *Second Annual Regional Conference on Russian, East European, and Central Asian Studies*, Seattle, WA, 20 April 1996

Brook, Daniel. "Doing Social Research: Modern Revolution in Czechoslovakia and Beyond", Paper presented at the 91st Annual Meetings of the American Sociological Association on *Social Change: Opportunities & Constraints*, New York, NY, 16-20 August 1996

Brook, Daniel. "Democratic Daydreams and Communist Party Nightmares", *Chinese Community Forum*, 5 February 1997

Brook, Daniel. "Comparisons of Coercion, Consent, and Change in China", *Chinese Community Forum*, 22 January 1997

Brown, Lester R. "China's Food Problem: The Massive Imports Begin", *World Watch*, 1995

Brown, Lester R. "Who Will Feed China?", *World Watch*, 1994

Brown, Lester R. *Who Will Feed China?* (Island Press, 1995)

Brown, Lester R. and Brian Halweil, "China's Water Shortage Could Shake World Food Security", *World Watch*, July/August 1998

Bugajski, Janusz. *Czechoslovakia: Charter 77's Decade of Dissent*

(Westport, CT: Praeger, 1987)

Burawoy, Michael. *Manufacturing Consent: Changes in the Labor Process Under Monopoly Capitalism* (Chicago, IL: University of Chicago Press, 1979)

Burawoy, Michael. "Two Methods in Search of Science: Skocpol Versus Trotsky", *Theory and Society*, November 1989

Burke, Edmund. *Reflections on the Revolution in France* [1789-90], J.G.A. Pocock, ed. (Indianapolis, IN and Cambridge: Hackett Publishing, 1987)

Caldor, Mary, ed. *Europe from Below: An East-West Dialogue* (London and New York: Verso, 1991)

Calvert, Peter. *Revolution and Counter-Revolution* (Minneapolis: University of Minnesota Press, 1990)

Capra, Fritjof. *The Tao of Physics* (New York: Bantam Books, 1975)

Castle-Kanerova, Mita, ed. *High Hopes: Young Voices of Eastern Europe* (London: Virago Press: 1992)

Chace, James. "'Managing' China's Ascent", *World Policy Journal*, Summer 1996

Chase-Dunn, Christopher K., ed. *Socialist States in the World System* (Beverly, CA, London, and New Delhi: Sage Publications, 1982)

"China's New Model Army", *The Economist*, 11 June 1994

Chirot, Daniel. "The East European Revolutions of 1989" in Jack A. Goldstone, ed., *Revolutions: Theoretical, Comparative, and Historical Studies*, Second Ed. (Fort Worth, TX: Harcourt Brace College Publishers, 1994)

Chirot, Daniel. *How Societies Change* (Thousand Oaks, CA: Pine Forge Press, 1994)

Chomsky, Noam. *What Uncle Sam Really Wants* (Berkeley, CA: Odonian Press, 1992)

Chomsky, Noam. *Secrets, Lies and Democracy* (Berkeley, CA: Odonian Press, 1994)

Chomsky, Noam. *World Orders Old and New* (New York: Columbia University Press, 1994)

Chomsky, Noam. *Hegemony or Survival* (New York: Metropolitan Books, 2003)

Chorley, Katherine C. *Armies and the Art of Revolution* (London: Faber & Faber, 1943)

Cohen, Jean and Andrew Arato. *Civil Society and Political Theory* (Cambridge, MA: MIT Press, 1992)

Colburn, Forrest, ed. *Everyday Forms of Peasant Resistance* (Armonk, NY: M.E. Sharpe, 1989)

Collier, David. "The Comparative Method" in Ada W. Finifter, ed., *Political Science: The State of the Discipline II* (Washington, D.C.: American Political Science Association, 1993)

Collins, Randall and David Waller. "What Theories Predicted the State Breakdowns and Revolutions of the Soviet Bloc?" in Louis Kriesberg and David R. Segal, eds., *Research in Social Movements, Conflicts and Change*, Vol. 14: The Transformation of European Communist Societies (Greenwich, CT and London: JAI Press, 1992)

Conference on Security and Co-Operation in Europe, Final Act, Helsinki, 1 August 1975, http://www.hri.org/docs/Helsinki75.htm

Costain, Anne N. *Inviting Women's Rebellion* (Baltimore, MD and London: Johns Hopkins University Press, 1992)

Coye, Molly Joel and Jon Livingston, eds. *China Yesterday and Today*, Second Ed. (New York: Bantam Books, 1975, 1979)

Crow Dog, Mary. *Lakota Woman* (New York: HarperPerennial, 1990)

Dahl, Robert A. *A Preface to Economic Democracy* (Berkeley and Los Angeles: University of California Press, 1985)

Dahrendorf, Ralf. *Reflections on the Revolution in Europe* (New York: Times Books, 1990)

Davies, James C. "Toward a Theory of Revolution", *American Sociological Review*, February 1962

Davies, R.W. "Gorbachev's Socialism in Historical Perspective", *New Left Review*, January-February 1990

de Condole, James. *Czechoslovakia: Too Velvet a Revolution?* (London: Institute for European Defense and Strategic Studies, 1991)

de Tocqueville, Alexis. *Democracy in America* [1835, 1840], Richard D. Heffner, ed. (New York: Mentor Books, 1956)

de Tocqueville, Alexis. *The Old Regime and the French Revolution* (New York: Anchor Books/Doubleday, 1955 [1856])

Debray, Régis. *Revolution in the Revolution?*, trans. Bobbye Ortiz (New York: Grove Press, 1967)

Deess, E. Pierre. "Social Change in the German Democratic Republic: The Role of Institutional Pre-Mobilization Practices (IPPs)", Paper presented at the 91st Annual Meetings of the American Sociological Association *Social Change: Opportunities & Constraints*, New York, NY, 16-20 August 1996

Deng Xiaoping. "The Four Modernizations" in Molly Joel Coye and Jon Livingston, eds., *China Yesterday and Today*, Second Ed. (New York: Bantam Books, 1975, 1979)

di Palma, Guiseppe. "Legitimation from the Top to Civil Society: Politico-Cultural Change in Eastern Europe", *World Politics*, October 1991

DiMaggio, Paul. "Culture and Economy" in Neil J. Smelser and Richard Swedberg, eds., *The Handbook of Economic Sociology* (Princeton, NJ and New York: Princeton University Press and Russell Sage Foundation, 1994)

Dix, Robert. "Why Revolutions Succeed and Fail", *Polity*, Spring 1984

Djilas, Milovan. *The New Class: An Analysis of the Communist System* (New York: Praeger, 1957)

Dorris, Michael. "Indians on the Shelf" in Calvin Martin, ed., *The American Indian and the Problem of History* (New York and Oxford: Oxford University Press, 1987)

Drabek, Zdenek, Kamil Janacek, and Zdenek Tuma. "Inflation in Czechoslovakia, 1985-91", World Bank Paper 1135, http://www.worldbank.org, April 1993

Du Bois, W.E.B. "The Revelation of Saint Orgne the Damned" [1938 commencement speech at Fisk University] in Philip S. Foner, ed., *W.E.B. Du Bois Speaks* (New York: Pathfinder, 1970)

Duke, Michael S. *The Iron House* (Layton, UT: Gibbs-Smith Publ., 1990)

Dunn, John. *Modern Revolutions* (London and New York: Cambridge University Press, 1972)

Durkheim, Emile. *Suicide: A Study in Sociology* (New York: Free Press, 1951 [1897])

Eckstein, Harry. "On the Etiology of Internal Wars", *History and Theory*, 1965

Editors of *Time Magazine*. *Massacre in Beijing: China's Struggle for Democracy* (New York: Time Inc. Books, 1989)

Edwards, Lyford P. *The Natural History of Revolution* (Chicago: 1927)

Ehrenreich, Barbara and John. *Long March, Short Spring* (New York and London: Monthly Review Press, 1969)

Einhorn, Barbara. "Where Have All the Women Gone?: Women and the Women's Movement in East Central Europe", *Feminist Review*, Winter 1991

Eisenstadt, S.N. "The Breakdown of Communist Regimes and the Vicissitudes of Modernity", *Daedalus*, Spring 1992

Ekiert, Grzegorz. "Democratization Processes in East Central Europe: A Theoretical Reconsideration", *British Journal of Political Science*, July 1991

Eley, Geoff. "What Produces Fascism: Preindustrial Traditions or a Crisis of a Capitalist State", *Politics & Society*, 1983

Elon, Amos. "Prague Autumn", *New Yorker*, 22 January 1990

Emirbayer, Mustafa. "Symbols, Positions, and Objects: Toward a New Relational Strategy of Historical Analysis", *Comparative & Historical Sociology*, Fall/Winter 1995

Engels, Friedrich. *Principles of Communism* [1847], #11, http://csf.colorado.edu/psn/marx/archive/1847-prin/main.htm

Fanon, Frantz. *The Wretched of the Earth* (New York: Grove Press, 1963 [1961])

Fanon, Frantz. *Toward the African Revolution* (New York: Grove Press, 1967 [1964])

Farhi, Farideh. *States and Urban-Based Revolutions: Iran and Nicaragua* (Urbana and Chicago: University of Illinois Press, 1990)

Fast, Howard. *The Jews: Story of a People* (New York: Dell Publishing, 1968)

Feffer, John. *Shock Waves: Eastern Europe After the Revolutions* (Boston, MA: South End Press, 1992)

Feigon, Lee. "Gender and the Chinese Student Movement" in Jeffrey N. Wasserstrom and Elizabeth J. Perry, eds., *Popular Protest and*

Political Culture in Modern China, Second Ed. (Boulder, San Francisco, and Oxford: Westview Press, 1992, 1994)

Feltenstein, Andrew and Jiming Ha. "An Analysis of Repressed Inflation in Three Transitional Economies", World Bank Paper 1132, http://www.worldbank.org, April 1993

Fenstermaker, Sarah, Candace West, and Don H. Zimmerman. "Gender Inequality: New Conceptual Terrain" in Rae Lesser Blumberg, ed., *Gender, Family, and the Economy: The Triple Overlap* (Newbury Park, CA: Sage Publications, 1991)

Ferree, Myra Marx. "The Political Context of Rationality: Rational Choice Theory and Resource Mobilization" in Aldon D. Morris & Carol McClurg Mueller, eds., *Frontiers in Social Movement Theory* (New Haven, CT and London: Yale University Press, 1992)

Finifter, Ada W., ed. *Political Science: The State of the Discipline II* (Washington, D.C.: American Political Science Association, 1993)

Fischhoff, Baruch and Ruth Beyth. "'I Knew It Would Happen': Remembered Probabilities of Once-Future Things", *Organizational Behavior and Human Performance*, February 1975

Foner, Philip S., ed. *W.E.B. Du Bois Speaks* (New York: Pathfinder, 1970)

Foran, John and Jeff Goodwin. "Revolutionary Outcomes in Iran and Nicaragua: Coalition Fragmentation, War, and the Limits of Social Transformation", *Theory and Society*, 1993

Foran, John. "Revolutionizing Theory/Theorizing Revolutions", *Contention*, Winter 1993

Foucault, Michel. *Discipline and Punish* (New York: Vintage Books, 1995 [1975])

Fox, Richard G. *Lions of the Punjab: Culture in the Making* (Berkeley and Los Angeles: University of California Press, 1985)

Franck, Thomas M. and Edward Weisband. *Word Politics: Verbal Strategy Among the Superpowers* (New York: Oxford University Press, 1972)

Frankland, Mark. *The Patriots' Revolution: How East Europe Won Its Freedom* (London: Sinclair-Stevenson, 1990)

Friedland, Roger and Robert Alford. "Bringing Society Back In: Symbols, Practices, and Institutional Contradictions" in Walter W. Powell and Paul J. DiMaggio, eds., *The New Institutionalism in Organizational Analysis* (Chicago, IL: University of Chicago Press, 1991)

Furet, Francois. "From 1789 to 1917 & 1989: Looking Back at Revolutionary Traditions", *Encounter*, September 1990

Gamson, William A. "The Social Psychology of Collective Action" in Aldon D. Morris & Carol McClurg Mueller, eds., *Frontiers in Social Movement Theory* (New Haven, CT and London: Yale University Press, 1992)

Geertz, Clifford. *The Interpretation of Cultures* (New York: Basic Books, 1993 [1973])

Gerth, H.H. and C. Wright Mills, eds. *From Max Weber: Essays in Sociology* (New York: Oxford University Press, 1946)

Giddens, Anthony. *Profiles and Critiques in Social Theory* (London: Macmillan, 1982)

Giddens, Anthony. *Sociology* (Oxford: Polity Press, 1989)

Giddens, Anthony. *The Constitution of Societies* (Cambridge: Polity Press, 1984)

Gilbert Rozman *et al.*, eds. *Dismantling Communism: Common Causes and Regional Variations* (Washington, D.C.: Woodrow Wilson Center Press & Baltimore, MD and London: Johns Hopkins

University Press, 1992)

Gilley, Bruce. "Vox Populi", *World Press Review*, March 1996 [*Far Eastern Economic Review*, 7 December 1995]

Gilley, Bruce. "The Sound of Silence", *Far Eastern Economic Review*, 18 April 1996

Gitelman, Zvi. "The Politics of Socialist Restoration in Hungary and Czechoslovakia" in Jack A. Goldstone, ed., *Revolutions: Theoretical, Comparative, and Historical Studies* (San Diego, CA: Harcourt Brace Jovanovich, 1986)

Gitelman, Zvi. "The Roots of Eastern Europe's Revolution", *Problems of Communism*, May-June 1990

Glenny, Misha. "Hungary Opposition 'has links to West'", *Guardian*, 4 May 1987

Glionna, John M. "An Icon, And Then He's Gone", *Los Angeles Times*, 4 June 2004

Golden, Miriam. "Historical Memory and Ideological Orientations in the Italian Workers' Movement", *Politics & Society*, March 1988

Goldfrank, Walter. "Theories of Revolution and Revolution Without Theory: The Case of Mexico", *Theory and Society*, January-March 1979

Goldstein, Steven, ed. *China Briefing, 1984* (Boulder, CO: Westview Press, 1985)

Goldstone, Jack A., ed. *Revolutions: Theoretical, Comparative, and Historical Studies* (San Diego, CA: Harcourt Brace Jovanovich, 1986)

Goldstone, Jack A. "Revolutions in Modern Dictatorships" in Jack A. Goldstone, ed., *Revolutions: Theoretical, Comparative, and Historical Studies*, Second Ed. (Fort Worth, TX: Harcourt Brace College Publishers, 1994)

Goldstone, Jack A. "The Comparative and Historical Study of Revolutions" in Jack A. Goldstone, ed., *Revolution: Theoretical, Comparative, and Historical Studies*, Second Ed.(Fort Worth, TX: Harcourt Brace College Publishers, 1994)

Goldstone, Jack A., ed. *Revolutions: Theoretical, Comparative, and Historical Studies*, Second Ed. (Fort Worth, TX: Harcourt Brace College Publishers, 1994)

Goldstone, Jack A. *Revolution and Rebellion in the Early Modern World* (Berkeley and Los Angeles: University of California Press, 1991)

Goldstone, Jack A. "Theories of Revolution: The Third Generation", *World Politics*, April 1980

Goldstone, Jack A. "The Coming Chinese Collapse", *Foreign Policy*, Summer 1995

Goldstone, Jack A., Ted Robert Gurr, and Farrokh Moshiri, eds. *Revolutions of the Late Twentieth Century* (Boulder, CO: Westview Press, 1991)

Goldstone, Jack A. "Introduction" in Jack A. Goldstone, Ted Robert Gurr, and Farrokh Moshiri, eds., *Revolutions of the Late Twentieth Century* (Boulder, CO: Westview Press, 1991)

Goldstone, Jack A. "Revolution, Theories of" in David Miller, ed., *The Blackwell Encyclopaedia of Political Thought* (Oxford and New York: Basil Blackwell, 1987)

Goldstone, Jack A. "Methodological Issues in Comparative Macrosociology", *Comparative Social Research*, Vol. 16 (1997)

Goldstone, Jack A. "An Analytic Framework" in Jack A. Goldstone, Ted Robert Gurr, and Farrokh Moshiri, eds., *Revolutions of the Late Twentieth Century* (Boulder, CO: Westview Press, 1991)

Goldstone, Jack A. "Gender, Work, and Culture: Why the Industrial Revolution Came Early to England But Late to China", *Sociological Perspectives*, Spring 1996

Goldstone, Jack A. "Theories of Revolution, Elite Crisis, and the Transformation of the USSR", Paper prepared for a conference on *Elite Change and Regime Change*, Santa Maria del Paular, Spain, 8 May 1996

Goldstone, Jack A. "Predicting Revolutions: Why We Could (and Should) Have Foreseen the Revolutions of 1989-1991 in the USSR and Eastern Europe", *Contention*, Winter 1993

Goodwin, Jeff. "A Case for Big Case Comparison", *Comparative & Historical Sociology*, Fall/Winter 1995

Gorbachev, Mikhail. *Perestroika: New Thinking for Our Country and the World* (New York: Harper & Row, 1987)

Gorbachev, Mikhail. *The Socialist Idea and Revolutionary Perestroika* (Moscow: Novosti Press, 1989)

Graham, Richard, ed. *Brazil and the World System* (Austin: University of Texas Press, 1991)

Gramsci, Antonio. *Selections from the Prison Notebooks* [1929-35], trans. by Quintin Hoare and Geoffrey Nowell Smith (New York: International Publishers, 1971)

Granovetter, Mark. "Economic Action and Social Structure: The Problem of Embeddedness", *American Journal of Sociology*, November 1985

Greene, Thomas H. *Comparative Revolutionary Movements: Search for Theory and Justice*, Second Ed. (Engelwood Cliffs, NJ: Prentice-Hall, 1984)

Grilli di Cortona, Pietro. "From Communism to Democracy: Rethinking Regime Change in Hungary and Czechoslovakia", *International Social Science Journal*, May 1991

Griswold, Wendy. *Cultures and Societies in a Changing World* (Thousand Oaks, CA: Pine Forge Press, 1994)

Groth, Alexander. *Revolution and Elite Access: Some Hypotheses on Aspects of Political Change* (Davis, CA: Institute of Government Affairs, 1966)

Guevara, Che. *Guerilla Warfare* (New York: Vintage Books, 1961)

Gurr, Ted Robert. *Why Men Rebel* (Princeton, NJ: Princeton University Press, 1970)

Gurr, Ted Robert. "Minorities in Revolution" in Jack A. Goldstone, ed., *Revolutions: Theoretical, Comparative, and Historical Studies*, Second ed. (Fort Worth, TX: Harcourt Brace College Publishers, 1994)

Gurr, Robert and Jack A. Goldstone. "Comparisons and Policy Implications" in Nikki R. Keddie, ed., *Debating Revolutions* (New York and London: New York University Press, 1995)

Guthrie, Douglas J. "Political Theater and Student Organizations in the 1989 Chinese Movement: A Multivariate Analysis", *Sociological Forum*, September 1995

Gwertzman, Bernard and Michael T. Kaufman, eds. *The Collapse of Communism* [a collection of *New York Times* articles] (New York: Times Books, 1990)

Habermas, Jürgen. *Legitimation Crisis*, trans. Thomas McCarthy (Boston, MA: Beacon Press, 1975)

Hagopian, Mark N. *The Phenomenon of Revolution* (New York: Dodd, Mead & Co, 1974)

Hall, John R. *Cultures of Inquiry* (Cambridge: Cambridge University Press, 1999)

Hall, John R. "The Partimonial Dynamic in Colonial Brazil" in Richard Graham, ed., *Brazil and the World System* (Austin: University of Texas Press, 1991)

Hallinan, Maureen. "The Sociological Study of Social Change",

Presidential Address to the 91st Annual Meetings of the American Sociological Association *Social Change: Opportunities & Constraints*, New York, NY, 17 August 1996

Harding, James. "China's Sleeping Giant Starts to Stir", *Financial Times*, 3 August 1999

Harrington, Michael. *Taking Sides* (New York: Holt, Rinehart and Winston, 1985)

Harrington, Michael. *The New American Poverty* (New York: Penguin Books, 1984)

Hasegawa, Tsuyoshi. "The Connection Between Political and Economic Reform in Communist Regimes" in Gilbert Rozman *et al.*, eds., *Dismantling Communism: Common Causes and Regional Variations* (Washington, D.C.: Woodrow Wilson Center Press & Baltimore, MD and London: Johns Hopkins University Press, 1992)

Havel, Václav. *Summer Meditations*, trans. Paul Wilson (New York: Alfred A. Knopf, 1992)

Havel, Václav. 1995 Harvard University Commencement Address, http://world.std.com/~awolpert/gtr19.html

Havel, Václav. "The Power of the Powerless" in Václav Havel, *et al. The Power of the Powerless: Citizens Against the State in Central Eastern Europe* (Armonk, NY: M.E. Sharpe, 1985)

Havel, Václav, *et al. The Power of the Powerless: Citizens Against the State in Central Eastern Europe* (Armonk, NY: M.E. Sharpe, 1985)

Herman, Edward S. and Noam Chomsky. *Manufacturing Consent: The Political Economy of the Mass Media* (New York: Pantheon, 1988)

Hill, Christopher. *Lenin and the Russian Revolution* (New York: Penguin Books, 1984 [1947])

Hirschman, Albert O. "The Search for Paradigms as a Hindrance to Understanding", *World Politics*, April 1970

Hirschman, Albert O. *Shifting Involvements: Private Interest and Public Action* (Princeton, NJ: Princeton University Press, 1982)

Hirschman, Albert O. "Exit, Voice, and the Fate of the GDR: An Essay in Conceptual History", *World Politics*, January 1993

Hirschman, Albert O. *Exit, Voice, and Loyalty: Responses to Decline in Firms, Organizations, and States* (Cambridge: Harvard University Press, 1970)

Hobsbawm, E.J. *Primitive Rebels: Studies in Archaic Forms of Social Movement in the 19th and 20th Centuries* (New York: W.W. Norton, 1959)

Hobsbawm, Eric and Terence Ranger, eds. *The Invention of Tradition* (Cambridge: Cambridge University Press, 1983)

Hoffer, Eric. *The Ordeal of Change* (New York: Harper & Row, 1963)

Hofheinz, Roy, Jr. "The Ecology of Chinese Communist Success: Rural Influence Patterns 1932-45" in A.D. Barnett, ed., *Chinese Communist Politics in Action* (Seattle, WA: 1969)

Hollander, Paul. "The Mystery of the Transformation of Communist Systems" in Louis Kriesberg and David R. Segal, eds., *Research in Social Movements, Conflicts and Change*, Vol. 14: The Transformation of European Communist Societies (Greenwich, CT and London: JAI Press, 1992)

Hoover, Kenneth and Todd Donovan. *The Elements of Social Scientific Thinking*, Sixth Ed. (New York: St. Martin's Press, 1995)

Huang, Ethan. "Disinformation in Democratic Society", *Chinese Community Forum*, 23 October 1996

Hunger Strike Announcement [originally printed at Tiananmen Square in *Xinwen daobao* (*News express*), 12 May 1989; reprinted in

Zhongguo zhichun (*China spring*) (New York) 75 (August 1989)] in Michel Oksenberg, Lawrence R. Sullivan, and Marc Lambert, eds., *Beijing Spring, 1989: Confrontation and Conflict: The Basic Documents* (Armonk, NY and London: M.E. Sharpe, 1990)

Hunt, Lynn, ed. *The New Cultural History* (Berkeley and Los Angeles: University of California Press, 1989)

Hunt, Lynn. "Introduction: History, Culture, and Text" in Lynn Hunt, ed., *The New Cultural History* (Berkeley and Los Angeles: University of California Press, 1989)

Huntington, Samuel P. *Political Order in Changing Societies* (New Haven, CT and London: Yale University Press, 1968)

Huntington, Samuel P. *The Third Wave: Democratization in the Late Twentieth Century* (Norman: University of Oklahoma Press, 1991)

Inglehart, Ronald. *Culture Shift in Advanced Industrial Society* (Princeton, NJ: Princeton University Press, 1990)

"Invasion from Cyberspace", *World Press Review*, March 1996 [*Asiaweek*, 8 September 1995]

Jackman, Robert W. *Power Without Force: The Political Capacity of Nation-States* (Ann Arbor: University of Michigan Press, 1993)

Jedlicki, Jerzy. "The Revolution of 1989: The Unbearable Burden of History", *Problems of Communism*, July-August 1990

Jenkins, J. Craig and Charles Perrow. "Insurgency of the Powerless: Farm Worker Movements (1946-1972)", *American Sociological Review*, April 1977

Jennings, James. *Understanding the Nature of Poverty in Urban America* (Westport, CT: Praeger, 1994)

Johnson, Chalmers. *Revolution and the Social System* (Stanford, CA:

Hoover Institution on War, Revolution, and Peace, 1964)

Johnson, Chalmers. *Revolutionary Change* (Boston and Toronto: Little, Brown, 1966)

Johnson, Chalmers. *Blowback: The Costs and Consequences of American Empire* (New York: Metropolitan Books, 2000)

Johnson, Chalmers. *Sorrows of Empire: Militarism, Secrecy, and the End of the Republic* (New York: Metropolitan Books, 2004)

Johnson, Owen V. "Mass Media and the Velvet Revolution" in Jeremy D. Popkin, ed., *Media and Revolution: Comparative Perspectives* (Lexington: University of Kentucky Press, 1995)

Joseph, Gilbert M. and Daniel Nugent, eds. *Everyday Forms of State Formation: Revolution and the Negotiation of Rule in Modern Mexico* (Durham, NC and London: Duke University Press, 1994)

Judt, Tony. "The Past is Another Country: Myth and Memory in Postwar Europe", *Daedalus*, Fall 1992

Judt, Tony R. "Metamorphosis: The Democratic Revolution in Czechoslovakia" in Ivo Banac, ed., *Eastern Europe in Revolution* (Ithaca, NY and London: Cornell University Press, 1992)

Judt, Tony. "Nineteen Eighty-Nine: The End of *Which* European Era?", *Daedalus*, Summer 1994

Kabeer, Naila. *Reversed Realities: Gender Hierarchies in Development Thought* (London and New York: Verso, 1994)

Kafka, Franz. "Reflections on Sin, Pain, Hope, and the True Way" [#6] in *The Basic Kafka* (New York: Pocket Books, 1979)

Kaplan, Robert D. "3 Views of the Atrocities of Bosnia—And Our Role", *San Francisco Examiner*, 8 March 1995

Karl, Terry Lynn and Philippe C. Schmitter. "Modes of Transition in

Latin America, Southern and Eastern Europe", *International Social Science Journal*, May 1991

Keddie, Nikki R., ed. *Debating Revolutions* (New York and London: New York University Press, 1995)

Keynes, John Maynard. "A Short View of Russia" [1925], *Daedalus*, Spring 1992

Kinnucan, Michael J. "Political Economy and Militarism", *PS: Political Science & Politics*, September 1992

Kiser, Edgar and Michael Hechter. "The Role of General Theory in Comparative-Historical Sociology", *American Journal of Sociology*, July 1991

Konrad, George. "From Communism to Democracy" in Mary Caldor, ed., *Europe from Below: An East-West Dialogue* (London and New York: Verso, 1991)

Koo, George. "An Asian American Perspective on China", *Asian Week*, 17 January 1997, reprinted in *Chinese Community Forum*, 29 January 1997

Koren, Leonard. *Wabi-Sabi: For Artists, Designers, Poets & Philosophers* (Berkeley, CA: Stone Bridge Press, 1994)

Korten, David C. When Corporations Rule the World (West Hartford, CT and San Francisco, CA: Kumarian Press and Berrett-Koehler Publishers, 1995)

Krejcí, Jaroslav. *Great Revolutions Compared* (New York: St. Martin's Press, 1983)

Kriesberg, Louis and David R. Segal, eds. *Research in Social Movements, Conflicts and Change*, Vol. 14: The Transformation of European Communist Societies (Greenwich, CT and London: JAI Press, 1992)

Kristof, Nicholas D. "Satellites Bring Information Revolution to China",

New York Times, 11 April 1993

Kristof, Nicholas D. "China's Hero of Democracy: Gorbachev" in Bernard Gwertzman and Michael T. Kaufman, eds., *The Collapse of Communism* [a collection of *New York Times* articles] (New York: Times Books, 1990)

Kristof, Nicholas D. "A Chinese Lesson in Polite Protest" in Bernard Gwertzman and Michael T. Kaufman, eds., *The Collapse of Communism* [a collection of *New York Times* articles] (New York: Times Books, 1990)

Kroeber, Clifton B. "Theory and History of Revolution", *Journal of World History*, Spring 1996

Kuhn, Thomas S. *The Structure of Scientific Revolutions*, Enlarged Second Ed. (Chicago, IL: University of Chicago Press, 1970 [1962])

Kumar, Krishan. "The Revolutions of 1989: Socialism, Capitalism, and Democracy" [1992] in Stephen K. Sanderson, ed., *Sociological Worlds: Comparative and Historical Readings on Society* (Los Angeles, CA: Roxbury Publishing, 1995)

Kundera, Milan. *The Joke*, Definitive Ed. (New York: HarperPerennial, 1982, 1992 [1967])

Kuran, Timur. "Sparks and Prairie Fires: A Theory of Unanticipated Political Revolution", *Public Choice*, April 1989

Kuran, Timur. "The East European Revolution of 1989: Is it Surprising that We Were Surprised?", *American Economic Review*, May 1991

Kuran, Timur. "Now Out of Never: The Element of Surprise in the East European Revolution of 1989", *World Politics*, October 1991

LaFeber, Walter. "Inevitable Revolutions", *Atlantic Monthly*, June 1982

LaFeber, Walter. *Inevitable Revolutions* (New York and London: W.W.

Norton, 1983, 1984)

Lakoff, George. "Bringing the Mind Into Intellectual Discourse", Paper presented at the conference honoring Pierre Bourdieu on *Fin-De-Siecle Intellectuals: Looking Back and Looking Forward*, UC Berkeley, Berkeley, CA, 5 April 1996

Lakoff, George. *Moral Politics*, 2nd ed. (Chicago: University of Chicago Press, 2002)

Lakoff, George. *Don't Think Of An Elephant* (White River Jct., VT: Chelsea Green Publishing, 2004)

Lakoff, George and Mark Johnson. *Metaphors We Live By* (Chicago, IL and London: University of Chicago Press, 1980)

Lambrose, R.J. "Department Stores", *Lingua Franca*, January/February 1994

Lange, Oskar. "On the Theory of Economic Socialism" in Benjamin Lippincott, ed., *On the Economic Theory of Socialism* (Minneapolis: University of Minnesota Press, 1938)

Leff, Carol Skalnik. "Could This Marriage Be Saved?: The Czechoslovak Divorce", *Current History*, March 1996

Lenin, V.I. *What Is To Be Done?* (Peking [Beijing]: Foreign Languages Press, [1902])

Lenin, V.I. *The State and Revolution* (Peking [Beijing]: Foreign Languages Press, 1970 [1917])

Lerner, Michael. *The Politics of Meaning* (Reading, MA: Addison-Wesley, 1996)

Lewis, Paul G., ed. *Eastern Europe: Political Crisis and Legitimation* (London and Sydney: Croom Helm, 1984)

Li Zijing. "Twelve Nightmares for Beijing", *World Press Review*, March 1996 [*Cheng Ming*, December 1995]

Lindesay, William. "The New Consumers", *National Geographic Traveler*, September/October 1998

Link, Perry. *Evening Chats in Beijing: Probing China's Predicament* (New York: W.W. Norton, 1992)

Lippincott, Benjamin, ed. *On the Economic Theory of Socialism* (Minneapolis: University of Minnesota Press, 1938)

Lippman, John. "Tuning in the Global Village: How TV is Transforming World Culture and Politics", *Los Angeles Times*, 20 October 1992

Lipsky, William E. "Comparative Approaches to the Study of Revolution: A Histiographic Essay", *Review of Politics*, October 1976

Little, Daniel. *Varieties of Social Explanation* (Boulder, CO: Westview Press, 1991)

Liu, Drew. "The Unfolding of Post-Deng Era: Reports from China", *China Backgrounder*, No. 2, http://www.ned.org/page_3/China/publ/backg/back2.html

Luers, William H. "Czechoslovakia: Road to Revolution", *Foreign Affairs*, Spring 1990

Luttwak, Edward. *Coup D'État: A Practical Handbook* (Cambridge: Harvard University Press, 1968, 1979)

Manion, Melanie. "Introduction: Reluctant Duelists: The Logic of the 1989 Protests and Massacre" in Michel Oksenberg, Lawrence R. Sullivan, and Marc Lambert, eds., *Beijing Spring, 1989: Confrontation and Conflict: The Basic Documents* (Armonk, NY and London: M.E. Sharpe, 1990)

Mao Tse-tung [Mao Zedong]. "We Must Learn to Do Economic Work" [10 January 1945] in *Quotations from Chairman Mao Tse-tung* (Peking [Beijing]: Foreign Languages Press, 1966)

Markham, James M. "Across a Divided Europe, An Ideology Under Siege", *New York Times*, 23 January 1989

Markoff, John. *Waves of Democracy: Social Movements and Political Change* (Thousand Oaks, CA: Pine Forge Press, 1996)

Marshall, Tyler. "TV a Star Player on the World's Political Stage", *Los Angeles Times*, 20 October 1992

Martin, Calvin, ed. *The American Indian and the Problem of History* (New York and Oxford: Oxford University Press, 1987)

Martin, Paul. "Face-Off in Tiananmen Square", *National Geographic Traveler*, January/February 2001

Marx, Karl. "The Possibility of Non-Violent Revolution" [8 September 1872] in Robert C. Tucker, ed., *The Marx-Engels Reader*, Second Ed. (New York: W.W. Norton, 1978)

Marx, Karl. "Critical Marginal Notes on the Article 'The King of Prussia and Social Reform'" [July 1844] in Robert C. Tucker, ed., *The Marx-Engels Reader*, Second Ed. (New York: W.W. Norton, 1978)

Marx, Karl. *Capital*, Vol. One [1867], trans. Ben Fowkes (New York: Vintage Books, 1977)

Marx, Karl. "The Eighteenth Brumaire of Louis Bonaparte" [1852] in Robert C. Tucker, ed., *The Marx-Engels Reader*, Second Ed. (New York: W.W. Norton, 1978)

Marx, Karl and Friedrich Engels. *The Manifesto of the Communist Party* [1847-48] in Robert C. Tucker, ed., *The Marx-Engels Reader*, Second Ed. (New York: W.W. Norton, 1978)

Marx, Karl. "Wage Labor and Capital" [1847, 1849] in Robert C. Tucker, ed., *The Marx-Engels Reader*, Second Ed. (New York: W.W. Norton, 1978)

McAdam, Doug. *Political Process and the Development of Black*

Insurgency, 1930-1970 (Chicago, IL and London: University of Chicago Press, 1982)

McAfee, Kathy. "Environment", *In Brief* [Oxfam America], 1992

McDaniel, Tim. "Rejoinder to Goodwin", *Theory and Society*, December 1994

McDaniel, Tim. *Autocracy, Modernization, and Revolution in Russia and Iran* (Princeton, NJ: Princeton University Press, 1991)

McDonald, Joe. "Miners Riot to Protest Layoffs as China Tries to Close Unprofitable State Companies", *Associated Press*, 5 April 2000

McDonald, Terrence J., ed. *The Historic Turn in the Human Sciences* (Ann Arbor: University of Michigan Press, 1996)

McMichael, Philip. *Development and Social Change: A Global Perspective* (Thousand Oaks, CA: Pine Forge Press, 1996)

Mead, Walter. "In the Shadow of History", *Worth*, September 1994

Meisler, Stanley. "'...All They Are Saying Is Give Prague a Chance'", *Smithsonian*, June 1993

Merton, Robert K. *Social Theory and Social Structure* (New York: Free Press, 1957)

Michels, Robert. *Political Parties* [1915], trans. Eden and Cedar Paul (New York: Collier Books, 1962)

Millar, James R. "The Little Deal: Brezhnev's Contribution to Acquisitive Socialism", *Slavic Review*, Winter 1985

Miller, David, ed. *The Blackwell Encyclopaedia of Political Thought* (Oxford and New York: Basil Blackwell, 1987)

Mills, C. Wright. *The Sociological Imagination* (London, Oxford, and New York: Oxford University Press, 1959)

Mills, C. Wright. *Listen, Yankee: The Revolution in Cuba* (New York: Ballantine Books, 1960)

Misztal, Barbara A. "Understanding Political Change in Eastern Europe: A Sociological Perspective", *Sociology*, August 1993

Moore, Barrington, Jr. *Social Origins of Dictatorship and Democracy* (Boston, MA: Beacon Press, 1966)

Moore, Barrington, Jr. *Injustice: The Social Bases of Obedience and Revolt* (White Plains, NY: M.E. Sharpe, 1978)

Morgan, Robin. *The Anatomy of Freedom, Feminism, Physics, and Global Politics* (Garden City, NJ: Anchor Books/Doubleday, 1984)

Morris, Aldon D. & Carol McClurg Mueller, eds. *Frontiers in Social Movement Theory* (New Haven, CT and London: Yale University Press, 1992)

Narayanswamy, Ramnath. "Causes and Consequences of the East European Revolutions of 1989", *Economic and Political Weekly*, 15 February 1992

Nelson, Daniel N. and Samuel Bentley. "The Comparative Politics of Eastern Europe", *PS: Political Science & Politics*, March 1994

"New Rumbles of Democracy", *World Press Review*, November 1997 [Marcus Gee, *Globe and Mail*, 17 September 1997]

Newman, Andrew E. "Escape from Flatland: Is Comparative-Historical Research Acontextual?", *Comparative & Historical Sociology*, Winter 1995

Nohria, Nitin and Ranjay Gulati. "Firms and Their Environments" in Neil J. Smelser and Richard Swedberg, eds., *The Handbook of Economic Sociology* (Princeton, NJ and New York: Princeton University Press and Russell Sage Foundation, 1994)

O'Connor, James. *The Fiscal Crisis of the State* (New York: St. Martin's

Press, 1973)

O'Donnell, Guillermo and Philippe C. Schmitter. *Transitions from Authoritarian Rule: Tentative Conclusions About Uncertain Democracies* (Baltimore, MD and London: Johns Hopkins University Press, 1986)

Oksenberg, Michel with Lawrence R. Sullivan. "Preface" in Michel Oksenberg, Lawrence R. Sullivan, and Marc Lambert, eds., *Beijing Spring, 1989: Confrontation and Conflict: The Basic Documents* (Armonk, NY and London: M.E. Sharpe, 1990)

Oksenberg, Michel, Lawrence R. Sullivan, and Marc Lambert, eds. *Beijing Spring, 1989: Confrontation and Conflict: The Basic Documents* (Armonk, NY and London: M.E. Sharpe, 1990)

Olson, Mancur, Jr. *The Logic of Collective Action* (New York: Schocken Books (Harvard University Press), 1965)

Otis, Eileen M. "Gender and the Politics of Chinese Nationalism", unpublished manuscript

Paige, Jeffery M. *Agrarian Revolution* (New York: Free Press, 1975)

Parenti, Michael. *Power and the Powerless* (New York: St. Martin's Press, 1978)

Parenti, Michael. *Blackshirts and Reds: Rational Fascism and the Overthrow of Communism* (San Francisco: City Lights Books, 1997)

Park, Robert. "The City: Suggestions for the Investigation of Human Behavior in the Urban Environment", *American Journal of Sociology*, 1916

Peet, Richard. "Cultural Production of Economic Forms in the New England Discursive Formation", unpublished manuscript

Perry, Elizabeth J. "Casting a Chinese 'Democracy' Movement: The Roles of Students, Workers, and Entrepreneurs" in Jeffrey N.

Wasserstrom and Elizabeth J. Perry, eds., *Popular Protest and Political Culture in Modern China: Learning from 1989* (Boulder, CO: Westview Press, 1992)

Pietraru, Dinu. "The Significance of a Classic Revolution. Romania 1989", Paper presented at the 91st Annual Meetings of the American Sociological Association on *Social Change: Opportunities & Constraints*, New York, NY, 16-20 August 1996

Piven, Frances Fox and Richard A. Cloward. *Poor People's Movements: Why They Succeed, How They Fail* (New York: Vintage Books, 1977)

Polanyi, Karl, Conrad Arensberg, and Harry Pearson, eds. *Trade and Market in the Early Empires: Economies in History and Theory* (Chicago, IL: Henry Regnery, 1971 [1957])

Polanyi, Karl. *The Great Transformation: The Political and Economic Origins of Our Time* (Boston, MA: Beacon Press, 1957 [1944])

Poole, Teresa. "The Long March to Affluence", *World Press Review*, March 1996 [*Independent on Sunday*, 31 December 1995]

Popkin, Jeremy D. "Media and Revolutionary Crises" in Jeremy D. Popkin, ed., *Media and Revolution: Comparative Perspectives* (Lexington: University of Kentucky Press, 1995)

Popkin, Jeremy D., ed. *Media and Revolution: Comparative Perspectives* (Lexington: University of Kentucky Press, 1995)

Powell, Walter W. and Paul J. DiMaggio, eds. *The New Institutionalism in Organizational Analysis* (Chicago, IL: University of Chicago Press, 1991)

Przeworski, Adam. "The 'East' Becomes the 'South'?: The 'Autumn of the People' and the Future of Eastern Europe", *PS: Political Science & Politics*, March 1991

Przeworski, Adam. *Democracy and the Market: Political and Economic*

Reforms in Eastern Europe and Latin America (Cambridge: Cambridge University Press, 1991)

Ragin, Charles C. and Howard S. Becker, eds. *What is a Case?: Exploring the Foundations of Social Inquiry* (Cambridge and New York: Cambridge University Press, 1992)

Ragin, Charles C. *The Comparative Method: Moving Beyond Qualitative and Quantitative Strategies* (Berkeley and Los Angeles, CA: University of California Press, 1987)

Ragin, Charles C. *Constructing Social Research: The Unity and Diversity of Method* (Thousand Oaks, CA: Pine Forge Press [Sage], 1994)

Ragin, Charles C. with Mary Driscoll. "Afterword: The Promise of Social Research" in Charles C. Ragin, *Constructing Social Research: The Unity and Diversity of Method* (Thousand Oaks, CA: Pine Forge Press [Sage], 1994)

Ramet, Sabrina P. "Eastern Europe's Painful Transition", *Current History*, March 1996

Rejai, Mostafa. "Survey Essay on the Study of Revolution", *Journal of Political and Military Sociology*, Fall 1973

"Report: Chinese Police Scuffle with Protesting Factory Workers", *Associated Press*, 5 November 1999

Rodriguez, Richard. *Hunger of Memory* (Boston, MA: David Godine, 1982)

"Romanian TV Becomes Soul of Revolution", *San Francisco Chronicle*,27 December 1989

Rosemont, Henry, Jr. "Why the Chinese Economic Miracle Isn't One", *Z Magazine*, October 1995

Rosemont, Henry, Jr. "China and U.S. Morality", *Z Magazine*, December 1995

Rosenau, Pauline Marie. *Postmodernism and the Social Sciences: Insights, Inroads, and Intrusions* (Princeton, NJ: Princeton University Press, 1992)

Rousseau, Jean-Jacques. *On the Social Contract* [1762]

Rueschemeyer, Dietrich, Evelyne Stephens, and John Stephens. *Capitalist Development & Democracy* (Chicago, IL: University of Chicago Press, 1992)

Sahlins, Marshall. *Stone Age Economics* (New York: Aldine Publishing, 1972)

Sahlins, Marshall. *Culture and Practical Reason* (Chicago, IL: University of Chicago Press, 1976)

Schattschneider, E.E. *The Semi-Sovereign People* (New York: Holt, Rinehart and Winston, 1960)

Schmemann, Serge. "In Hope and Dismay, Lenin's Heirs Speak" in Bernard Gwertzman and Michael T. Kaufman, eds., *The Collapse of Communism* [a collection of *New York Times* articles] (New York: Times Books, 1990)

Schneider, Kirk J. and Rollo May, eds. *The Psychology of Existence* (New York: McGraw-Hill, 1995)

Schock, Kurt. *Unarmed Insurrections: People Power Movements in Nondemocracies* (Minneapolis: University of Minnesota Press, 2005)

Schumacher, E.F. *Small Is Beautiful: A Study* of Economics as if People Mattered (London: Abacus, 1973)

Scott, James C. *Domination and the Arts of Resistance: Hidden Transcripts* (New Haven, CT and London: Yale University Press, 1990)

Scott, James C. *The Moral Economy of the Peasant* (New Haven, CT and London: Yale University Press, 1976)

Scott, James C. "Foreword" in Gilbert M. Joseph and Daniel Nugent, eds., *Everyday Forms of State Formation: Revolution and the Negotiation of Rule in Modern Mexico* (Durham, NC and London: Duke University Press, 1994)

Scott, James C. *Weapons of the Weak* (New Haven, CT and London: Yale University Press, 1985)

"Self-Sufficiency in Grain Ensured", *Beijing Review*, 28 October-3 November 1996

Sewell, William H., Jr. "Three Temporalities: Toward an Eventful Sociology" in Terrence J. McDonald, ed., *The Historic Turn in the Human Sciences* (Ann Arbor: University of Michigan Press, 1996)

Sewell, William H., Jr. "A Theory of Structure: Duality, Agency, and Transformation", *American Journal of Sociology*, July 1992

Sewell, William H., Jr. "Collective Violence and Collective Loyalties in France: Why the French Revolution Made a Difference", *Politics & Society*, December 1990

Shambaugh, David. "China's Fragile Future", *World Policy Journal*, Fall 1994

Shanin, Teodor. *The Roots of Otherness: Russia's Turn of the Century*, Vol. 2: Russia, 1905-1907, Revolution as a Moment of Truth (New Haven, CT and London: Yale University Press, 1986)

Skilling, H. Gordon and Paul Wilson, eds. *Civic Freedom in Central Europe: Voices from Czechoslovakia* (New York: St. Martin's Press, 1991)

Skocpol, Theda, ed. *Social Revolutions in the Modern World* (Cambridge and New York: Cambridge University Press, 1994)

Skocpol, Theda. "Sociology's Historical Imagination" in Theda Skocpol, ed., *Vision and Method in Historical Sociology* (Cambridge: Cambridge University Press, 1984)

Skocpol, Theda. "Reflections on Recent Scholarship about Social Revolutions and How to Study Them" in Theda Skocpol, ed., *Social Revolutions in the Modern World* (Cambridge and New York: Cambridge University Press, 1994)

Skocpol, Theda. "Emerging Agendas and Recurrent Strategies in Historical Sociology" in Theda Skocpol, ed., *Vision and Method in Historical Sociology* (Cambridge: Cambridge University Press, 1984)

Skocpol, Theda. *States and Social Revolutions: A Comparative Analysis of France, Russia, and China* (Cambridge: Cambridge University Press)

Skocpol, Theda. "France, Russia, China: A Structural Analysis of Social Revolutions" in Jack A. Goldstone, ed., *Revolutions: Theoretical, Comparative, and Historical Studies* (San Diego, CA: Harcourt Brace Jovanovich, 1986)

Skocpol, Theda, ed. *Vision and Method in Historical Sociology* (Cambridge: Cambridge University Press, 1984)

Smelser, Neil J. *Theory of Collective Behavior* (New York: Free Press, 1962)

Smelser, Neil J. and Richard Swedberg, eds. *The Handbook of Economic Sociology* (Princeton, NJ and New York: Princeton University Press and Russell Sage Foundation, 1994)

Smelser, Neil J. and Richard Swedberg. "The Sociological Perspective on the Economy" in Neil J. Smelser and Richard Swedberg, eds., *The Handbook of Economic Sociology* (Princeton, NJ and New York: Princeton University Press and Russell Sage Foundation, 1994)

Snyder, David and Charles Tilly. "Hardship and Collective Violence in France, 1830 to 1960", *American Sociological Review*, October 1972

Somers, Margaret R. "Narrating and Naturalizing Civil Society and

Citizenship Theory: The Place of Political Culture and the Public Sphere", *Sociological Theory*, November 1995

Somers, Margaret R. "What's Political or Cultural about Political Culture and the Public Sphere?: Toward an Historical Sociology of Concept Formation", *Sociological Theory*, July 1995

Sorel, Georges. *Reflections on Violence* (New York: Collier Books, 1961 [1950])

Staal, J.F. "Sanskrit and Sanskritization", *Journal of Asian Studies*, 1963

Stacey, Judith. *Patriarchy and Socialist Revolution in China* (Berkeley and Los Angeles: University of California Press, 1983)

Stephen K. Sanderson, ed. *Sociological Worlds: Comparative and Historical Readings on Society* (Los Angeles, CA: Roxbury Publishing, 1995)

Sterling, Bruce. "Triumph of the Plastic People", *Wired*, http://www.hotwired.com/wired/3.01/features/prague.html, January 1995

Stouffer, S.A. *et al. The American Soldier*, Vol. 1 (Princeton, NJ: Princeton University Press, 1949)

Support Democracy in China and Christus Rex et Redemptor Mundi. "Tiananmen, April-June 1989", http://www.christusrex.org, revised 29 May 1995

Swanson, Guy. "Frameworks for Comparative Research" in Ivan Vallier, ed., *Comparative Methods in Sociology* (Berkeley: University of California Press, 1971)

Swidler, Ann. "Culture in Action: Symbols and Strategies", *American Sociological Review*, April 1986

Szasz, Andrew. *EcoPopulism: Toxic Waste and the Movement for Environmental Justice* (Minneapolis: University of Minnesota Press, 1994)

Szelenyi, Ivan, Katherine Beckett, and Lawrence P. King. "The Socialist Economic System" in Neil J. Smelser and Richard Swedberg, eds., *The Handbook of Economic Sociology* (Princeton, NJ and New York: Princeton University Press and Russell Sage Foundation, 1994)

Tarrow, Sidney. *Power in Movement: Social Movements, Collective Action and Politics* (Cambridge and New York: Cambridge University Press, 1994)

Tarrow, Sidney. "'Aiming at a Moving Target'": Social Science and the Recent Rebellions in Eastern Europe", *PS: Political Science & Politics*, March 1991

Taylor, Michael, ed. *Rationality and Revolution* (Cambridge: Cambridge University Press, 1988)

Thomas, Daniel C. "Social Movements and the Strategic Use of Human Rights Norms: A Comparison of East European Cases", http://hdc-www.harvard.edu/cfia/pnscs/f94thoma.htm, 9 November 1994

Thompson, E.P. "The Moral Economy of the English Crowd in the Eighteenth Century", *Past and Present*, February 1971

Tilly, Charles. *European Revolutions, 1492-1992* (Oxford and Cambridge, MA: Blackwell Publishers, 1993)

Tilly, Charles. *From Mobilization to Revolution* (Reading, MA: Addison-Wesley, 1978)

Tilly, Charles. "Macrosociology, Past and Future", *Comparative & Historical Sociology*, Fall/Winter 1995

Tilly, Charles. *Big Structures Large Processes Huge Comparisons* (New York: Russell Sage Foundation, 1984)

Tilly, Charles, ed. *The Formation of Nation States in Western Europe* (Princeton, NJ: Princeton University Press, 1975)

Tilly, Charles. "Food Supply and Public Order in Modern Europe" in Charles Tilly, ed., *The Formation of Nation States in Western Europe* (Princeton, NJ: Princeton University Press, 1975)

Traugott, Mark. "Capital Cities and Revolution", *Social Science History*, Spring 1995

Trimberger, Ellen Kay. *Revolution From Above* (New Brunswick, NJ: Transaction Books, 1978)

Trotsky, Leon. *The History of the Russian Revolution* [1932], trans. Max Eastman (Ann Arbor: University of Michigan Press, 1957)

Trotsky, Leon. *The Revolution Betrayed* (London: Faber & Faber, 1937)

Tuck, Christopher. "Is the Party Over?", *World Press Review*, March 1996 [*Contemporary Review*, May 1995]

Tucker, Nancy Bernkopf. "China as a Factor in the Collapse of the Soviet Empire", *Political Science Quarterly*, Winter 1994-95

Tucker, Robert C., ed. *The Marx-Engels Reader*, Second Ed. (New York: W.W. Norton, 1978)

Ulc, Otto. "The Bumpy Road of Czechoslovakia's Velvet Revolution", *Problems of Communism*, May-June 1992

Vallier, Ivan, ed. *Comparative Methods in Sociology* (Berkeley: University of California Press, 1971)

Van Luyn, Floris-Jan. "Will China Eat Up the World?", *World Press Review*, March 1996 [*NRC Handelsblad*, 26 October 1995]

Veyne, Paul. *Writing History: Essay on Epistemology*, trans. Mina Moore-Rinvolucri (Middletown, CT: Wesleyan University Press, 1984 [1971])

Volgyes, Ivan. "Political Socialization in Eastern Europe: A Comparative Framework", *Journal of Political and Military Sociology*, Fall 1973

Walker, Martin. "China and the New Era of Resource Scarcity", *World Policy Journal*, Spring 1996

Wallerstein, Immanuel. *The Modern World System*, Vols. 1-3 (New York: Academic Press, 1974, 1980, 1989)

Walton, John. *Reluctant Rebels: Comparative Studies of Revolution and Underdevelopment* (New York: Columbia University Press, 1984)

Walton, John. *Western Times and Water Wars: State, Culture, and Rebellion in California* (Berkeley and Los Angeles: University of California Press, 1992)

Walton, John. "Making the Theoretical Case" in Charles C. Ragin and Howard S. Becker, eds., *What is a Case?: Exploring the Foundations of Social Inquiry* (Cambridge and New York: Cambridge University Press, 1992)

Wang Dan. "The Star of Hope Rises in Eastern Europe" [4 March 1989] in Mok Chiu Yu and J. Frank Harrison, eds., *Voices from Tiananmen Square: Beijing Spring and the Democracy Movement* (Montreal and New York: Black Rose Books, 1990)

Wang, Li-Cheng. "Chinese Military Expenditures in the 1990s", *Stanford Journal of International Affairs*, Spring/Summer 1995

Wasserstrom, Jeffrey N. and Elizabeth J. Perry, eds. *Popular Protest and Political Culture in Modern China: Learning from 1989* (Boulder, CO: Westview Press, 1992)

Wasserstrom, Jeffrey N. "Mass Media and Mass Actions in Urban China, 1919-1989" in Jeremy D. Popkin, ed., *Media and Revolution: Comparative Perspectives* (Lexington: University of Kentucky Press, 1995)

Wasserstrom, Jeffrey N. and Elizabeth J. Perry, eds. *Popular Protest and Political Culture in Modern China*, Second Ed. (Boulder, San Francisco, and Oxford: Westview Press, 1992, 1994)

Watson, Rubie S. "Memory, History, and Opposition Under State Socialism: An Introduction" in Rubie S. Watson, *Memory, History, and Opposition Under State Socialism* (Santa Fe, NM: School of American Research Press, 1994)

Watson, Rubie S. *Memory, History, and Opposition Under State Socialism* (Santa Fe, NM: School of American Research Press, 1994)

Watson, Peggy. "Eastern Europe's Silent Revolution: Gender", *Sociology*, August 1993

Weber, Max. "The Social Psychology of the World Religions" [1922-23] in H.H. Gerth and C. Wright Mills, eds., *From Max Weber: Essays in Sociology* (New York: Oxford University Press, 1946)

Weber, Max. "Politics as a Vocation" [1918] in H.H. Gerth and C. Wright Mills, eds., *From Max Weber: Essays in Sociology* (New York: Oxford University Press, 1946)

Weber, *Max. The Protestant Ethic and the Spirit of Capitalism* [1904-05], trans. by Talcott Parsons(London: Unwin Paperbacks, 1987)

Welch, Sharon. "Populism and the 1996 Elections", *Tikkun*, September/October 1996

West, Candace and Don H. Zimmerman. "Doing Gender", *Gender and Society*, 1987

Wheaton, Bernard and Zdenek Kavan. *The Velvet Revolution: Czechoslovakia, 1988-1991* (Boulder, CO: Westview Press, 1992)

Whipple, Tim D., ed. *After the Velvet Revolution: Václav Havel and the New Leaders of Czechoslovakia Speak Out* (New York: Freedom House, 1991)

Whyte, Martin King. "The Social Sources of the Student Demonstrations in China, 1989" in Jack A. Goldstone, ed., *Revolutions: Theoretical, Comparative, and Historical Studies*, Second Ed.

(Fort Worth, TX: Harcourt Brace College Publishers, 1994)

Wickham-Crowley, Timothy. *Guerrillas & Revolution in Latin America: A Comparative Study of Insurgents and Regimes Since 1956* (Princeton, NJ: Princeton University Press, 1992)

Wickham-Crowley, Timothy. "Structural Theories of Revolution", unpublished manuscript

Wei Liming, "Are You On Line?", *Beijing Review*, 30 November-6 December 1998

Weiner, Rebecca. "Grassroots Conservatism Comes of (New) Age: The Falun Gong Phenomenon", *Tikkun*, January/February 2000

Wolchik, Sharon L. "Czechoslovakia's 'Velvet Revolution'", *Current History*, December 1990

Wolchik, Sharon L. *Czechoslovakia in Transition: Politics, Economics & Society* (London and New York: Pinter Publishers, 1991)

Wolf, Eric. *Peasant Wars of the Twentieth Century* (New York: Harper & Row, 1969)

Wolfe, Alan. *The Limits of Legitimacy* (New York: Free Press, 1977)

Wright, Mark. "Ideology and Power in the Czechoslovak Political System" in Paul G. Lewis, ed., *Eastern Europe: Political Crisis and Legitimation* (London and Sydney: Croom Helm, 1984)

WuDunn, Sheryl. "150,000 Lift Their Voices for Change" in Bernard Gwertzman and Michael T. Kaufman, eds., *The Collapse of Communism* [a collection of *New York Times* articles] (New York: Times Books, 1990)

Yu, Mok Chiu and J. Frank Harrison, eds. *Voices from Tiananmen Square: Beijing Spring and the Democracy Movement* (Montreal and New York: Black Rose Books, 1990)

Zeitlin, Irving M. *Ideology and the Development of Sociological Theory*,

Second Ed. (Englewood Cliffs, NJ: Prentice-Hall, 1981)

Zinn, Howard. *A People's History of the United States* (New York: Harper & Row, 1980)

Zolberg, Aristide R. "Moments of Madness", *Politics and Society*, Winter 1972

Author Biographical Sketch

Daniel Brook earned a self-designed B.A. in Socio-Political Economy from Clark University in Worcester, Massachusetts, an M.A. in Political Science from San Francisco State University, and an M.A. and Ph.D. in Sociology from the University of California, Davis. He has also been trained in Civil Disobedience as well as Community Mediation. Dan has taught at various schools, teaching preschool to English as a Second Language to university, including at most of the public universities in the San Francisco Bay Area, where he lives with his wife and son. Besides writing haiku and other poetry, Dan also publishes widely, having articles in various media from the *American Journal of Economics and Sociology* to *Peace Review* to *Z Magazine* in addition to being interviewed on KDVS and KPFA. He is also active in various actions and movements for progressive change, environmental sustainability, and social justice. Dan's CV can be viewed at www.brook.com/dan; he maintains *CyberBrook's ThinkLinks* at www.brook.com/cyberbrook; and has created *Eco-Eating* at www.brook.com/veg, *The Vegetarian Mitzvah* at www.brook.com/jveg, and *No Smoking?* at www.brook.com/smoke. Dan may not always be an optimist, but he is always an anti-pessimist.